Sky Over Scapa
1939-1945

Gregor Lamb

BYRGISEY

ISBN 0 9513443 2 3

This book is typeset in 10pt Palatino by Jeremy Willis, Haselbury Plucknett, Somerset

Printed and bound in Great Britain

FRONTISPIECE
771 Squadron Twatt Pilots Johnny Treloar and Charlie Buxton in the snow, January 1945 – PEMBERTON

Dedicated to all those who sojourned among us

Contents

ACKNOWLEDGEMENTS

I am not sure that I should thank Orkney farmer Sandy Scarth for his initiative in suggesting that the Control Tower of Twatt airfield should be preserved. He made a lot of work for me! Had I put the same effort for four years into breeding beef cattle I would have a fine herd by this time and might have made a lot of money but then a piece of Orkney history would have vanished. Orcadians owe him a sincere debt of gratitude.

My first duty is to acknowledge the help of Ronald Gilbert, Chief Executive of Orkney Islands Council who, though on holiday, made special arrangements to prevent the demolition of the Control Tower of Twatt airfield in Orkney and, unwittingly, set in motion a wide ranging research project which has culminated in this book. Tom Eggeling, Director of Planning to Orkney Islands Council must also be congratulated for his foresight in seeing in the wartime eyesores which lie scattered throughout the Orkney landscape, some things worthy of preservation to commemorate the huge impact which war had on these islands.

I would especially like to thank Captain 'Hank' and wife Deborah Rotherham of Canada who, on hearing of a plan to preserve something of the Royal Naval Air Station at Twatt, flew to Orkney to give the project their blessing. Without their initial input of enthusiasm, the book would have remained a dream. Hank has an outstanding memory and carefully typed out for me detailed notes of his experiences in Orkney to supplement the material in his own book, *"It's Really Quite Safe"*. Many initial contacts were made through Hank especially a close friend of his, Duncan Hamilton of Somerset who, by showing me his wonderful collection of photographs of war-time Hatston, gave me the idea of building up a Photographic Archive. Duncan was most generous in his support and is a most convivial host who has spared much of his time to help. He loved Orkney and devoted a long and very amusing chapter to his time at Hatston in his autobiography *Touch Wood.*

Nicholas Horne was a photographer at RAF Skeabrae and, after the war, continued in this profession. On his retirement he cleaned out a lot of chaff and was uncertain what to do with a useless album of photographs of Skeabrae. By good fortune he happened to mention this to a close friend, Ralph Faulkner, an ex-Fleet Air Arm man who had come to retire in Orkney. In this way unique photographs of this station were saved. There is a great shortage of wartime RAF photographs throughout Britain: some squadrons disappeared without leaving any photographic record so we are particularly fortunate in this regard. Sadly there are no squadron photographs in the collection but nevertheless, we do have a fine record of life on this famous wartime station and I should like to thank sincerely Ralph and Nicholas for presenting the album to Orkney Archives.

A rich collection of photographs was also loaned by Patrick Hill and Michael Hill, sons of Lt.Cdr. Peter Hill, head of photography at Twatt. The collection included rare colour ciné film shot in Orkney during the war and therefore valuable archival material. Also from the same Photograph Section at Twatt, Wren Photographer Celia Pemberton (née Green) loaned an album in which the Wrens were well represented. The Royal Navy was very proud of the high standard of photography in this department and, judging by the evidence this is very true.

Mrs. Anne Bell and David Richardson, librarians at the Fleet Air Arm Museum at Yeovilton in Somerset provided every facility at their disposal, (including coffee!), to assist with the tracking down of Scapa related photographs in their very fine library. Dr. Graham Mottram of the Museum there has also shown keen interest in the project and was intimately connected with the identification of war-time aircraft on the seabed off Orkney. By way of gratitude to these members of the Museum it gives me much pleasure to be able to donate copies of the whole collection of Fleet Air Arm photographs to the Museum. Scapa Flow is now well represented there!

Among the other large private photograph collections which have been loaned I must acknowledge the help of Lt. Keith Remmington and Wren Muriel Wears of Gosport who were stationed at Twatt. They met there and later married. In common with all those couples who spent their war time years in Orkney, they have vivid memories of life there and were able to provide a tape for Orkney Sound Archive. Chief Petty Officer

Pilot Eric Haslam and Wren Peggy Harrison of Oxford also met at Twatt and provided many unusual photographs and very helpful notes on the station. New Zealander, Cyril Burke, latterly CO of 771 Squadron at Twatt and now resident in Australia sent his whole album - at enormous expense - to Orkney to be copied. Cyril also very kindly donated, unsolicited I might add, £25 to the project. This was handed over to Tom Eggeling, Director of Planning, as unofficial trustee of project funds. From Canada unique photographs were sent by Jean-Paul Fournier. French-Canadian, Jean-Paul, was the Royal Navy's first helicopter pilot. It does not appear to be recorded in Naval history that the Royal Navy's first operational helicopter was assembled and flown in Orkney at Twatt airfield, consequently such photographs are most valuable. I was particularly pleased to be contacted by John Molyneux, son of Commander H Molyneux, CO of 771 Squadron at Twatt: for copying, John very kindly loaned the family album which contained many rare and fine photographs.

Air Commodore 'Cyclops' Brown was a pilot at Skeabrae and made a return visit to the islands in 1989. He called on me and expressly asked for the RAF to be represented in any museum or interpretation centre likely to be established. He gave me a copy of his vignette of life in Orkney as seen through the eyes of a young Hurricane pilot. It is beautifully written and I hope, one day it will be published in its own right. I have used several extracts from Cyclop's paper in this book, quite moving descriptions of Orkney which help us see a fighter pilot in a different light. Cyclops was so interested in the Orkney project that he undertook to write up a history of Skeabrae based on the Station Diary in the Public Record Office at Kew. This was of inestimable help to me in the early stages of the research and I am most appreciative of the contribution made by Cyclops to this study.

Bill Reid, a pilot with 771 Squadron at Twatt from 1942 until 1943 wrote for me a brief reminiscence. "My memories of Twatt after so long are largely of wind, red hot cast iron stoves, more wind, the Balfour and Beatty men, still more wind - and Highland Park Whisky". So many references were made to Balfour Beatty, the firm of constructional engineers who did so much to mould war-time Orkney that I contacted them to let them know they had not been forgotten. I was delighted to receive a letter from Mr. A J Wivell, Director and General Manager who replied to say that two of his office colleagues began their Civil Engineering careers in Orkney and that his father also worked there. He sent good wishes for the success of the project and an interim goodwill contribution of £150! I should like to thank Mr. Wivell for this generous contribution and acknowledge the enormous war-time effort of Balfour Beatty who, among other projects, undertook the building of the Churchill Barriers to block off the eastern approaches to Scapa Flow. Balfour Beatty, a name familiar to many in Britain today for its association with major roadworks is still a household name in Orkney today but for another reason.

TAGs (Telegraphic Air Gunners) are well represented in my list of contributors and I should like to thank Doug Cole of Norwich, Secretary of this organisation for rustling up so many useful contacts for me. Many others have written reminiscences and have loaned photographs and personal mementoes all of which have helped to create a picture of life in Orkney for the serviceman and woman during the war. I have kept detailed notes of all other service contributors but if I have omitted any, may I please be forgiven. Sincere thanks to:- Con Ardern (neé Watson), Bournemouth, Wren, Twatt: Lt. Cdr. J W Armstrong, Cambs., Hatston: W Atherton, Clwyd, Air Fitter Twatt: K Baylis, Hampshire, Hatston: Margaret Boden (neé Baikie), Cornwall, Wren, Hatston: Sqdn.Ldr. Ian Blair, Essex, 602 Squadron Pilot, RAF, Skeabrae: Margaret Bramwell (neé Bennett), Salisbury, Wren, Twatt: Lt. Alan Bristow, Surrey, 771 Squadron helicopter Pilot, Twatt: Capt. Eric Brown, Sussex, 802 Squadron Pilot, Twatt: Norman Brown, Orkney, Observer, 700 Squadron, Twatt: Lt.Cdr. Cyril Burke, Australia, CO 771 Squadron, Twatt: Glyn Clayton, Pembroke, pilot, 840/841 Squadron, later 856 Squadron, Hatston: D Coll, Herts, Met. Officer, Twatt: Lt.Cdr. John Cooper, Surrey, Pilot, 809 Squadron Twatt, later CO, 882 Squadron, Twatt, Hatston: Pat Conder, Wren, Hatston: J Crooks, Hull, Twatt: Cdr. Michael Crosley, Isle of Wight Pilot, 800 Squadron, Hatston, 804 Squadron, Hatston, Twatt; CO 880 Squadron, Skeabrae, Grimsetter: E Trevor Dole, Signals, Twatt: Leading A/M G F Edwards, Southampton, Twatt: E M Evans (neé Dunnett), Bolton, WAAF, Skeabrae: Capt. H St.J Fancourt, Hampshire, CO Hatston: PO Ralph Faulkner, Orkney, 856 Squadron, Hatston: R G Fletcher, Suffolk, 845 Squadron, Hatston: Lt. Jean-Paul Fournier, Canada, helicopter Pilot, 771 Squadron, Twatt: Barbara Fry (neé Murray), Dorset, Wren Twatt: E J Gilberd, New Zealand, Pilot, 771 Squadron, Twatt: P Godley, Devon, 771 Squadron, Twatt: T Halhead, Lancashire, TAG 771 Squadron, Hatston: Douglas Haskey, Pilot/Observer, Orkney, 821 Squadron, Hatston: Bernard Hazelton, Essex, TAG, Twatt: Lt. Donald Hewlett, Kent, Met. Officer, Hatston: Ruby Heymans-Nicoll, Netherlands, Wren, Twatt: Leading Stoker Jack Holden, Orkney, Twatt: Sub.Lt. Ian Houghton, Ross-shire, Pilot, 771 Squadron, Twatt: PO Ron Howarth, Wigan, TAG, Swordfish Squadron, Hatston: Arthur Howes, Sutton Coldfield, TAG, 846 Squadron, Hatston: Lt. C G Hyde, Dorset, Pilot, 771 Squadron, Twatt: Air Mechanic Leslie Jessett, Norfolk, 771 Squadron, Twatt: R I Kennedy, Bristol, 771 Squadron, Hatston and Twatt: Ken Knowles, Leicester, TAG, Twatt: Eric Lambeth, Norwich, 771 Squadron TAG, Twatt: Cmdr. J R Lang, Hampshire, 835 Squadron, Hatston: W C Larkins, Canada, 771 Squadron,

Twatt: Mick Lawrence, Secretary, Fleet Air Arm Officers' Association, London: Petty Officer Barbara Ledger-Lomas (neé Hayward), Liverpool, Wren, Twatt: Leif Lyssand, Norway, pilot, 331 Squadron, Skeabrae: Catherine Mair, Cheltenham, NAAFI, Twatt: Norman Mills, Gwynnedd, 823 Squadron, Hatston, G C Marley, Hampshire, Hatston: General Helge Mehre, Norway, pilot and CO, 331 Squadron, Skeabrae: Harald Meltzer, Norway, pilot, 331 Squadron, Skeabrae: Pat Molony, Herts, 771 Squadron TAG, Twatt: Norman Mills, Air Frame Fitter, Gwynedd, 823 Squadron, Hatston: J Newbery, Junior Clerk to Admiralty, Skeabrae: Professor J O'Connel, Huddersfield, PO Radio Mechanic, Twatt: Lt. Leonard Page, Canada, 771 Squadron helicopter Pilot, Twatt: Iris Page (neé Turner, Canada, Wren, Twatt: Celia Pemberton (neé Green), London, Wren Photographer, Twatt: William Pitman, Wiltshire, Air Mechanic, 809 Squadron, Twatt; Lt. Bill Reid, Surrey, Pilot, 771 Squadron, Twatt; Eleanor Robertson (neé Irvine), Shetland, WAAF, Skeabrae, Grimsetter: Sam Sephton, Hull, Twatt: Arthur (Tiny) Small, Suffolk, Radio Operator, Twatt: Barry Smith, Norfolk, RAF Hatston and Twatt: Dick Stark, Nottingham, 771 Squadron TAG, Twatt: Harry Stephens, Surrey, Radio Mechanic, 700 Squadron, Twatt: Roy Stevens, Hampshire, 800 Squadron, Hatston: Beryly Strouts (neé Turner), U.S.A., Wren, Twatt: Gretta Taylor, Sutherlandshire, WAAF, Skeabrae: John Thompson, Nottingham, Chief Air Radio Officer, Hatston: Sonia Thorpe (neé Morrison), Nottingham, Leading Wren Air Mechanic, Twatt: Mary Treby, Essex, Wren, Twatt: Fl/Lt. Mike Walker, Herts, Signals Officer, Skeabrae: Syd Vincent, Hon. Secy., FAA, New Zealand: Commander D C B White, former Director, Fleet Air Arm Museum, Yeovilton: G R S Williams, South Glamorgan, Radar Mechanic, Twatt and Hatston: Trevor Wiren, brother of Lonsdale Wiren, New Zealand, 878 Squadron, Hatston: Frank Wyles, Cleveland, Leading Air Fitter, Hatston.

The very fine collection of photographs which were loaned to me by servicemen and women were meticulously copied by David Mackie, photographer with the Department of Archives of the Orkney Library. I should like to thank David and Alison Fraser, Head of Archives for their unfailing patience in dealing with such a mass of specialist material when there were so many other calls upon their time. With their help Orkney now has an archive of photographs of military aviation unequalled outside major British museums.

I should like to single out for special mention three people not directly concerned with Orkney but who have been very helpful. Ray Sturtivant's *The Squadrons of the Fleet Air Arm* is an outstanding reference book and has been of great value to me in piecing together the history of the Fleet Air Arm in Orkney. I sincerely acknowledge the assistance I have received from this book and from Ray Sturtivant personally. Ron Pankhurst of Exeter is an authority on Fleet Air Arm casualties and very generously supplied me with all the data relating to Orkney during World War II. Keith Bryers of Ross-shire shares an interest in aircraft accidents and he too provided me with all his relevant research.

Three Orcadians deserve special mention. Alec Strutt of Kirkwall is an experienced diver and came by chance upon a Grumman Avenger aircraft on the seabed off Hatston. A Royal Naval expedition confirmed this and photographed the find - which, by the way, still remains a mystery. So far no reference has been found of this aircraft ditching off Hatston. This discovery sparked off in Alec a great interest in war-time military aircraft. I thank Alec for his interest in the project. It is recorded that five aircraft were raised from the seabed in Scapa Flow during the war but I can assure Alec that there are many more lying out there and waiting to be discovered. I would also like to thank Orcadian farmer Tom Johnston of Bryameadow Farm, Twatt. Tom has lived all his life alongside the 'drome' as it is known locally and is a great authority on the history of the station. He has woven a spider's web round the airfield and succeeds in catching any unsuspecting serviceman or woman who tries to creep back unobtrusively. Through Tom I have made many valuable contacts. Without him, this book would have been the poorer. The third is Orcadian by adoption, Jack Holden of Stenness. Jack spent all the war years with the Fleet Air Arm at Twatt and loved the islands so much that he decided to move from Kent and settle here in the 1950's. He was a superb artist but his talent as a writer is less well known. Jack showed great interest in the project and wrote some extremely amusing pieces for us to enjoy. It is my deepest regret that he did not live to see the completion of this book.

A number of extracts have been used from the references quoted in the bibliography and I should like to thank the publishers of the following works for generous permission to quote:- **Churchill, Winston**: *The Gathering Storm*, Curtis Brown Ltd., New York; **Clostermann, Pierre**: *The Big Show*, Chatto and Windus, London, 1951; **Crosley, Cmdr. R Mike**: *They gave me a Seafire*, Airlife Publishing Ltd., Shrewsbury, 1986; **Gordon, Dr. T. Crouther**: *Early Flying in Orkney: seaplanes in World War I*, BBC Radio Orkney, 1985; **Hamilton, Duncan**: *Touch Wood*, Duncan Hamilton & Co. Ltd., Bagshot, Surrey, 1990; **Partridge, R T (Major)**: *Operation Skua*, Fleet Air Arm Museum, Yeovilton, Somerset, 1983; **Rotherham, Capt. Hank:** *"It's Really Quite Safe"*, Hangar Books, Canada; **Scott, Desmond**: *One More Hour*, Random Century (New Zealand) Ltd, 1989. I also acknowledge permission from **The Times** of London to use the article *Return to the Orkneys* printed in that newspaper in May 1946. Copyright to the poem *The Bloody Orkneys*, published by

Faber and Faber in **Verse and Worse** is held by the author, Captain Hamish Blair. With the help of the publishers, all reasonable steps have been taken to find Captain Blair but with no success. All photographs are credited; my very special thanks to the Fleet Air Arm Museum, Yeovilton, the Trustees of the Imperial War Museum, the Public Records Office and Orkney Archives for permission to publish photographs from their collections.

The Scottish Arts Council provided a travel grant to cover the cost of the many journeys undertaken to the Public Record Office in Kew and to the Imperial War Museum in London to research the history of the flying services in Orkney. I am very grateful to the Council for this financial assistance.

The onerous task of proof reading was undertaken by Air Commodore Cyclops Brown, Duncan Hamilton and Dr. Graham Mottram all of whom, accumulatively, pin-pointed many errors. I remain extremely indebted to them for their help, advice and encouragement.

Gregor Lamb,
South Waird,
Marwick,
Birsay,
Orkney

8 November 1990

Introduction

In October 1986, at a meeting of the Community Council of the parish of Birsay in Orkney, Councillor and farmer Sandy Scarth drew the attention of the members to the fact that, next day, the Control Tower of Twatt Aerodrome was to be blown up. He was of the opinion that, since this was one of the last vestiges of World War II still extant, it was of historical interest and should be preserved. The Council concurred and it was agreed that steps should be taken immediately to prevent its demolition. It fell to the writer, also a member of the Council, to act on behalf of the Community Council and appeal to Orkney Islands Council to preserve the Control Tower of the Royal Naval Air Station at Twatt as testimony to the enormous contribution made to the war effort by the Fleet Air Arm in Orkney. Ronald Gilbert, Chief Executive of Orkney Islands Council, was sympathetic to the Council's request and instructions were given to the army demolition team to preserve the Control Tower. The arrival of the messenger was timely for holes had already been drilled into the tower and the charges implanted.

The Community Council was now left to decide what to do with the building. Civil Engineer, Mike Austin, established that it was structurally sound but even simple refurbishment was far beyond the budget of the Community Council. Little was known of the history of the Tower or indeed of the Airfield and, again, on behalf of the Council, the writer offered to undertake some simple research. An approach was made to the Director of the Fleet Air Arm Museum at Yeovilton in Somerset with a hint that the Orkney site might make a small museum or interpretation centre. From here a message was passed on to Captain Hank Rotherham a retired naval officer living in Quebec, Canada. Hank Rotherham was the first permanent Station Commander at Twatt and he had just recently written a book about his naval experiences, devoting a considerable amount of space to his time spent in Orkney. Hank was very excited about the project and made arrangements to fly to Orkney with his wife.

Thus the Orkney Fleet Air Arm Museum became airborne. A brief news item in the *Daily Telegraph* brought in some letters of encouragement and several photographs. Word got round through service magazines and at service reunions and a file of correspondence built up including letters from Australia, New Zealand and Canada. By coincidence a local diver, Alec Strutt, found an intact Grumman Avenger at the bottom of Kirkwall Bay and the prospect of this aircraft being the centrepiece of a display gave new life to the project.

In the summer of 1988 the writer had a visit from Air Commodore Cyclops Brown, a former Skeabrae pilot. Cyclops had heard of the project and made the not unreasonable suggestion that, since RAF Skeabrae was very close to Twatt and there had been a high degree of cooperation between these two stations during the war, the project might perhaps be extended to include reference to the Royal Air Force as well. From this point onwards the net was spread wider and contact was made with RAF personnel. By doing so interest was increased twofold and the writer was particularly pleased to make contact with members of the Norwegian Hurricane Squadron which had been based in Orkney during the war. The project now took a new turn: to accumulate as much material as possible relating to the flying services in Orkney during World War II.

Meanwhile the photographic collection built up. At the beginning of the project there was only one photograph in Orkney Archives relating to the flying services in World War II and arrangements were made for Archives to copy any which were loaned to the writer. In this way a superb collection of over 600 photographs has been made, mostly copied from private collections but 70 were very generously donated by the Fleet Air Arm Museum at Yeovilton. Others were purchased from the Public Records Office at Kew and from the Imperial War Museum.

Orkney Islands Council meanwhile had begun to establish an Interpretation Centre at Lyness, the administrative headquarters of Scapa Flow during World War II and accordingly Birsay Community Council approached Orkney Islands Council to enquire whether the Islands Council had had a change of heart over the future of certain war-time buildings. The Council replied positively indicating that they saw the project envisaged at Twatt as being complementary to their own scheme at Lyness. The Lyness Interpretion Centre would focus on warships, the Twatt Centre on military aircraft. This was followed immediately by a proposal to buy not only the Control Tower but also nine acres of the surrounding land, the aim being to recreate, piecemeal, certain features of the old station.

Cooperation from all parties had been so great that the writer decided to bring together many wartime reminiscences and photographs and weave them into a history of the *Sky over Scapa, 1939-45*. It was in this way that the book had its beginnings. The book is intended to complement that excellent reference book *This Great Harbour, Scapa Flow*, by William Hewison. Unlike William Hewison the writer has no particular qualifications to write a book of this nature. He was only two years old when war broke out. As a student he did help to dismantle the giant Torpedo Building at the Royal Naval Base at Lyness and translated correspondence between the contractors, Tait of Dounby and a German firm in Lübeck to where, ironically, the building was to be transported. The only other qualification of marginal relevance possessed by the writer is a certificate to say that he had failed the officer training course at the Britannia Royal Naval College, Dartmouth!

A chronological approach has been adopted within each chapter with the exception of the chapter entitled *A Posting to Orkney* where chronology is less significant. It is important for the reader to realise that this book does not vaunt war. Set in a European perspective, it merely tells the story of airmen and islanders in six tragic years of history. Without Scapa Flow, its deep-water anchorage, the war would have passed Orkney by. Instead it became, at one point, the focus of interest in Europe and, as the war progressed, well over a hundred thousand men and women from all three services must have passed through the islands, playing a part in their defence or taking temporary advantage of the enormous support structure which had been established there. If the reader can visualise from the pages of this book, something of the bustle and excitement of war and its effect on a small island community but at the same time give thought to the private, sometimes agonised lives of those who came to Scapa, then the writer will have succeeded in his aim.

Time is like a river made up of the events which happen, and its current is strong;
no sooner does anything appear than it is swept away, and another comes in its place, and will be swept away too.

Marcus Aurelius, Meditations, IV. 43

Chapter One

Early Aviators

It is not generally known that, in World War II conflict began not in the south of England, as one might expect, but in the island group to the north of Scotland known as Orkney. In his introduction to *Action Stations* (No.7), David Smith writes, "The Battle of Orkney was fought and won long before the Battle of Britain began". In the war, this small group of islands played a part out of all proportion to its size. Why was this so?

In the 14th. century, Orkney and parts of Northern Germany whence the threat now came, had been part of the same kingdom and their peoples, loyal subjects of the King of Denmark. Now fate had ranged them on opposing sides. Orkney had been given in bond to the Scottish Crown and, with the Union of the Crowns and Parliaments had become part of Great Britain. Schleswig-Holstein and Lower Saxony had become *länder* of the German State and later, of the German Reich. On 3 September 1939 Britain declared war on the Reich and already the small island community of Orkney had begun a series of preparations which were to leave no part of the islands undefended and would eventually swell its population to a remarkable 60,000. Within a year the islands had been turned into an impenetrable fortress: no other part of Britain of similar size was protected with such rigour.

To understand the frenetic activity in the air over Scapa Flow in World War II we have to look briefly at the history of Orkney. In the 1930's Orkney had a population of 22,000. It was a farming community with an economy based on beef cattle and it was known nationally for its egg production. It had no manufacturing industry, no minerals, no part of its land surface was of any strategic value and, as part of Britain, it was about as far away from Germany as it was possible to get. At first sight it would appear to be of little value to Germany - or indeed to any enemy. Despite these negative attributes, the islands had played a significant part in European history and indeed pre-history. There had been dense settlement here in Neolithic, Bronze Age and Iron Age times and even today the landscape is studded with monumental remains of highly organised societies who vied for territorial control of these low, windswept islands. Harassed

Norsemen settled here and established an Earldom, which, at its height, controlled most of the north of Scotland and western Britain. What brought these people here? For all those who have left their mark in the history of Orkney, the principal attraction must have been, not the land, good as it is, but the water. The islands offered rich fishing grounds and, in an otherwise hostile coastline, shelter.

Although the first record of warships in Orkney dates from the 12th. century, Orkney must have been associated with navies from the earliest times. The historian Adam Bede speaks of the subjugation of Orkney by the Romans and, if true, this could have been achieved only through an impressive display of naval power for it is known that the Picts themselves had a considerable fleet of warships. For these fleets, the place of assembly must have been Scapa Flow, the vast natural anchorage in the south of Orkney encircled by the Mainland of Orkney to the north and a profusion of islands to the south, east and west. 'Scapa' takes its name from the narrow neck of land to the north-east of this stretch of water and 'Flow' is the Old Norse word *flói* which we find used for bays in Iceland. The first written record of warships in Scapa Flow dates from the year 1154 when Earl Rognvald and Earl Harald brought a fleet of fourteen into the north-east corner of the anchorage. Meanwhile, to the south-east, another smaller fleet of seven warships commanded by Sweyn Asleifsson slipped in and prepared to do battle. More than a hundred years pass before we find our next record, a fleet of 120 Norse vessels anchored in Scapa Flow. In the flagship *Kristsuthin* was King Håkon Håkonsson of Norway hosted by the Earl of Orkney, taking stock of men and materials, recruiting volunteers and hiring ships in preparation for the showdown with King Alexander of Scotland over the disputed territories in the west of Scotland.

After a period of 500 years, Scapa Flow came to the fore again. During the Napoleonic Wars a marine surveyor's report looked seriously at Scapa Flow as a fine roadstead where battleships could rendezvous but there is no evidence that his proposals received consideration. However extensive use was made of Scapa Flow by merchant shipping. The reason for this was plain. Britain had two enemies: to the west the rebel colonists of North America and, to the east, France. Unarmed British merchant shipping vessels hugged the coast as far as possible to avoid the attentions of American and French privateers but, for deep water journeys, they wisely waited for naval escorts. The Compulsory Convoys Act of 1803 was introduced to protect merchant shipping and for voyages in northern Europe where timber and forest products made up much of the trade, merchantmen gathered in Longhope, a long arm of Scapa Flow and cast anchor. To guard the vessels in the bay, two defensive points which took the form of Martello Towers were built and a battery of guns erected. When the man-of-war appeared, the vessels would slip their moorings and the journey eastwards in convoy begin.

By the beginning of this century, there was intense rivalry between the navies of Britain and the rising German nation. The report of the 18th. century marine surveyor which recommended Scapa Flow as a Fleet Anchorage was brought down and dusted. Gradually there were occasional visits of naval vessels to Scapa Flow but not until April 1909 could it be truly said that 'The Fleet's in'. Under the command of Admiral Sir William May, the battleship HMS *Dreadnought* led into Scapa Flow a fleet of 82 ships, not insignificant vessels by any means, for more than half of them were destroyers. Here they remained for a month. At a stroke the population of the islands was increased by almost 70%. Wherever possible, victualling was done from the islands themselves and, for the first time, Orkney merchants were to experience the booms and slumps which have been a feature of commercial activity in Orkney in the 20th. century. The following year the Fleet returned, this time with 90 warships.

The arrival of this enormous British Fleet in Scapa Flow coincided with two remarkable feats of aviation both of which, in the long term, were to bring great changes to the islands. The one occurred, by default, at home. Three German balloonists lifted off from Munich on a December day for a short flight but, getting caught in a violent south-easterly gale, they were whipped across Europe and over the North Sea. After a journey of 1,000 miles they made landfall in the east of Orkney but not before they had lost one of their crew by first hitting the open sea. The survivors made history by being the first to arrive in Orkney by air.

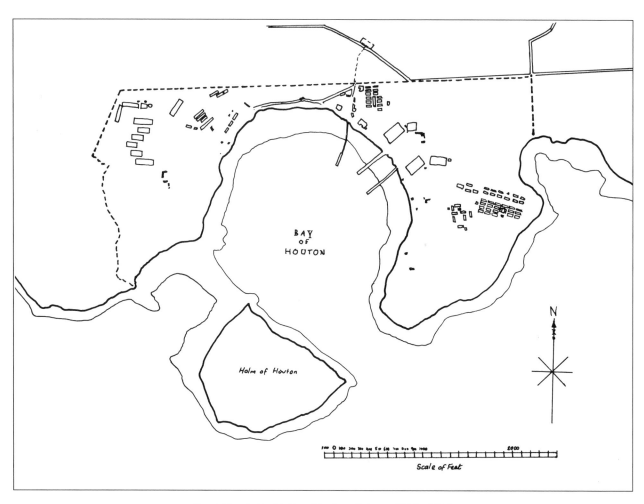

Royal Naval Air Station, Houton, Orkney, 1918 – PRO

The other feat occurred 3000 miles away in Chesapeake Bay, USA where American Eugene Ely made the first successful flight from a ship at sea. A year later he landed on a specially adapted cruiser and in this way opened up new possibilities for naval warfare. But the landing on was still technically a very risky operation and, meanwhile it was the development of the so called *hydroaeroplane* which was favoured by the American and British governments. In 1912 Lt. C R Samson RN in a Short S.27 floatplane took off from a specially extended platform over the foredeck of the battleship HMS *Africa* in Sheerness Harbour, and made a successful landing at Eastchurch. Later the aircraft landed in the sea beside the parent vessel, was winched back on board and prepared for another flight. This was the modest beginning of what later became the catapult flights of 700 Squadron of the Royal Navy which reached their peak in the middle years of World War II.

The year 1911 brought Winston Churchill to the office of First Lord of the Admiralty. The success of Samson's flight led him to believe there was a considerable future for naval aviation but Churchill considered the first obstacle in the way of its development was the name *hydroaeroplane* or,

sometimes, *hydroplane*. Churchill suggested the name seaplane and the name stuck. The Royal Flying Corps was formed in 1912, consisting of a Military Wing, a Naval Wing and a Central Flying School and in the same year the old light cruiser HMS *Hermes* was converted as a parent ship for seaplanes with platforms fore and aft for launching and stowing. In August 1913 HMS *Hermes* was in Scapa Flow with two aircraft embarked, one of British manufacture, the other French and Orcadians watched with great interest the comings and goings of the heavier than air machines, the first of many hundreds to fly over Scapa Flow. Winston Churchill, in his capacity as First Lord of the Admiralty, was in Scapa Flow at the time and was privileged to view the anchorage from above when he had a flight round Scapa Flow in one of *Hermes'* seaplanes.

On 1 August 1914, with war now inevitable, the Fleet, consisting this time of 96 warships, took refuge in Scapa Flow and was later joined by a flotilla of 18. At this time Scapa Flow was anything but a safe haven and the Fleet remained extremely jittery until all the anti-submarine booms and blockships had been put in place. Joining the Grand Fleet as it came to be known on the outbreak of war,

Airship sheds from SE – Caldale Air Station, Orkney – KENT

Observers in a basket suspended below a Kite Balloon: the observer on the right is using a telephone – copyright unknown.

Houton Kite Balloon Station, Orkney 1918 – KENT

five aircraft arrived, 3 seaplanes and two aeroplanes. They were aircraft of the newly formed Royal Naval Air Service which had grown out of the earlier so called Naval Wing. A Fleet Aircraft Repair Base was set up near the farm of Nether Scapa in the North-East corner of the anchorage but in the most exposed place possible, wide open to gales from the south-west. Within three months one such gale struck the islands doing extensive damage not only to the temporary buildings but also to the aircraft. A more sheltered repair facility was sought and this led to the construction of a base at Houton in the north of Scapa Flow although it did not become operational until 1917.

Another development in aerial reconnaissance made its mark in Orkney. This was the so called 'kite balloon'. It was merely an extension of the long established observation post on the crow's nest. A balloon, beneath which hung a basket with an observer, was secured to a ship with a long hawser. At Caldale to the west of Kirkwall, huge hangars, originally intended to house and maintain airships were adapted to service and inflate these balloons. Balloons of a type used to protect warships from aerial attack were also serviced here: towards the end of the war this establishment had a staff of almost 200. The remains of this large station is still in evidence. Yet another kite balloon station was built at Houton in Orphir. Apparently an attractive proposition from the observer's point of view, kite observation balloons were not a success. They could scarcely ever be flown in windy Orkney and, moreover, could be lethal when an electrical storm threatened since the storm tended to discharge through the balloon which of course was hydrogen filled. Several were ignited by lightning in Scapa Flow, though the observers, remarkably, survived. One observer was less fortunate: the hawser supporting the kite sheared in the strong wind and balloon, basket and observer disappeared into the northern mists. Although a parachute was a standard piece of equipment in such balloons in case it was brought down by gunfire, the heavy clothing worn by the observer to protect him against atmospheric cold would have made survival in the cold North Sea impossible.

Meanwhile seaplane development continued apace with the commissioning of HMS *Campania* as an aircraft carrier in 1915. At first capable of carrying six seaplanes she was later modified to carry twelve and her inclined deck extended to 200 feet. Much of the early experimental work with this carrier was carried out in Scapa Flow. Seaplanes were clumsy, slow and unmanoeuvrable compared with aeroplanes and it was an experiment by Royal Naval pilots in Scapa Flow itself which was, much later, to spike the development of the seaplane as a ship-borne aircraft.

In Scapa Flow in 1917, one of the most significant advances in naval aviation was made. HMS *Furious* had been launched in 1916 as a light battle cruiser and during later construction, was modified as an aircraft carrier though initially the facilities she offered aviators were extremely primitive being equipped only with a flying-off deck forward. When *Furious* arrived in Scapa, pilots in their Sopwith Pups could now get plenty of practice flying off but there was one great handicap. There

Fellow pilots holding back the aircraft as Squadron Commander Dunning in a Sopwith Pup lands safely on HMS Furious in Scapa Flow in 1917. This was the first ever landing on a vessel underway – copyright unknown

Despite desperate attempts by fellow officers, Squadron Commander Dunning goes over the side and is killed while attempting a second landing on HMS Furious in Scapa Flow – copyright unknown

was no airstrip anywhere in Orkney where naval aeroplanes (as distinct from seaplanes) could land. The only choice for the Sopwith pilot was to ditch or to find a reasonably flat piece of land where he could park his aeroplane until it was retrieved. To facilitate more flexible use of aeroplanes, the urgent need for a land base became apparent and a small naval airfield was established at Smoogro on the north coast of Scapa Flow. Pilots were able to get much needed flying practice from this airfield for the Fleet was in Scapa Flow for long periods of time. Now *Furious* was a fast warship, capable of a top speed of 31 knots in the open sea and it occurred to the Smoogro pilots that, if the carrier sailed into a reasonably strong natural wind of around 25 knots, it might be possible to land on the flying-off deck. It was decided to attempt something which had never been done anywhere in the world before - a landing on the deck of a moving carrier. *Furious* was not the ideal vessel to land on for the deck was after all a flying off deck and was of course placed immediately in front of the funnels. The aviator would have not only to negotiate the funnels but also to pilot his frail craft through the extreme turbulence around that part of the vessel. Neither was Scapa Flow the ideal place for such an experiment. The maximum stretch of water was a little over ten miles and it would have taken some time for the carrier to get up speed - and some time for it to slow down. Moreover the anchorage was crowded with warships. At least wave height in the anchorage was normally fairly low and there would have been little heave on *Furious'* landing platform. Ideally the experiment should have been conducted in the open sea but this would have run the risk of a U-boat attack.

On 5 August 1917 aircraftmen prepared Squadron Commander Edwin Dunning's Sopwith Pup for the epic flight. Carrier arrester wires were still unheard of so grappling ropes were fixed to the wing struts to enable the deckhands to restrain the aircraft if it touched down. Conditions were not ideal when he took off from Smoogro: the natural wind speed was only 21 knots and, to make his task more difficult, *Furious'* maximum attainable speed was only 26 knots. He did however land on successfully with the help of the grappling party and history was made. Tragically, in a second attempt five days later his aircraft went over the side and he was drowned. His experiment had not been in vain however. A Committee of Enquiry into Naval Aviation meeting in 1917 recommended that the minimum length of a

Houton Seaplane Station – KENT

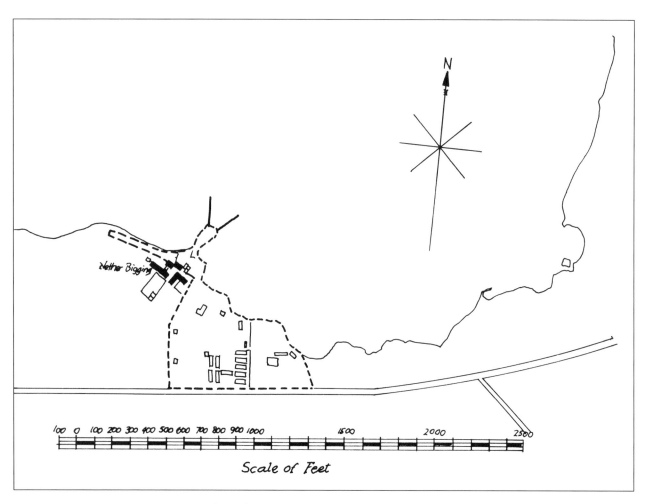

Royal Naval Air Station, Stenness, Orkney, 1918 – PRO

landing deck should be 300 feet (91.4m) and no less than the full width of the vessel. Thus was born the first flush-deck carrier, the *Argus* and the way was open for development of Royal Naval aeroplanes which were faster, lighter, more manouevrable and with longer endurance.

The Royal Navy still considered that the seaplane had a vital role to play as a land-based aircraft and consequently two seaplane bases were built in Orkney, one in Stenness, the other in Orphir. The Stenness base was established on the southern shore of the Stenness Loch beside the farm of Netherbigging. Flights 309, 310 and 311, consisting of 18 Felixstowe F3 seaplanes operated from here and the staff of 200 were billeted partly in the Standing Stones Hotel and partly in a hutted camp. The hotel became the Headquarters of the Royal Naval Air Service serving Scapa Flow. However the Stenness Loch proved too shallow and too exposed for a seaplane base and eventually the more sheltered base at Houton in Orphir on the edge of Scapa Flow was favoured. Originally intended only as a repair and maintenance base, Houton, when fully developed had slipways, hangars, concrete aprons, repair shops, its own generating plant and accommodation for a staff of 600. Apart from a

good number of Short seaplanes, 36 Large America type Curtiss flying boats were planned for this station: at one point 25 flying boats could certainly be mustered though they were not by any means always serviceable. The presence of so many of these massive machines with wing-spans of almost 100 feet (30m.) must have been an impressive sight at Scapa in these early days of aviation. After the seaplane base was moved to Houton, the Standing Stones Hotel in Stenness, though now inconveniently placed, was retained as the Headquarters of the Naval Air Service.

The purpose of the seaplane base was to provide anti-submarine patrols in the waters to the north of Orkney, between North Ronaldsay and Fair Isle. To counter the menace of German U-boats, an anti-submarine boom had been placed across the English Channel and now to gain access to the Atlantic, U-boats took the northern route through the Fair Isle Channel. Usually in the faint light of dusk or dawn, they would break water and check their compasses by Fair Isle since their compasses were still not gyroscopic. To monitor the reported positions of U-boats, a large map of the North Atlantic covered the wall in the Operations Room at the Headquarters in Stenness, and on it were plotted the positions of British and enemy submarines. The Headquarters was commanded by Captain Oliver Swan, (later Air Vice-Marshal), a pioneer of seaplane development. Curtiss and Felixstowe flying boats were used on patrols, some of which lasted more than five hours. Few could have envied the lot of the pilots of these frail aircraft in open cockpits, usually in inclement weather, their only lifeline initially being the two obligatory pigeons which they carried with them in a basket and which, in an emergency, flew back to the pigeon loft at Houton. Flight Lieutenant T. Crouther Gordon records a not untypical entry in his diary:-

12 September (1918): The Admiral at Longhope called for patrols and two flying boats were despatched but it was a dreadful day for flying. The sea was rough, the wind was high and the air was very bumpy. In addition there was no U-boat to be seen. Four hundred gallons of petrol and nothing to show for it! The language of the pilots was not suitable to be recorded in my diary.

The stormy weather wreaked havoc on land too: despite the relatively sheltered position of Houton, a storm on 6 October 1918, lifted a brand new flying boat worth £14,000 (an enormous amount of money at that time) off its cradle and completely destroyed it. The planes seemed to have had little success in finding their quarry despite numerous reports of enemy submarine presence in the Fair Isle Channel. Naval aviation being in its infancy, the appropriate infrastructure to maintain an operational fleet of seaplanes had yet to be established. On one occasion there was only one flying boat available for anti-submarine patrol and an old Short seaplane had to be brought into use as well.

It is well known that, apart from its engagement with the German Navy at Jutland in 1916, the Grand Fleet rarely left the anchorage in Scapa Flow, nevertheless development of the Royal Naval Air Service in the islands went ahead. Towards the end of the war, a new airfield at Swanbister in Orphir on the northern edge of Scapa Flow was begun and, even after the Armistice, work was still progressing there. Considerable progress was made in Naval Aviation during the war and there is no doubt that Scapa Flow played a large part not only in developing roles for aircraft but also in developing new roles for warships with the advent of aerial warfare. There was still some prejudice in the Senior Service against aviators: indeed there was still evidence of this in World War II but, despite this, aircraft clearly had operational value at sea and were here to stay. The Royal Navy had 2,900 aircraft in 1918, the same year in which the world's first

Seaplanes continued to appear in Scapa in the inter-war years: here a Supermarine Southampton III, S1058 lies on the beach near the old Royal Naval Air Station at Nether Scapa in 1930 – KENT

purpose-built aircraft carrier the *Hermes* was laid down and, ironically, the same year in which the Royal Naval Air Service merged with the Royal Flying Corps to form the Royal Air Force.

By 1918 elements of the Grand Fleet had moved south to Rosyth though Scapa Flow continued to be maintained fully as a naval base. However, by November in that same year many of the warships were back again, on this occasion shepherding upwards of 70 warships of the German *Hochseeflotte* which, under the terms of the Armistice were to be interned in an Allied port. It was a remarkable assemblage of warships. Overhead flew an escort of Royal Naval planes from the Air Station at Houton. As the world was soon to learn, the German warships were, before long, to disappear beneath the surface of Scapa Flow. There was no further need for a Grand Fleet presence in the anchorage and gradually it moved south once more to Rosyth with its accompanying aircraft. At times, 100,000 Royal Naval personnel had been based in Scapa Flow and Orcadian farmers and merchants had fed them. The prosperity brought by war had now gone. Between 1922 and 1923 what had been the old Royal Naval Air Service Stations were sold off and a blighted landscape of concrete and iron remained. No one could have predicted that, within 15 years, the whole cycle would begin again with even greater intensity.

Chapter Two

The Military Airfields of Orkney

Four hundred and forty four military airfields were built in Britain during World War II. Four of these airfields were established in Orkney and five 'dummy dromes', altogether quite a number for such a small area. The Orkney airfields were extremely busy and, at their height, could launch 15 squadrons of aircraft. In this chapter we trace the convoluted evolution of these stations and their post-war history.

Early in 1938, the Directorate of the Naval Air Division suggested that a survey of sites suitable for the location of a military airfield should be undertaken in Orkney in view of the fact that Scapa Flow was intended to be used as a base for the Home Fleet in the event of possible hostilities with Germany. By August 1938, twenty-nine sites had been examined in Orkney by the Air Ministry and, of these, it was considered that Skeabrae was possibly the only suitable location. Between 15 and 21 September 1938, the Admiralty visited Orkney and considered four sites. These were Skeabrae, Hatston, Wideford near Kirkwall and Quoyburray in Tankerness. Wideford, at that time used by Scottish Airways, was considered incapable of expansion. Quoyburray was low lying, wet, and had little to recommend it. Hatston had the advantage that it could be developed in the dual role of aerodrome and seaplane base. Skeabrae might also be developed in this way, the seaplane base being established in the north end of the Harray Loch. The decision was taken to establish the first purpose built military airfield at Skeabrae and, accordingly, Mr. James Wood the proprietor of the farm of Garson in Sandwick, and Mr. John Kirkness of the farm of Hammerclait, were given verbal notice by military surveyors that their lands were to be immediately requisitioned. They were visited again in mid September by the Admiralty for an on-site assessment of the alternatives. There was no further immediate action and we find both these farmers writing to the Air Ministry in October 1938 anxious about their future. Mr. Wood was unsure whether to buy sheep to make up his breeding stock: he had no desire to buy in sheep and have to resell them immediately at a loss. Mr. Kirkness wanted an assurance that his property

would no longer be required 'now that peace seems assured'. The proprietors were not to know that, as a result of the September visit, doubts were cast in the minds of the Admiralty experts about the suitability of Skeabrae. Its remoteness from Kirkwall and the difficulties in establishing a seaplane base at the north end of the Harray Loch counted against it. Moreover Kirkwall clearly needed a proper civil airport, the Wideford site often being fogbound and incapable of extension. The intention of Scottish Airways to develop Hatston as an alternative civil airport seemed to weigh heavily in favour of this site. In December 1938, plans to develop Skeabrae were abandoned and Hatston was chosen as the first purpose-built Royal Naval Air Station in Great Britain. The Sandwick farmers could not have been very happy about the two months' delay in the reply to their letter only to be told then that their lands were no longer wanted.

The lands of Hatston extending to 320 acres were purchased by the Admiralty for £25,000 and in February 1939, work was begun on the construction of the airfield. Unlike Skeabrae, it had the added advantage that seaplanes, at that time very important in naval aviation, could land alongside. What appeared at first sight to be a difficulty - the main Kirkwall to Stromness road passed through the middle of the site - was to be used to advantage as one of four runways to be constructed. Because of the climate and the nature of the underlying soil, all runways were to have tarmacadam surfaces and, in what was surely to be a unique arrangement, the local council was contracted to construct them. For the first pilots who landed at Hatston, hard runways came as a great surprise to them for the norm at that time was the grass landing strip. Hatston was one of the first aerodromes in Britain to have a tarmacadam surface but not the first as quoted in David Smith's *Action Stations*. Gosport and Odiham in England already had bitumen surfaces in 1938. The main road was to be diverted, at the Admiralty's expense, to the south of the station. Four Bellman hangars were planned along with workshops, storage space, compass swinging bases, a magazine and tanks for 50,000 gallons of

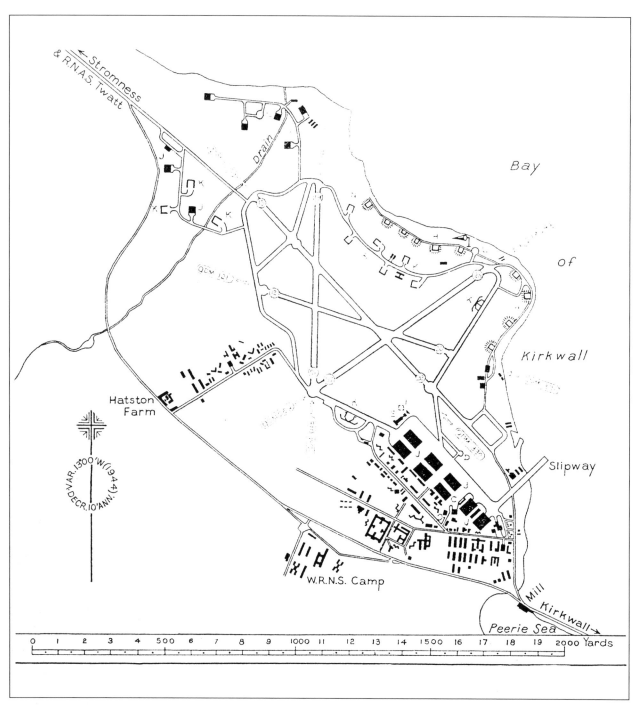

Royal Naval Air Station, Hatston – FAAM

aviation fuel. To man this station the requirements were 70 officers, 38 Chief Petty Officers, 36 Petty Officers and 290 other ratings, a complement of 434, for all of whom hutted accommodation had to be provided. All in all it was a major project for Hatston started from scratch.

On 25 August 1939, Hatston runways were considered operational and Fleet Requirement Unit, 771 Squadron moved in to begin its long association with Orkney. The very next day 800 Squadron Skuas disembarked from *Ark Royal*, the first of seventy two Royal Naval squadrons to do so in the following six years. On 2 October, the station was commissioned as HMS *Sparrowhawk*. At the

commencement of hostilities, the Royal Navy, in terms of aviation, was reasonably prepared. Churchill was not happy that there was no RAF presence to protect the Fleet in its Home Base but seemed satisfied that the Navy itself would provide two squadrons of fighter aircraft when the Fleet was in Scapa and a visit to the anchorage on 14 September 1939 confirmed his impression that this was adequate. The dramatic turn of events in October which resulted in the penetration of the Scapa defences by a U-boat and the later bombing of the Fleet caused an immediate reassessment of the position. As Churchill says in his *The Gathering Storm*,

Aerial photograph of Hatston under snow: shows clearly the main Kirkwall/Stromness road which served initially as the main runway – FAAM

These events showed how necessary it was to perfect the defences of Scapa against all forms of attack before allowing it to be used . . . On October 31st., accompanied by the First Sea Lord, I went to Scapa* to hold a second conference on these matters in Admiral Forbes' flagship. The scale of defence for Scapa upon which we now agreed included . . . substantial fighter protection . . . organised both in the Orkneys and at Wick on the mainland.

*it was in fact the Clyde [G.L.]

The immediate outcome of this was the proposal to build in Orkney a second airfield for the Royal Navy and two landing strip aerodromes for the RAF. In November 1939, the Admiralty immediately took up its option on Skeabrae and so, almost a year after they had been told their land was not wanted, the farmers of Garson, Hammerclait and Grind in Sandwick were given very short notice to leave their properties. On 8 December, the bulldozers moved in, in some cases before the farms were properly vacated. Plans for the new Skeabrae station were modest - the construction of a one squadron (12 aircraft) site. As for the RAF, the Air Ministry, Aerodrome Branch, considered sites at Grimsetter, Twatt and Birsay. Birsay was eliminated as being too exposed: Twatt was considered too near the Royal Naval Air station being developed at Skeabrae. The decision was taken to construct a station at Grimsetter in

Control Tower, Hatston with Avenger in foreground – PRO

Tankerness on the East Mainland. In the interim, RAF Coastal Command at Wick took over operational control of the northern Royal Naval squadrons - 803 Skuas and Rocs at Wick and 804 Gladiators at Hatston.

With the return of the Fleet to Scapa in March 1940, the German bombers returned too, this time in force. On 16 March, the whole of 804 Squadron from Hatston got airborne in the gathering darkness to intercept a bombing raid on Scapa Flow and, indeed, on their own station. They failed to make contact with any enemy aircraft and had great difficulty in returning to base. On Monday 8 April upwards of two dozen German bombers attacked the Flow and this time RAF Hurricanes of No.605 Squadron from Wick came to the aid of the defences. On Wednesday 10 April, the day after the German invasion of Norway, 60 enemy bombers made a determined raid on Scapa and again the Wick Hurricanes went into action. In this great air battle over Orkney, seven enemy bombers were brought down.

Despite the threat of more and bigger attacks on Scapa, perhaps even an invasion, there was still no RAF presence in Orkney and no immediate prospect either, pending the completion of

Grimsetter scheduled for the Autumn. There was a desperate need for the faster RAF fighters to be stationed locally and immediately. A solution was found by transferring the new Royal Naval Air Station at Skeabrae to the Royal Air Force. On 2 May 1940 it was handed over, in an incomplete state, to the RAF. Despite the transfer, the RAF was still dithering about the development of Skeabrae for we find that, on 14 May, a directive was sent to the Admiralty to the effect that Skeabrae was no longer needed since Castletown in Caithness was now operational. The outcome of that message is not recorded. Castletown did receive its first squadron, No.504 Hurricanes on 21 June but development of Skeabrae went ahead nevertheless, plans being modified to make it into a station capable of handling two Fighter Squadrons. Runways of Royal Naval air stations were a mere 30 yards wide and this meant extending them in width to the standard 50 yards required by the RAF. These modified plans, coupled with acute labour shortages in the islands meant that it was 15 September before the first aircraft landed at what was still a very incomplete station. By this time the Battle of Britain was at its height and so, though the RAF station was at last operational, no RAF

Hatson was situated right at the edge of the sea and the rescue launch was frequently required! Air Mechanics on board the launch in Kirkwall Bay – HAMILTON

squadrons could be spared! 804 Squadron of the Royal Navy with Grumman Martlets was called upon to fill the gap and took over the defending role. They had to wait until 7 January 1941 before they were at last relieved of their duties by No.3 Squadron of the Royal Air Force.

The Royal Navy, now one airfield short was, in turn, hard pressed to carry out its duties. Between 23 and 24 May 1940, Admiralty surveyors were already in the islands looking at the alternative sites available and, the following month, it was decided to construct a new station at Twatt in the parish of Birsay with plans to accommodate one reinforcing fighter squadron but this was very soon changed to accommodate one and a half squadrons. The landowners concerned got even less warning than their Sandwick counterparts. The farm of Hyval was to be immediately demolished followed by Festigarth, Skogar, Newhall and North Newhall. The RAF was not happy about the Royal Navy choosing a site in such close proximity to Skeabrae, the airfields being barely two miles distant. It was considered that, without some measure of Flying Control, it was inevitable that, with the wind blowing from a north-westerly or south-easterly direction aircraft landing at one station would collide with aircraft taking off at the other. The RAF proposed that it be responsible for Flying Control in the immediate area of both stations. The Royal Navy objected most strongly to this and thus began between these two services, a series of sharp exchanges. The Royal Navy could not, understandably, tolerate a situation in which a junior officer in Flying Control at Skeabrae might countermand the order of a carrier Admiral to embark his squadrons immediately. The RAF felt so strongly about the issue that they suggested the Royal Navy move to their station at Grimsetter! The argument was never resolved. Both services controlled their aircraft independently and, as a matter of fact, the only collision which occurred over Skeabrae during the war involved RAF aircraft and the only incident at Twatt was a mid-air collision between two Royal Navy planes.

Twatt was commissioned on 1 April 1941 as HMS *Tern*, a satellite of Hatston and the first aircraft, a detachment of four Sea Hurricanes of 880 Squadron landed on. At first it acted as an overflow for frontline squadrons disembarked at Hatston but, with the arrival of USS *Wasp* in Scapa Flow in April 1942 and the disembarkation of three of her squadrons for an extended period while she ferried

Walrus taxying up slipway, Hatston, 1941: in background can be seen neutral shipping brought into Kirkwall Harbour from the North Atlantic by the Royal Navy to check on contraband materials bound for Germany – FANCOURT

King George VI at Hatston, 1941: note famous Maryland in background – FANCOURT

Spitfires to beleaguered Malta, Twatt assumed a new role. Fleet Requirements Unit 771 was transferred to Twatt and was subsequently joined two months later by 700 Squadron. Previously, on 31 March, Twatt had been elevated to an independent command. Meanwhile, in the East Mainland, RAF Grimsetter became operational on 17 October 1940 as a satellite of Skeabrae and all Fighter Operations shed their Coastal Command control and were transferred from Wick to RAF Headquarters in Kirkwall. Grimsetter was used regularly by squadrons based at Skeabrae but it was not until 11 June 1942 that the first squadron, No.132 moved in.

Five decoy airfields were also constructed in Orkney during the war. On The Mainland, two were established in the parish of Birsay at Deasbreck and at the Burn of Grid. The other 'dummy dromes' were built on the island of Sanday on the Plain of Fidge, at Sacquoy Head in Rousay and at Cot-on-Hill in the south-east of Shapinsay. All these dummy airfields relied on flare paths as means of deceit and individual generating stations had to be provided. Even the large RNAS Station at Twatt did not have its own flare path until the end of the war! Some decoy stations also had dummy

fires which could be lit to deceive the enemy into believing that important targets had been hit. The enemy showed no interest in these decoy airfields: although an enormous amount of effort had gone into their planning, we find that, by September 1942, the Sanday and Rousay sites had already been abandoned. In December 1942, in Army manoeuvres, the Deasbreck facilities were accidentally shelled and destroyed. Not only did the enemy show no interest in the decoys, they showed surprisingly little interest at all in Orkney airfields. Only Hatston saw a little enemy action - and that was in the early stages of the war: Grimsetter was bombed once. Skeabrae and Twatt were left untouched.

As the war shifted its focus in Europe the functions of the stations changed. There was no likelihood of further aerial bombardment and even less of airborne invasion. The RAF, having wanted only one station in Orkney in the first place found themselves with two, one of which, Grimsetter, was, by 1943, considered surplus to their requirements. The Royal Navy on the other hand found itself from time to time hard pressed for squadron accommodation. Hatston regularly had to accommodate five squadrons of disembarked aircraft and the runways were considered inadequate for the new 845 and 846 Avenger Squadrons which were about to arrive. Twatt, with 700 Squadron and 771 Squadron both of which had the largest number of aircraft of any of the Royal Naval squadrons was crowded with aircraft and could rarely accept front line disembarkations. Consequently, on 6 July 1943, Grimsetter was transferred to the Royal Navy, initially as a satellite of Hatston but on 15 August became an independent command when it was commissioned as HMS *Robin* and a major rebuilding programme begun which would equip the Station to cope with three disembarked squadrons. The first opportunity to use the station came in September when Hatston was again swamped by aircraft, this time from the American carrier *Ranger* which joined the British Fleet at Scapa. 846 Squadron with its twelve Avengers were displaced from Hatston and took up residence at Grimsetter. By October the Royal Navy had upgraded the station with the addition of new officers' quarters, recreational block and galleys. The inadequacy of Hatston as an airfield became increasingly apparent as the war went on and with the Royal Navy now operating from three stations there was a real need to rationalise. On 30 March

1944 the proposal was made to develop Twatt as the only suitable airfield in Orkney where disembarked squadrons of Home Fleet aircraft could train together. After the arrival of 771 Squadron, Twatt had already been expanded from a one and a half to a three squadron station. New proposals included demolition of the Control Tower and the construction of a superior Fearn type tower, more squadron hangars, workshops, offices and upgrading of the accommodation to accept 1,872 personnel including 438 WRNS. A large frontline training unit accommodating three squadrons of Fighters, each with fourteen aircraft and two squadrons of Torpedo Bombers with twelve aircraft each was envisaged. To make this possible, the whole of the Fleet Requirements Unit, 771 Squadron, the largest squadron in the Royal Navy and now combined with 700 Squadron was to move to a new station. In July, the former Coastal Command station, Dounreay in Caithness was acquired for this purpose and established as a satellite of Twatt as HMS *Tern II* but as the war progressed attention shifted to the Far East and, as a consequence, the huge expansion plans for Twatt were barely implemented. On 5 December 1944 the plans were abandoned and it was decided merely to

Duke of Kent visiting Hatston, 16.05.41; being met by Capt. Fancourt and Commander Rotherham: the aircraft is a Lockheed Hudson I, N7263 – FANCOURT

make some minor cosmetic changes to the station. With the cessation of hostilities in Europe on 8 May 1945, the writing was already on the wall for Orkney's military airfields. In their quick demise there were echoes of their tortuous beginnings. No squadrons were based at Grimsetter after April 1945 and, at the end of July, the Royal Navy was happy to transfer it back to the Royal Air Force to become a satellite of Skeabrae. 846 Squadron Avengers, the last operational squadron to be based at Hatston left on 19 July for Twatt and two weeks later Hatston became a satellite of Twatt as HMS *Tern II*. With the departure of No. 451 Squadron from Skeabrae in September, Skeabrae itself came under the wing of Twatt and, for a short time the commander of Twatt was responsible for the control of four stations, Grimsetter, Skeabrae and Dounreay, in addition to his own! Hatston was soon however to become Kirkwall's first civilian airport, a position it held to 1948 when, with the arrival of Dakotas, it became necessary to transfer the airport to Grimsetter which eventually came to be known as Kirkwall Airport. Hatston airfield was taken over by Kirkwall Town Council and the Officers' and Ratings'

Skeabrae; aerial photograph from 5,000 feet; 29.04.43: at that time No. 66 Spitfire Squadron, No. 234 Spitfire Squadron and 1476 Anson Advanced Ship Recognition Flight were based there – HORNE

RAF Skeabrae showing, encircled, defended positions – HORNE

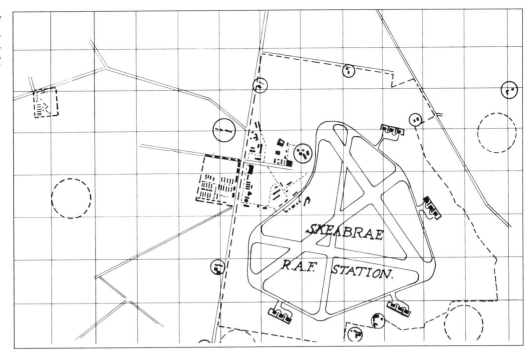

Aerial photograph of Grimsetter, 12.02.45 – FAAM

accommodation was used to solve the town's immediate post-war housing problem. Some of the hangars were converted to civilian use and the idea gradually developed of Hatston as Orkney's first Industrial Estate. Twatt became a reserve station under Lossiemouth until 1949 when both it and its satellite Skeabrae were placed on a Care and Maintenance basis. But an end was in sight. With the announcement in June 1956 of the closure of Scapa Flow Royal Naval Base, there was clearly no future for the Royal Naval Air Stations. Both Skeabrae and Twatt were sold off in 1957. All timber and Nissen buildings were removed and the land reverted to what could only be described as limited agricultural use because of the vast amount of concrete and brickwork left on the airfields. But Skeabrae and Twatt were not dead by any means - only apparently unconscious for in the 1970's military surveyors again appeared warning the new proprietors and indeed the contiguous proprietors that their lands were to be requisitioned for a new airfield which this time would combine both the old RAF and Fleet Air Arm Stations. At that time relations between Britain and Iceland were strained over fishing rights, the so called 'Cod War' and it was feared that NATO was to be asked to pull out of its base at Keflavik. The new NATO base was to be in Orkney. The fishing dispute was finally solved and the plan to redevelop Skeabrae and

Twatt abandoned. Shortly afterwards with the advent of North Sea oil both airfields came to the fore again when it was planned to construct a huge airfield there to handle trans-Atlantic oil-related freight. Like the many schemes which mushroomed at this time, the trans-Atlantic air freight port came to nothing. In the mid 1980's when oil prices were high and the development of the fields to the west of Orkney became a real possibility, the British Helicopter Advisory Board recommended that Twatt be considered as a helicopter base. Unfortunately the price of oil dropped steeply curtailing further offshore exploration and so Twatt airfield, the first British proving ground of helicopters, was denied a new lease of life. Meanwhile memories of Skeabrae airfield are kept alive by those dissatisfied with the present civil airport at Grimsetter. As a site for a civil airport, Grimsetter was a bad choice, its only advantage being proximity to Kirkwall. A serious disadvantage is experienced in April and May when the warmer waters of the Atlantic meet the cold North Sea and a dense bank of fog creeps in over the eastern part of the archipelago closing Kirkwall Airport. Meanwhile Skeabrae and, indeed, Twatt, to the west of the long chain of hills which act as a barrier to the fog, bask in sunshine! The cost of a new civil airport serving only the islands would be prohibitive and it seems that, despite this

RNAS Grimsetter – FAAM

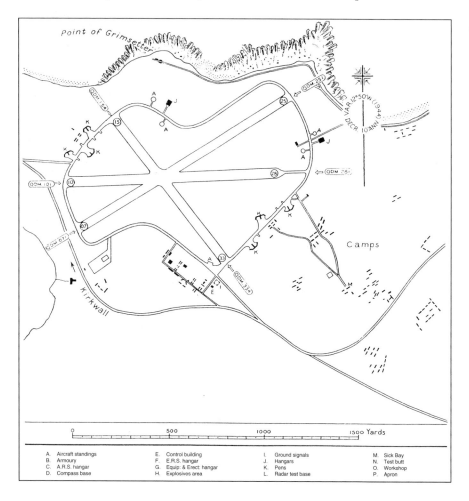

A.	Aircraft standings	E.	Control building	I.	Ground signals	M. Sick Bay
B.	Armoury	F.	E.R.S. hangar	J.	Hangars	N. Test butt
C.	A.R.S. hangar	G.	Equip: & Erect: hangar	K.	Pens	O. Workshop
D.	Compass base	H.	Explosives area	L.	Radar test base	P. Apron

Aerial photograph of Twatt Royal Naval Air Station. – FAAM

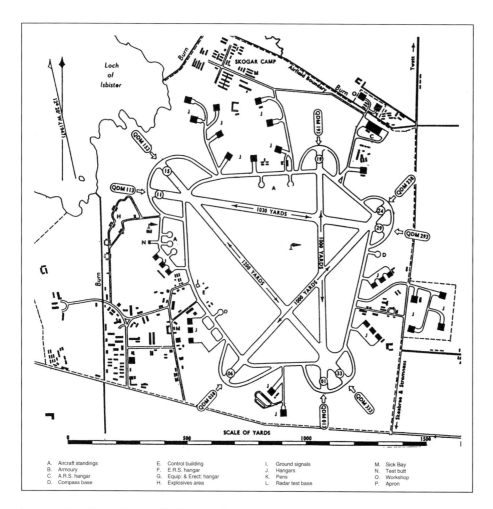

A. Aircraft standings   E. Control building   I. Ground signals   M. Sick Bay
B. Armoury   F. E.R.S. hangar   J. Hangars   N. Test butt
C. A.R.S. hangar   G. Equip: & Erect: hangar   K. Pens   O. Workshop
D. Compass base   H. Explosives area   L. Radar test base   P. Apron

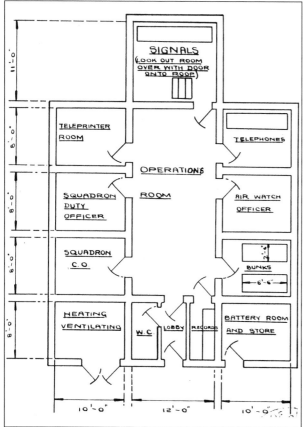

*Plan of Control Tower (Protected Control Building or 'PCB'),
Twatt, 1940 – PRO*

handicap, the airport is likely to remain to the east of Kirkwall.

In 1986 Government monies could be directed to the removal of wartime relics and consequently, with the permission of the new landowners, the final demolition process was begun. Ironically what had been an eyesore for forty years was, by this time, being seen by some people in a completely new light. So, when the parish of Birsay, a community which had been totally involved in the war objected to the demolition of Twatt airfield, the Orkney Islands Council was taken aback. An appeal was made for the retention of the Control Tower at least to form the basis of a small museum. A sympathetic Council agreed and, at the eleventh hour, when the demolition charges were already implanted, a stay of execution was granted. This triumph was followed by an immediate reversal of Council policy. The Control Tower was to be preserved as an Interpretation Centre to commemorate the work of both the Royal Navy and the RAF in Orkney and, on the surrounding nine acres of land, parts of the station were to be reconstructed, piecemeal. This generous gesture by the Islands' Council meant that few tears were shed when, half a century after its stormy birth, the Control Tower of nearby Skeabrae, the last remaining structure on that airfield, was razed to the ground.

Control Tower, Twatt, January 1945: it was a PCB or Protected Control Building: underneath lay a mass-concrete Communications Block: the two flags flying are the Affirmative Flying flag and the Negative Flying flag: when flown together in this photograph it was interpreted by pilots and TAG's as "You can fly if you don't want to"! The chequered vehicle is a crash tender –
PEMBERTON

Twatt Airfield 1945, looking South-East: the Control Tower is on the extreme right: there are four Boston bombers on the tarmac – HILL

Wrens inside the Control Tower, Twatt, 10.06.45: standing, with the field glasses is L/Wren Radio Mechanic Iris Turner who married Len Page, helicopter pilot – PAGE

Result of a mid-air collision at Twatt between Roc piloted by Lt. Tony Thackard and Henley piloted by Sub/Lt. Ted Gilberd: what appears to be a wing of the Roc is in fact the tail plane of the Henley: 12.03.43 – BURKE

Flying Control Officer Sub.Lt. Paul Congdon in Control Tower, March 1944 – PEMBERTON

Four Blackstone Diesel engines in the Power Station at Linklater in Sandwick: this station served both Skeabrae and Twatt – HILL

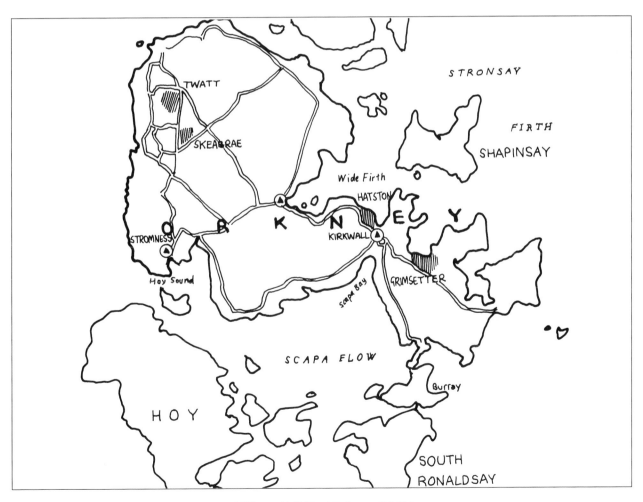

Military Airfields of Orkney – FAAM

In the Front Line

The harbingers of war knocked early on Orcadian doors. In 1936 surveyors on the island of Hoy explored the possibilities of siting fuel tanks there and a year later surface tanks with 100,000 gallon capacity were constructed near Lyness. In June 1938, the first submarine booms were placed in position in Scapa Flow and in September the Commander-in-Chief of the Home Fleet, Admiral Forbes, hitherto in a position to choose between Rosyth and Scapa Flow as the base of the Home Fleet, cast the die in favour of Scapa Flow. Farmers in the parish of Sandwick were told that their lands were to be immediately requisitioned for an airfield.

To Orcadians it was clear that Britain was on a war footing but, despite the obvious preparations, life went on in its usual unhurried style, after all wasn't Orkney just about as far away from German soil as it was possible to get? So, in their customary leisurely way, Orkney County Council started to convert a main road into the Royal Navy's first purpose-built runway and Orcadians went about their age old crafts of raising cattle, cutting peat, mowing meadow hay, buying and selling. In the endless summer days of 1939, little did they know that the Air Staff now predicted that the Luftwaffe were capable of dropping over 400 tons of bombs in Orkney in one day and, before long, Orcadians would be in the front line.

800 Squadron Skua, L2533 taking off from Ark Royal, 1939 – STEVENS

By 25 August 1939, Hatston airfield was considered operational: 771 Squadron Fleet Requirements Unit moved in and, the next day, Skuas of 800 Squadron disembarked from HMS *Ark Royal*. By 31 August there were 44 warships in Scapa Flow and, with the invasion of Poland on 1 September, most of them put to sea including the *Ark Royal* with its Skua squadron: the pawns in the war game were taking up position. On Sunday 3 September, war was declared. There was little stir among Orcadians: the story is told that when a venerable Stromnessian learned of the outbreak of war, he remarked, "My, thir gotten a graand day fur hid". By contrast there was a flurry of activity around the great battleship HMS *Nelson* which had been left to guard the Flow. A crated consignment was lowered into an awaiting drifter which ploughed through a choppy Flow to Scrabster. A heavily guarded truck drew up and sped the case to Thurso where the vaults of the National Bank were already open and waiting. The doors were firmly shut: at least the uniform of Admiral Nelson was safe!

At 10 pm on 5 September, Churchill held a conference on Scapa Flow. In his book *The Gathering Storm* he says:-

There were now in 1939 two dangers to be considered: the first, the old one of submarine incursion; the second, the new one of the air. I was surprised to learn at my conference that more precautions had not been taken in both cases to prepare the defences against modern forms of attack . . . The new danger from the air had been almost entirely ignored. Except for two batteries of anti-aircraft to defend the naval oil tanks at Hoy and the destroyer anchorage, there were no air defences at Scapa. One airfield near Kirkwall was available for the use of naval aircraft when the Fleet was present, but no provision had been made for immediate RAF participation in the defence and the shore radar station, although operative, was not wholly effective. Plans for basing two RAF fighter squadrons at Wick had been approved but this measure could not become effective before 1940. I called for an immediate plan of action. Our air defence was so strained, our resources so limited, and our vulnerable points . . . including all vast London - so numerous, that it was no use asking for much. On the other hand protection from air attack was now needed only for five or six great ships, each carrying a powerful anti-aircraft armament of its own. To keep things going, the Admiralty undertook to provide two squadrons of naval fighter aircraft whilst the Fleet was in Scapa . . . I felt it my duty to visit Scapa at the earliest moment . . .

and so he did on 15 and 16 September. His heart must have sunk when he arrived back in London to be told that the aircraft carrier HMS *Courageous* had been torpedoed in the Bristol Channel with the loss of 500 lives. Worse was to come.

Two weeks later, on 1 October 803 Squadron equipped with Skua fighter dive-bombers flew off *Ark Royal* and took up station at Hatston to protect Scapa Flow against aerial attack. On 6 October they were inspected by King George VI who, earlier in the day, had sped into the safety of Scapa Flow in the cruiser HMS *Aurora* with a large destroyer escort. But was Scapa really safe? Between 9 and 12

October, vapour trails criss- crossing the sky high above Scapa signalled the arrival of German reconnaissance aircraft. Dönitz had requested intelligence on the number of warships in the base and the aerial photographs showed an aircraft carrier, five heavy ships and ten cruisers. On October 14, tragedy struck and Orcadians heard the resounding booms of German munitions only half a mile from their shores. U-47 under the command of Lieutenant-Commander Günther Prien, had slipped into the anchorage through a partially blocked channel and one hour later the battle cruiser HMS *Royal Oak* went to the bottom of Scapa Flow with the loss of over 800 men. Most of the Home Fleet with the exception of HMS *Iron Duke*, the flagship of the Admiral commanding Orkney and Shetland, quickly put to sea and dispersed, seeking shelter in a variety of Scottish sea lochs and estuaries. Despite all the lessons learned in World War I Scapa Flow defences could be breached from the sea. Was it safe from air attack?

On 17 October the Luftwaffe struck. It was no Air Show by any means. Only four Junkers 88 bombers of this massive army of the air made the 900 mile journey from Sylt. Diving in from 11000 feet they bombed and sank HMS *Iron Duke* but not without loss. The first enemy aircraft of the war to fall to anti-aircraft fire was shot down by Orkney gunners over Hoy and the only surviving member of the crew taken prisoner. Three hours later a more threatening formation of 15 high level bombers arrived and released their bombs over Scapa Flow, narrowly missing the 12000 ton accommodation liner *Voltaire*. At this stage in the war only military targets were attacked but one bomb fell, by mistake, on the island of Hoy, the first part of the British Isles to be hit by a German bomb in World War II. From this small beginning, it was difficult to believe that, in under a year, with the Battle of Britain at its height, 372 bombers escorted by 642 fighters would attack London . . . Mercifully Orkney was far beyond fighter support range. But what of the Royal Navy's own fighters in this engagement? The slow Skuas of 803 Squadron at Hatston made no contact with the enemy.

On 31 October Churchill held a conference with Admiral Forbes at his temporary Headquarters in the Clyde. Both were resolved to retain Scapa as the base of the Home Fleet: new defence measures included, among other things:

substantial fighter protection . . . organised both in the Orkneys and at Wick on the mainland.

As a matter of fact Churchill was not making any new request. He had previously asked for two fighter squadrons to defend Scapa and so far only one, which had proved to be completely inadequate, had been provided. Another month was to pass before the second squadron, 804 with

Gladiators was formed at Hatston. Meanwhile, in a juggling operation, 803 Squadron was moved alternately between RNAS Hatston and RAF Wick on the other side of the Pentland Firth until finally they both came together at Hatston in early February 1940.

Reinforcement of Scapa Flow defences went on apace. November gales were the first enemy to test the structures. Radar and wireless masts were blown down. Referring to this gale Captain Loriston-Clarke R.N. in his short history of Hatston written for the Flag Officer, Orkney at the end of the war writes wryly,

It was a matter of departmental pride that the Meteorological Hydrogen Balloon Filling Tent was the last to become airborne.

As for the squadrons, they were persistently airborne maintaining regular patrols in case, in the absence of warships, the defences themselves, especially the submarine boom nets and Hatston airfield came under attack. Squadron readiness still left something to be desired. The pilots of 804 Squadron lived in the luxury of an hotel in a narrow street a mile from the station, an altogether hopeless arrangement. Imagine the enemy pounding away at the naval base while the pilots cycled to the airfield! Some luxury was sacrificed when the whole squadron moved on to the airfield but it was then possible to have a flight of three at immediate readiness, one at readiness, one at stand-by and the fourth off duty. Sightings of German aircraft were few but on 22 November 1939 a reconnaissance aircraft passed low over Hatston station!

In December 1939 Wick became a Sector Station with headquarters in a primary school classroom. It controlled all fighter operations over Scapa Flow including the Royal Navy squadrons at Hatston. On 28 December the first accident involving British aircraft occurred when two Sea Gladiators of 804 Squadron collided and the Commanding Officer, Captain R T Partridge had to bale out when his aircraft became uncontrollable. The first fatal accident occurred two weeks later when a Skua of 803 Squadron spun in off a turn near Stronsay killing the midshipman pilot and his air gunner.

In January, anticipating a return of the Fleet, German reconnaissance was stepped up and when weather conditions were right, almost daily flights appeared, unfortunately far beyond the interception capabilities of 803 and 804 Squadrons. On the ground, British squadron strength was increasing with the arrival of 800 Squadron disembarked from HMS *Ark Royal* in mid February and the positioning of two squadrons of RAF aircraft, Nos. 43 and 605 at Wick. To guard against dive-bombers, 950 Barrage Balloon Squadron of the RAF moved to Scapa: initially capable of flying over fifty balloons this squadron grew to become the largest in Britain with a capability of flying over 80 balloons most of which

were based on land but others were on trawlers which were anchored at strategic points in Scapa Flow. Anti-submarine patrols were also stepped up in early 1940 when a number of merchant ships were torpedoed in Orkney waters. Off Copinsay the U-57 sank the 5000 ton steamer *Loch Maddy* bound from Vancouver to Leith with a cargo of wheat. Later the same submarine and in the same location torpedoed the *Daghestan*, a merchant vessel of 5000 tons. The U-23 torpedoed the 10000 ton Danish tanker *Danmark* as she lay at anchor in Inganess Bay. Despite frequent patrols there were no successful spottings of submarines by the Skua and Sea Gladiator squadrons based at Hatston.

By early March, every defensive precaution considered necessary had been taken. On 6 March HMS *Hood* arrived at Scapa from Rosyth and, the next day, Churchill embarked on the flagship HMS *Rodney* in the Clyde for the voyage back to the base of the Home Fleet. It must have been an impressive sight as five capital ships, a cruiser squadron and twenty destroyers sailed north through the Minches. But any doubts Churchill might have had about the reduced capabilities of the Luftwaffe in the highly defended Scapa area were immediately dispelled when German aircraft dropped mines in the approaches to the base and brought the Fleet to a standstill off Orkney for twenty four hours. Churchill had to transfer to a destroyer for a speedy passage to Scapa and in the middle of this operation an air raid warning went and the warships swung into action stations. Churchill was impressed . . .

the whole ship flashed into activity as all the ack-ack batteries were manned and other measures were taken.

In the event the aircraft did not appear but the Premier must have been left in no doubt that he was in the front line.

Churchill was impressed by the security at Scapa too. Orkney had been turned into a so called 'Protected Area': it was impossible for any civilian to enter or leave the islands without a special pass. In addition to the barrage balloons, the five squadrons of fighter aircraft at the ready and the Fleet's own guns, two new airfields were under construction, 52 Heavy Anti-Aircraft guns and 20 Light Anti-aircraft guns were in position and manned by almost 10000 troops. In his *The Gathering Storm* Churchill wrote,

more than six months of constant exertion and the highest priorities had repaired the peace-time neglect.

It took German intelligence one week to assess the new military situation and adopt counter measures. The Allies had no knowledge at the time of Germany's intention to invade Norway and the absolute necessity for the enemy to destroy not only the Home Fleet but the base itself which, with the occupation of Norway, would lie a mere three hundred miles from German territory.

Meanwhile in Orkney, the week ending Saturday 16 March had been windy and practically all the barrage balloons had been grounded. This was unfortunate because in the gathering darkness Shetland radar picked up what was clearly a formation of enemy aircraft approaching Orkney from the east. Ten minutes later they flew in low over Scapa Flow and Hatston Royal Naval Air Station. Estimates put the number of aircraft as high as 35, mostly Heinkel 111's, but because of the twilight conditions, it was difficult to be precise. A hundred high explosive and incendiary bombs fell on land, half of them in error in the parish of Stenness where James Isbister, the first of many British civilians to die in the war, was killed. Most of the other bombs fell near Hatston blasting eight foot wide craters and miraculously just missing the bomb dump. The only casualty was one of the ground crew of 800 Squadron, Hatston, out walking a mile from base who was hit in the head by shrapnel. The attack on the Scapa Flow was more successful. The cruiser HMS *Norfolk* was hit and holed, three of her officers were killed and six ratings injured. Three days later Whitleys and Hampdens of Bomber Command launched a retaliatory attack on a German land target striking at the minelaying seaplane base at Hörnum on the island of Sylt. These were the opening shots in bombing campaigns which would soon engulf most of Europe.

The attack on the Scapa area lasted three quarters of an hour. Despite extensive anti-aircraft fire from the Fleet and the shore batteries supported by searchlights, no enemy aircraft were shot down. As for the fighter defences, their performance was very poor. The RAF squadrons from Wick made no contact at all. The Gladiators and Skuas from Hatston were scrambled with the same lack of success. In his book *Operation Skua*, Major R T Partridge wrote,

The whole squadron (804) got airborne but, in the gathering darkness, no contacts were made and we all had a hell of a job landing back at the airfield as there were no flares or runway lighting.

Both the Royal Navy and RAF blamed inadequate cover from Netherbutton Radar Station which was not surprising because in his November conference with Admiral Forbes the C-in-C of the Home Fleet, Churchill had attached the lowest priority to radar. The defences had been tested and had been found to be inadequate: clearly the capabilities of the Luftwaffe had been underestimated. On 19 and 20 March, Admiral Forbes received instructions to put to sea with the whole of the Home Fleet because of the danger of a night attack when the moon was full.

A solution to aerial bombardment, now apparently the most serious threat, was immediately sought.

Until shore based radar could be improved, a warship linked to the shore batteries and Fighter Control and with up-to- date radar was to be positioned in Scapa Flow. The guns of the Fleet and shore stations, instead of aiming at individual targets were now to fire a three minute barrage, virtually a continuous wall of shellfire on the approach of enemy aircraft. Thus was born the famous 'Scapa Barrage', probably the loudest sustained noise that has ever been heard in Britain! Meanwhile German aircraft kept their distance but the staff of Hatston Royal Naval Air Station feared the worst when a series of horrendous explosions rocked their establishment and the nearby town of Kirkwall. Believing it to be another German attack the whole airfield was in confusion as riggers scrambled to get their aircraft ready. But the unseen enemy on this occasion was the Orkney wind. Two Air Fitters had been returning bombs to the bomb dump: apparently the wind had turned the vanes of one to make it live and the whole dump with nineteen 100lb. bombs and one 500 lb. bomb had gone up. One fitter was killed instantly and the other had a miraculous escape.

Scapa Barrage was tested on 2 April when 12 Heinkel bombers approached Scapa Flow again at dusk. The formation immediately broke up on meeting the wall of fire. The attack lasted a mere ten minutes and no damage was done. Six days later on 8 April yet another twilight attack was made, on this occasion with 24 bombers flying between 12000 and 20000 feet to avoid the barrage. By this time the new radar was in place and the aircraft were picked up 80 miles out to sea. They were intercepted first by No.43 Squadron Hurricanes from Wick and in the ensuing dogfights three Heinkels were shot down. The remainder succeeded in reaching Scapa where they attempted to bomb Lyness and the boom defences but intense gunfire brought down another four, one of the Heinkels limping to Wick airfield where it force-landed with two dead crewmen. This raid was a prelude to the invasion of Norway though no one knew it at the time. The position of Orkney and Scapa Flow now assumed critical importance. The front was moving nearer. On 10 April, the boot was on the other foot. An attack on the German Fleet in Norway was planned, not on this occasion at the highest level in the Admiralty but in the Operations Room at Hatston Royal Naval Air Station by Lieutenant William Lucy, Officer Commanding 803 Squadron at Hatston. A fearless officer he was clearly sick of the endless routine of convoy patrols and of chasing enemy aircraft which he had no hope of catching. He had read intelligence reports of a German cruiser in Bergen harbour and succeeded in persuading Major R T Partridge, who was by this time Officer Commanding 800 Squadron to take part in a dive bombing raid on Bergen. The Commanding Officer of the station gave his approval and, at 5am on the morning of 10 April, 16 heavily armed Skuas took off from Hatston on an extremely risky mission. Meeting only light anti-aircraft fire the 16 aircraft made a simultaneous attack on what turned out to be the cruiser *Königsberg* in Bergen harbour. Fortunately the attack was completely successful. The raid made history for the *Königsberg* was the first major warship ever to be sunk by aircraft. The mission was not without loss. Roy Stevens, an armourer attached to 800 Squadron writes:-

It was a long time before we were warned to stand by to receive our aircraft back at Hatston. They arrived in formation, circled and took up approach positions, touching down in turn and taxying up to the hangar. Two Skuas were missing. One which returned had had a large chunk of its starboard tail-plane shot away - by its own gunner! In another, the observer had just stood up over the target area to mark the bomb's effect when a bullet came up through the seat and made its exit through the roof. He was a lucky chap. One of the missing Skuas had not been seen since the attack went in: the other had disappeared from the formation in cloud during the return journey so both were presumed lost. We did our rearming jobs and hung round just in case one or both turned up. Time went by and eventually the fitters said that the Skua's endurance limit had gone so we might as well pack up and leave. Then we heard it - a Skua's engine - and there it was a Skua coming towards Hatston. Straight in it came on to the grass and before it could taxi to the hangar, the engine stopped for lack of petrol. This was the aircraft which got lost over Bergen. The other was never seen again. This raid, the first of many, cost us one aircraft and its gallant crew.

Type 277S Radar, South Ronaldsay – PRO

Although the operation was successful, the timing was unfortunate because the Germans had plans of their own for 10 April. Several German reconnaissance aircraft arrived in the late afternoon flying quite low. Both 800 and 803 Squadrons were resting after their mission and it fell to 804 Squadron Gladiators from Hatston and No.605 Squadron Hurricanes from Wick to intercept. 804 Squadron diary for 10 April reads:-

A tremendous day for HMS *Sparrowhawk*, the first and we hope by no means the last. 804 Squadron began their fun at 16.05 hours when Yellow Section flew off to Copinsay. There were a great many plots on the board, the weather fine with layers of cloud varying in density up to about 10,000 feet. About 16.40 hours, P/O Sabey saw a Do17 and the section gave chase. Sub.Lt. Fell got in a burst at about 500 yds. as the Do17 disappeared into the cloud but followed him in. P/O Peacock went in above the cloud and as he came out so did the Do17, 400 yds. away. Peacock got in a burst before the enemy aircraft dived away back into the clouds. We were later informed that Do17 was crying SOS with a leaking petrol tank and did not reach his base.

At 16.45 hours Red Section was sent to patrol between Copinsay and Burray. As soon as it got there, Carver saw a Heinkel 111K about ten miles east going north-east. Hot pursuit was begun and as the Section followed, Hurricanes could be seen on the cloud-dodging Heinkel's tail. After a few minutes the enemy aircraft began climbing, twisting and diving. By the time Red Section arrived and got within range, 43 Squadron had done their job. The enemy aircraft's motors were idling and he dived down to 20 feet over the sea. For two or three miles, he held at 20 feet with a dark oil streak trailing behind him on the sea and finally flopped, port wing first. Six Hurricanes and Red Section flew around the wreck as three of the crew swam for it.

At dusk the radar picked up formations of 60 German bombers coming in from the east. They turned out to be He 111's and Ju88's. Again 800 and 803 Squadrons were out of commission and 804 Squadron Gladiators went out to meet the attackers. The Squadron diary records the contribution of the Fleet Air Arm in this, the greatest of the air battles over Orkney:-

At 20.45 hours, the evening blitzkrieg began. Red were scrambled to Copinsay where 15 - 20 enemy aircraft were reported approaching from the east at 18,000 feet between Copinsay and Burray. By 21.00 hours all Sections were in the sky and the party had started, the guns putting up an ugly barrage. Yellow had the first chase after an enemy aircraft which was in a long dive towards Kirkwall and which peppered Kirkwall and Hatston with front guns. Yellow Section could not, unfortunately, keep pace though P/O Sabey optimistically gave the enemy aircraft a burst at very long range in order to ease his repressed fighting spirit.

At 21.00 hours Red Section dived down to 11,000 feet about four miles east of Burray. Unfortunately Red 2 was left behind in the dive. As soon as they flattened out, a bomber crossed 200 yds. ahead from port to starboard. Carver and Ogilvy turned, pursued and loosed off nearly all ammunition, gradually closing in from 300 to 200 yards. The enemy fired back narrowly and finally turned and dived away to the south-east, with smoke coming from his starboard motor.

During this party, Blue Section were lurking further west and came galloping up on seeing the shooting.

Plenty of enemy aircraft were coming in so Smee chose a back one and stuffed himself under its tail. He and his Section rattled away

Swordfish at Hatston, 1941: the aircraft in the foreground appears to be V4356 – FANCOURT

with such good effect that the enemy aircraft was last seen in a flat right hand spiral going down towards South Ronaldsay. Unfortunately no wreckage was found and so the very probable result could not be confirmed. By 21.50 hours the party was over and 11 Gladiators returned. The 12th. was one of Blue Section who, shortly afterwards, could be heard calling, "Where am I?" Nifty* told him and led him back to Wick where he spent the night.
(* Fighter Control, Wick)

No.605 Squadron from Wick were quickly on the scene again. In the interception they shot down two and probably damaged another four. The enemy formations were broken up yet, despite this, 20 aircraft ran the gauntlet of the Scapa Barrage where another three were shot down. Those that did get through dropped 500lb. and 1000 lb. bombs aimed mainly at the boom nets. The cruiser HMS *Suffolk* was hit and several of the crew killed but the vessel itself sustained only minimal damage. The whole engagement lasted about an hour. For the very first time all the defensive measures had worked well. Had the two Skua squadrons been in action there is no doubt that the enemy casualties would have been much heavier. The Skuas had been immediately rearmed after the Bergen sortie but, fortunately for the Germans, the aircraft remained on the ground, their crews exhausted from the early morning mission. No damage was done to the

RAF reconnaissance photograph of Bismarck at Bergen: 21.05.41: this famous early reconnaissance photograph was taken by Pilot Officer Michael Suckling, flying from Wick and refuelling at Sumburgh – FANCOURT

boom nets and Scapa remained a safe haven. The enemy had failed again in its attempt to smash the Home Fleet and its base and both remained a piercing thorn in the German side throughout the war. It was the last mass bombing raid to take place over Scapa. The Battle of Orkney had been won. Offensive missions continued to be conducted by both sides, the Royal Navy continuing to use Hatston for this purpose. Single Skuas of 800 Squadron were despatched with the simple brief 'hit anything of military value'. There were a number of such missions in April supported by Blenheims of No.254 Squadron of the Royal Air Force which was based temporarily at Hatston. All these raids proved to be quite ineffectual and jeopardised the lives of highly skilled pilots who were badly needed elsewhere and were therefore discontinued. Only three further offensive operations were conducted from Hatston. In May 1940, 806 Squadron Skuas took part in a bombing operation on Bergen, the targets being oil tanks and coastal shipping and in the same month, Swordfish of 821 and 823 Squadron took off from Hatston for a revenge attack on the German battleship *Scharnhorst*

steaming south at high speed off the Norwegian coast. The *Scharnhorst* and *Gneisenau* had earlier sunk the aircraft carrier HMS *Glorious* on passage from Norway to Scapa and among the considerable losses was half of 823 Squadron which had been aboard at the time. Unfortunately the torpedo attack was unsuccessful, the *Scharnhorst* accounting for yet another Swordfish. The last Skua raid against Bergen from Hatston was around October 1940. All subsequent operations against the enemy in Norway were carrier based with the exception of a brilliant piece of reconnaissance work in May 1941 which was again conceived at Hatston.

On 21 May 1941, Pilot Officer Michael Suckling flying from Wick in a long-range reconnaissance Spitfire located in a fjord just south of Bergen the *Bismarck*, the most powerful battleship in the world. There was fear among the Allies that she would strike out into the Atlantic where she could do untold damage. For two months Captain H. St.J. Fancourt, Commanding Officer of Hatston had been training 828 Squadron Albacores for this great moment. He asked the RAF for another reconnaissance to confirm that the *Bismarck* was still

Maryland AR 717 at Hatston: with Noel Goddard as Pilot and Hank Rotherham as Observer, this was the aircraft which flew from Hatston to Bergen and confirmed that the Bismarck had sailed into the Atlantic: Noel Goddard was, in peacetime, Chairman of the Gloucester Flying Club: foreground left Lt. Martin: standing highest on the wing, Lt. Duncan Hamilton, Senior Engineer, Hatston – HAMILTON

in the fjord but, because of poor weather, they were unable to comply. Not to be outdone, he asked for volunteers from the Station's own 771 Fleet Requirements Unit to attempt such a reconnaissance. It was not all part of 771 Squadron's duties to conduct reconnaissance and certainly not at such a distance but the Commanding Officer of 771 Squadron, Noel Goddard, a most experienced pilot, volunteered along with his TAG, J W Armstrong and Air Gunner Milne. There was no experienced Observer available and, to fill the breach, Lieutenant Commander Hank Rotherham, the Station Executive Officer and trained Observer, stepped in. Their charge was a Maryland bomber AR717, one of two attached to 771 Squadron at Hatston. 828 Squadron Albacores meanwhile moved to Sumburgh in Shetland ready for the torpedo strike.

The reconnaissance was a complete success. The Maryland came through almost unscathed to transmit the urgent message "Battleship and cruiser have left".

The Fleet slipped its moorings in Scapa and headed for the Atlantic. Station Commander Fancourt was not disappointed that his Albacore Squadron was untested. He writes:-

When they had established that the *Bismarck* had sailed, there was nothing more I could do from Hatston. I am glad to say that I did not send in the Torpedo Bomber Squadron. It would have been a very difficult operation in the circumstances.

The importance of this daring mission was recognised by the Admiralty who awarded Rotherham as Captain of the aircraft an immediate DSO, Goddard an immediate DSC and Armstrong a DSM. Rotherham gives an excellent account of this reconnaissance in his book, *"It's Really Quite Safe"*.

After the air battle of 10 April 1940, German initiatives in the Scapa area were sporadic and half-hearted. Radar installations in Sanday and Deerness were bombed and minelaying operations around the coast continued. RAF Wick, outside the area of the Scapa Barrage was less fortunate. It was bombed several times. Aircraft and hangars were destroyed and there were several casualties including 11 civilians in Wick itself. Reconnaissance patrols in and around the islands continued, the lone aircraft sometimes appearing completely by surprise. On 25 December 1940 a Ju88 suddenly appeared over the West Mainland of Orkney. 804 Squadron equipped with their new Grumman Martlets were by this time stationed at Skeabrae and took off in pursuit of the intruder. The Station Diary has this entry:-

25 December first blood was drawn, an enemy aircraft, a Junkers 88

JU88 shot down by 804 Sqdn. Skeabrae in Sandwick, 25 December 1940 – FANCOURT

was sighted two miles west of base by 804 patrol, Lt.Commander Carver, just after the men had finished their Christmas Dinner: after an interesting and exciting chase, Sub.Lt. Parke put a burst from the stern in the starboard engine and white and black smoke was seen to come from it. After the fourth pass, the enemy aircraft was seen to be flying on only one engine and Carver noticed the enemy aircraft losing height after each burst and after the last burst, the aircraft landed with the undercarriage retracted. The crew of four, one of whom was injured, was taken to Kirkwall for interrogation: all the guns of the enemy machine showed stoppages.

The Junkers was brought down in a field near Flotterston in Sandwick, the first enemy aircraft of the war to be shot down by a British pilot flying an American aircraft. The aircraft suffered only minimal damage and was stored in a hangar at Skeabrae for some time before being transferred south.

Although the threat of aerial bombardment declined, there was no let up in security. After the invasion of Norway, airborne invasion was considered imminent. To add to the inconvenience already experienced by Orcadians with the introduction of the special pass required for travel to or from Orkney, a 11pm. to 5pm. curfew was introduced in July 1940 when fear of airborne invasion was at its height. Large troop

concentrations in Norway betokened the worst and considerable relief was felt when they turned eastwards into the Soviet Union. At last the pressure was off.

There is little doubt that the war in the north prepared the services well for the terrible events of the Autumn of 1940. Many lessons must have been learned and copious amendments made to service manuals. So far however civilian targets had been immune. A report on air attacks involving the civilian population of Orkney up to 1944 said,

In all, 228 bombs and two parachute mines have fallen on land in the county in 16 attacks. Hoy has suffered the largest number of attacks, having been bombed five times but other islands in and around Scapa Flow have also suffered. South Ronaldsay has been bombed three times, Flotta twice and Burray once. The North Isles have not escaped: Sanday has been bombed twice and Shapinsay once. At Auskerry the lighthouse came under attack and, to the west of Orkney, Sule Skerry light was also bombed. Casualties have been remarkably light - altogether three people in Orkney have been killed, 11 seriously injured and five slightly injured.

Civilians in the northern front line had come out well. When the Luftwaffe turned its attention to the south of England and the destruction of non-military targets was considered legitimate, the outcome was rather different.

Blockships proved inadequate to protect the Home Fleet in Scapa Flow: after the sinking of the Royal Oak, the eastern approaches to Scapa Flow were sealed off by a causeway which came to be known as the Churchill Barriers – BALFOUR.BEATTY

Chapter Four

The Resident Squadrons

Eight days before war broke out, the arrival of 'X' Flight of 771 Squadron at Hatston heralded the first of 91 squadrons of aircraft to use the military airfields of Orkney between 1939 and 1945. Almost all these squadrons were based in Orkney: only a few were in transit or diverted through bad weather. Though based in Orkney, these squadrons were not necessarily resident. A resident squadron was a squadron posted to Orkney to perform particular duties, be it, for example, target towing, interception, air-sea rescue, convoy protection or communications. All 19 RAF squadrons were resident. Of the 72 Royal Naval Squadrons, it would be generally true to say that all aircraft disembarked from carriers were not resident but this is only a rule of thumb. Some squadrons such as 801, 828 and 1770 flew to Orkney and trained for long periods before embarking on a carrier: in the early years of the war others such as 800 and 801 disembarked from carriers to play a role for many months in the defence of Orkney when RAF fighters were fully committed to the South of England. These were, properly, front-line squadrons and are considered under disembarked aircraft. Of Royal Naval squadrons, there were, in reality, only three squadrons resident in Orkney. As might be expected, these were squadrons in the 700 non-combative series, 771 Squadron, Fleet Requirements Unit which spent the whole of the war in Orkney, 700 Squadron, the Headquarters of all catapult flights, which spent most of the war years there and 712 Squadron, a Communications Squadron formed at Hatston in 1944 to replace the reduced communications facility available when 700 Squadron merged with 771 Squadron in March 1944. 712 Squadron was a small squadron flying Expeditor, Dominie, Sea Otter and Traveller aircraft and whose principal role was to ferry high ranking officers and, sometimes, urgent supplies from Orkney to the Scottish Mainland and will not be discussed here.

If there is any squadron which can lay claim to a long association with the Orkney Islands, it must surely be 771 Squadron of the Royal Navy. The complete Squadron was in residence at Hatston by 28 September 1939 flying in from Portland and Lee-on-Solent, in the case of the latter station, a timely move for, within a year, Lee-on-Solent was to be devastated by Stuka dive-bombers. When Hatston was chosen as the Royal Navy's first purpose built airfield, it could scarcely be envisaged that five squadrons of aircraft would frequently be disembarked there in addition to the busy 700 Squadron and 771 Fleet Requirements Unit Squadron. The disembarkation of front-line Fighter and Torpedo Bomber Squadrons received the highest priority and this meant that the resources of Hatston were usually stretched to the limit. A real crisis occurred in April 1942 when the carrier USS *Wasp* was loaned to Britain to ferry Spitfire aircraft to Malta. Three of *Wasp's* four squadrons of aircraft

Lt. Cdr. Michael Le Fanu, Fleet Gunnery Officer, Scapa: Twatt photographers have decorated him suitably: how were they to know that he was to rise to the rank of Admiral of the Fleet! – MOLYNEUX

Skua towing a drogue over Hatston – HAMILTON

Chesapeake streaming a drogue, Twatt, 31.03.45 – HILL

had to be disembarked somewhere in Britain for five weeks and the aircrew's rigorous training programmes had to be continued in that time. The only station capable of maintaining the crews at the highest standard of war-readiness was Hatston. Consequently, to make room for the Americans, it was decided that 771 Squadron should move to the new Royal Naval Air Station at Twatt which had been coping with the overspill of fighters from Hatston for almost a year. Here 771 Squadron remained until 25 July 1945 when it once again made the long journey south, on this occasion to Zeals in Wiltshire.

771 Squadron was an FRU or Fleet Requirements Unit. Its duties were multifarious but its primary role was in training, especially in providing gunnery practice for the Fleet in Scapa Flow or for the Naval A.A. Range, the so called Northern Range, at Yesnaby to the north of Stromness. Drogues and, later, winged targets were towed behind a variety of aircraft. Initially Swordfish, Skuas and Rocs were used for this purpose but later Chesapeake, Defiant and Martinet were introduced. 771 Squadron pilots logged up long hours of flying for, in busy Scapa Flow, there were few days when some ship or other did not require practice. CPO Pilot Haslams's log records the names of 83 ships with which he exercised in the last 18 months of the war, many of them allied. These exercises were not without risk. Many pilots refer to the experience of training the gunners on the Soviet battleship *Arkhangelsk*. This battleship had originally been the British *Royal Sovereign* but was transferred to the Soviets in July 1944. Admiral Levchenko and some

of the new crew arrived at Scapa from the Soviet Union in early May aboard the carrier *Fencer* as part of convoy RA59. The Soviets came armed with many crates of vodka and with such a cargo they received a rapturous welcome. Attitudes changed however after the first sea to air gunnery practice when the Twatt pilots saw the shells bursting in <u>front</u> of their aircraft instead of around the drogue which was streaming 6000 feet behind them! Nevertheless the training given the Soviet crew by the Twatt pilots proved very useful for, shortly after the battleship arrived in the Soviet Union, a direct hit was scored in its first encounter with an aircraft. Unfortunately the aircraft was American! By this time *Arkangelsk* was lying in Vaenga Bay a few miles below Murmansk.

The American pilot had been on a special mission to Norway from Scotland and, damaged by enemy fire, had sought what he thought was the friendly airfield at Graznaya! The Soviets, seeing the aircraft fly from the direction of occupied Norway naturally assumed it was an enemy aircraft.

A similar function of 771 Squadron was to provide air to air firing practice for both embarked and disembarked squadrons. Again drogues were used and streamed to a length of 1000 feet, such exercises being carried out at sea outside shipping lanes. There were also throw-off shoots when the big guns of the naval ships were offset 20° and practice shells fired at aircraft making simulated attacks. Ciné photography was used to evaluate such exercises and 771 Squadron at Twatt established one of the finest photographic departments in the Royal Navy.

Miles Martinet target towing aircraft over Orkney – HAMILTON

16 foot winged target towed by a Martinet in flight over Orkney – HASLAM

32 foot winged target at Twatt – HASLAM

Colour ciné of World War II activities in Orkney originated here at Twatt and is now valuable archival material. There were similar Army Cooperative exercises. Huge Army Artillery garrisons were stationed in Orkney throughout the war and since it was their principal duty to ensure that no enemy aircraft reached Scapa Flow, they needed constant practice. Approximately one third of all sorties made by 771 Squadron were for the benefit of the Army. Once a month there was an exercise code-named *Chutney* when as many aircraft as serviceable got airborne together and attacked the Home Fleet at anchor in Scapa Flow. The exercises consisted of dummy high-level bombing, dive-bombing, strafing and torpedo attacks. Accidents were not uncommon. In one such exercise on 14 August 1944 a pilot pulled up too late from a dive and his aircraft, a Miles Martinet, hit the superstructure of one of the capital ships and crashed into the sea. Both he and his TAG were killed. Perhaps one of the strangest incidents of the war occurred on the island of South Ronaldsay on 22 October 1943 when the crew of a Blackburn Roc of 771 Squadron at Twatt were rescued by the enemy! The Roc was on a dive-bombing and fighter direction exercise with HMS *Royalist* when the engine failed. Having a young midshipman on board, the pilot decided to crash land his aircraft rather than bale out. TAG Doug Cole relates what happened:-

We braced ourselves for what we knew was going to be a pretty heavy landing. The next I can recall is seeing very swarthy looking men with axes hacking round my head. They were dressed in strange clothing with huge red discs on their backs and they were jabbering away in a foreign language. In my stupor I thought this couldn't be any place on earth. Next I remember lying on the grass and a lady appearing from nowhere and offering me a cigarette. I asked her who these people were who got me out and she replied that they were Italian prisoners of war!

These Italian prisoners of war were employed in building what came to be known as the Churchill Barriers, the causeway which was built to link all the islands to the east of Scapa Flow to prevent the intrusion of enemy submarines.

In the twelve months leading up to D day, the official history of Twatt Air Station written up at the end of the war by a Wren officer records that 771 Squadron carried out over 4000 exercises and flew almost 11,000 hours so it does not surprise us to learn that, in their time in Orkney, this squadron had 40 recorded accidents and probably many more unrecorded. Altogether 18 aircrew lost their lives in Squadron operations in Orkney.

Few Royal Naval pilots had the opportunity to fly multi-engined aircraft during the war, but for 771

'The CO's compliments, and – er – he says please can we have our winged target back?' – HOLDEN

Squadron pilots this was commonplace. As early as October 1940, two Martin Maryland bombers, originally intended for the French Air Force, were attached to 771 Squadron at Hatston. By early 1945 the Squadron at Twatt could boast six bombers. One important use of these aircraft was in the checking of Radar Calibration, the size of the bombers giving a very good radar response. Cruisers and battleships were fitted with Air Warning radars which gave range, bearing and height and it was the function of 771 Squadron bombers to make passes at nine levels between 200 and 40,000 feet to check the accuracy of the radars. This service was a particularly valuable one not only for HM ships but also for the Station itself which, in keeping with its training role, established its own Radar Station at Hesta Geo on the north coast of Birsay on 10 May 1943 and, one week later, opened its Fighter Direction School with associated Link Trainer and Fisher Gun Trainer facilities. The purpose of the School was to exercise fighter aircraft and also ship's fighter director teams. In this it was highly successful for more than 1000 officers and 3000 ratings passed through this School in its two years' existence.

The cruiser HMS Newfoundland, steaming at 18 knots off Orkney: photographed by Twatt aircraft – HILL

Gladiator, 771 Sqdn. Twatt, 1943 – MOLYNEUX

Early morning 'Met' flights were a feature of every station: TAG Richard (Dick) Stark ready for the flight with a rather bulky barometer! – STARK

A 771 Sqdn. pilot looks down on the cruiser HMS Ceylon off Orkney – HASLAM

With such heavy commitments, it isn't surprising to learn that 771 Squadron was the largest in the Royal Navy. In July 1942 it already had 19 aircraft: by May 1945 increasing workload had raised the total to 51 which included 23 Martinet target towing aircraft, 16 Corsair single seater fighters, 6 Boston bombers, 3 Blenheim bombers and 3 helicopters. After November 1942 Twatt was considered too crowded to accept disembarked front-line fighters and from then on most of the overspill went to RAF Grimsetter or RAF Skeabrae. Eventually the problem was solved in July 1943 by transferring Grimsetter to the Royal Navy.

Pilots had to be very adept at handling a great variety of types of aircraft. Between January 1943 and August 1945, Cyril Burke RNZNVR, CO of the squadron, logged up 537 flying hours in 14 different types of aircraft 30% of that being multi-engined experience. There was little time to study the niceties of each machine. CPO Pilot Eric Haslam writes that, with single seater aircraft, he was given pilot's notes to read about an hour before the first flight. On his third Hurricane flight, exercising with HMS *Nelson* and HMS *Argonaut*, he crashed on landing due to a ground loop but was excused from blame due to inexperience on type. In accident enquiries this judgement was common. There was

even little time for accident enquiries and there was probably more than a grain of truth in the notice displayed in a Commander (Flying)'s Office:

> I sometimes feel that, if I could stop the paperwork caused by accidents, I could then stop the accidents which caused this paperwork which now prevents me stopping accidents.

In addition to its many fixed-wing aircraft, it is a little known fact that 771 Squadron was the first squadron in the Royal Navy to experiment with helicopters, indeed the Royal Navy's first operational helicopters were assembled and flown at Twatt. On 8 May 1944, three R-4 Sikorsky helicopters had arrived in Britain for evaluation by the Royal Navy at MAP (Ministry of Aircraft Production). One of these crashed due to mechanical failure but trials continued with the other two. The trials showed that the helicopter was of some value to the Royal Navy and the first operational machines were attached to 771 Squadron at Twatt. Lt. Jean-Paul Fournier RCN qualified as a fixed wing pilot in the Fleet Air Arm and after serving in TBR squadrons ashore and on the carrier HMS *Indomitable* was posted to the US Coastguard Station at Floyd Bennett, New York, for a course on helicopters. There he became the first

As part of an Army Co-operative Exercise, Lt. Cdr. Molyneux plans a flight with Norwegian Army Officers in Blenheim, Twatt, July 1943 – MOLYNEUX

In the Petty Officers' Mess: Twatt, 16.03.45 – HILL

Formation of 18 Corsairs of 771 Squadron, Twatt, lining up for attack on Home Fleet – HILL

Canadian to solo on helicopters. On completion of his course he returned to the UK and, in January 1945, was posted to Twatt where he found five or six crated R-4 Sikorsky helicopters and a maintenance crew of six or seven already there. The helicopters were assembled and test flown there but this development was so innovative that he had no terms of reference and initially was at a loss to know what to do. The machines were looked on as toys with little practical use.

In this honeymoon period there were pleasure trips in which the pilot landed on the gun-turret of the battleship HMS *Duke of York* and flew Admiral Tovey, C-in-C of the Home Fleet, to a local stream to do some fishing. That was a success. When the Captain of the battleship HMS *King George V* went for a joy ride in Scapa Flow, things did not go so well. The helicopter with floats was unserviceable so, at the last minute, the wheeled version was substituted. The helicopter landed on the front gun turret of the battleship and took its captain aboard for a short local flight. Unfortunately, on the return flight, the engine cut out but fortunately the blades continued to turn and the helicopter landed softly on the water close to the battleship. Without floats it began to submerge slowly. The pilot and the Captain released themselves, came to the surface, and were picked up by the ship's boat. The Captain was subsequently piped aboard, soaked to the skin, in front of all his crew! A signal to Twatt confirmed that he wasn't very pleased. The Station itself found a valuable use for the helicopter when the CO gave permission for the pilot to go round the farms collecting eggs!

Two 771 Sqdn. Corsairs on dispersal at Twatt, 1944 – HASLAM

Bristol Blenheim IV R2782 flying over Sma Geo, Marwick, Birsay, 31.03.45 – REMMINGTON

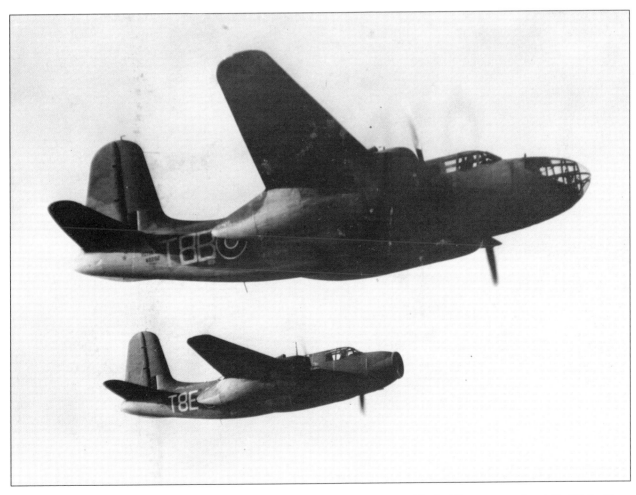

Boston and Havoc in flight over Orkney, 31.03.45: the Havoc (with a flat nose) was, like the Liberator, experimentally fitted with a searchlight known as a Turbanlite which gave a broad flat beam to pin-point targets – REMMINGTON

Getting a Boston ready: heating the engines: Twatt, January 1944 – MOLYNEUX

Hesta Geo, Birsay: Fighter Direction School, transmitting and receiving station – PRO

In the Fighter Direction School, Twatt, January 1945: 3rd. Officer Sheila Tucker and Johnny Treloar plotting – PEMBERTON

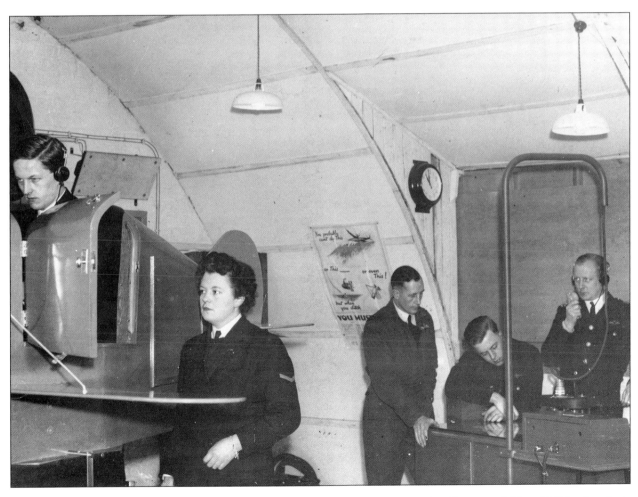

In the Link Trainer, Twatt, 26.01.45: Chris Morrish, Lesley Fowler-Johnson, Ron Heap, Tom Bennett and 'Crem '(talking in mike to Chris) – PEMBERTON

Very English landscape in the Link Trainer room, Twatt! 26.01.45 – HILL

Truck taking pilots of 771 Sqdn. to dispersal for take off, 1944: Left to Right – Sub/Lt. Playford, CPO Pilot Frank Daly, Not Known, Sub/Lt. Pilot . . . ? – HASLAM

Twatt Officers July 1945
Back Row: Sub/Lt. Hoppitt, F/O Ream, Sub/Lts. Barnwell, Treloar, Bennett, Fearnley, F/O Munro, Sub. Lts. Bentley, Jones
Front Row: Sub/Lts. Buxton, Scott, Moon, Lts. Mence, Remmington, Linstead, Lt. Cdr. Burke, Lt. Wright-Anderson, Prentice,
F/O Heap, Lt. Middleton, Sub/Lts. Woodhead, Hunt – REMMINGTON

Swordfish write off near Craigiefield, Kirkwall: pilot switched from gravity to main fuel tanks but, unfortunately, he had forgotten to
check that the main tanks were full before take off: unhurt, he walked away from the wreck! – HAMILTON

Albacore BF743 comes to a sudden halt! – HAMILTON

Pranged Boulton Paul P.82 Defiant TT.1, DR932 used for fire drill at Twatt – HILL

Grumman Wildcat FN270 which crash landed in a turnip field, Orkney, being towed out by the recovery vehicle – HAMILTON

Supermarine Seafire IIc, MB175 (884 Sqdn. Victorious) coming back from North Africa: being unloaded at Scapa for transport to Hatston Workshops: notice the sand cowl fitted to the front of the aircraft; Lt. Duncan Hamilton at head of stairway and Lt. Marney behind – HAMILTON

Normally civilians were kept well away from crashed aircraft but when a Grumman Martlet came down near Fiold in Westray in April 1943, where there was no Royal Naval recovery vehicle, the help of the local population had to be enlisted! The tractor drivers are Jack Hewison and George Rendall – HAMILTON

German U-Boats in Loch Eriboll after surrender, 23.05.45: photographed by Twatt aircraft – BURKE

King George V getting ready to hoist up her Walrus – REMMINGTON

Wren Air Mechanics working on a damaged Martinet, Twatt, 10.06.45 – PAGE

Fairly Fulmar in Hatston Workshops – HAMILTON

Grumman Wildcat FN270 arrives at the Hatston Workshops on a Bedford low-loader – HAMILTON

Lift-off, R-4 Sikorsky, Twatt: Lt. Jean-Paul Fournier RN with Senior visiting Wren officer, 6.4.45 – FOURNIER

Helicopter pilot Lt. Jean Paul-Fournier with his technicians in the Petty Officers' Mess at Twatt – FOURNIER

R-4 Sikorsky helicopter with floats: appears to be a trick photograph – both the same machine! – HILL

Twatt R-4 Sikorsky helicopter landing at Rinnigill on the island of Hoy – PRO

Jean-Paul Fournier was, after a month, joined by a second helicopter pilot who, during a demonstration flight, had the great misfortune to collide with a parked Blenheim. The machine was a write-off. However it was ingeniously set up by the workshops as a demonstration unit with cut-out opened sections of gear box and engine for the benefit of mechanics and pilots. With the arrival of the replacement helicopter pilot, Alan Bristow, later to become an international figure in the helicopter world, Fournier set about a proper evaluation of the helicopter in the Royal Navy. Soon it was found that the helicopter, though not giving such good radar response, was invaluable for Ship Radar and Fire Control Calibration because of its high degree of manoeuvrability. It also began to show its value in direct ship to shore communications a capability which battleships and cruisers lost after the demise of the Catapult Squadrons of 700 Squadron. Its Air-Sea Rescue potential was yet to be discovered but by landing an engineer on isolated Stroma in the Pentland Firth to attend to a faulty radar responder it showed its value in reaching isolated areas speedily and efficiently. The photographic possibilities of the helicopter were seen quickly by the excellent Photographic Section who, among other things, produced a magnificent diorama of RNAS Twatt, from a hovering helicopter, surely a unique visual record of a war-time RNAS station. To maintain such big and complex squadron of aircraft required workshop facilities of a very high standard. An engine repair shop, aircraft repair shop and general engineering shop, all capable of work up to major inspections of engines and major repairs to aircraft were established at Twatt. Truly of 771 Squadron could be said "You bend it, we mend it". In the last year of the war, 70 aircraft were repaired in the Twatt workshops but even from the very beginning when the squadron was based at Hatston the workshops there were kept extremely busy. Aside from the job of repairing aircraft, it was also the job of 771 Squadron to salvage and transport crashed aircraft. 56 Royal Naval crashes are recorded on land in Orkney during the war years though doubtless there were many more: as many off shore ditchings occurred. 771 Squadron were also required to repair aircraft damaged in deck-landing crashes at sea. For this the RNAS stations in Orkney were very poorly equipped, the damaged aircraft being landed at Scapa Pier, hoisted by a hand-worked crane and then transported over narrow twisting roads to the workshop.

One of the last tasks of 771 Squadron was to escort, triumphantly, the surrendering German U-boats which made their way to Scapa or Loch Eriboll in Sutherland. On the cessation of hostilities in Europe the Fleet moved east to the Pacific theatre. There

was no further need for aircraft whose main duty was to support the Fleet and so, on 24 July 1945, this massive squadron became airborne and headed off in stages to the south of England.

700 Squadron of the Royal Navy formed at Hatston on 21 January 1940, and was one of a number of Royal Naval squadrons which formed there during the hostilities. 700 Squadron was not, however, a completely new Squadron but a bringing together, under one command, of the widely scattered 700 Series of Flights which had been formed in mid July 1936. The new Squadron included all of 701, 702, 705, 711, 712, 713, 714, 715, 716, 718 and 720 Flights equipped with Walrus, Seafox and Swordfish. Such an amalgamation created, at that time, the biggest squadron in the Royal Navy with 65 aircraft. However, unlike the usual Naval Squadrons which normally kept together, the aircraft of 700 Squadron, by their very nature, came together only by chance. These were catapult aircraft embarked on cruisers and battleships and would disembark at Hatston whenever the parent ship was in Scapa Flow. The Squadron was large on paper only but there were occasions when large numbers of the Home Fleet and ships working up for other stations were present in Scapa and at such times, 700 Squadron aircraft were catapulted off to the shore station to avoid damage to the rigging of the aircraft during gunnery practice. Thus, in early 1942, no less than 21 Walrus aircraft, complete with flying and maintenance crews, were mustered at Hatston.

A Headquarters Flight of 700 Squadron, equipped principally with Walrus and later, Sea Otter aircraft was permanently shore based in Orkney. Their duties included Air-Sea Rescue and Anti-Submarine Patrol and in these duties they were joined by Walrus disembarked from capital ships and cruisers. 700 Sqdn. was constantly on call to pick up the crews of ditched aircraft. Sometimes they had to be rescued themselves. In April 1941, an Albacore of 828 Squadron, Hatston, crashed into the sea 50 miles east of Orkney and a Dutch submarine in the vicinity picked up the pilot, the only survivor. A 700 Squadron Walrus was catapulted from HMS *Shropshire* in Scapa Flow to fly the pilot to hospital in Kirkwall and although it rendezvoused successfully with the submarine it could not, because of deteriorating weather, take off again. The solution to this problem presented one of the oddest spectacles of the war. The submarine towed the Walrus to more sheltered waters near Orkney and it took off successfully again! On 25 April 1944, Sea Otter JM761 of 700 Squadron, on a Flight from Abbotsinsch to Twatt plunged into Hoy Sound and, just before the plane sank, the crew were saved by High Speed Rescue launch from Stromness, directed from Hatston which had picked up the distress signal. Others were less fortunate. On 24

April 1940, Walrus L2316 on Anti-Submarine Patrol from Hatston, disappeared without trace in the Fair Isle Channel presumably shot down by enemy aircraft which had been reported in the vicinity. On 24 September 1942, in a tragic accident all six members of Walrus L2329 of Twatt Flight and Walrus X9418 of *Sheffield* Flight were killed in a mid-air collision over Scapa Flow. This was one of several mid-air collisions which occurred during the war in Orkney's busy air space.

Pilots' and Observers' logs of 700 Squadron record ceaseless hours of Anti-Submarine Patrol. After the catastrophic sinking of the *Royal Oak* in the second month of the war, this duty was absolutely vital to protect the comings and goings of the Fleet. But, for the crews, it could be boring in the extreme since U-boats gave the well defended Orkney waters a wide berth, particularly at the end of the war. Norman Brown, Observer in 700 Squadron, is not proud today of what the crew did to relieve the monotony:-

In the absence of enemy submarines, the pilot would obligingly bank low over a basking shark to give the air gunner some practice. I'm ashamed to think of that now, but some terrible things were done in war time. I've seen detachments of the Fleet engage Stack Skerry with 6 inch guns, the shells bursting on the cliff face. Thousands of seabirds must have died. Today we would all hold up our hands in horror at the thought.

Apart from Air-Sea Rescue and Anti-Submarine Patrol work, the squadron also acted as communication channel between ship and shore. Aircraft were catapulted off but, on return, the only way to get back on board was to land beside their ship and to be hoisted on board by crane. This could be an extremely difficult operation in windy Scapa Flow. Bill Larkins, a pilot with 771 Squadron much admired the pilots of 700 Squadron whom he described as 'intrepid airmen who used to fly in amongst the balloon cables in Scapa Flow, to communicate back and forth with their parent ships'. Up to 85 balloons could be flown in Scapa Flow at any one time and presented a nightmarish obstacle to the uninitiated. The balloon area was, of course, out of bounds to all other squadrons, and pilots who transgressed there rarely came out unscathed. A Hurricane of 771 Squadron landed at Twatt minus a wing tip and, more dramatically, Boulton Paul Defiant DR937, lost most of its port wing but, in spite of this, the pilot made a successful belly landing.

Aircraft of the Headquarters Flight often had to travel much further afield, frequently to the Faroe Islands, a hazardous journey, for these islands were frequently fogbound and in the event of not being able to land, the aircraft did not have enough fuel for the return journey. On March 1 1944, in a flight lasting more than four hours, a Sea Otter from Twatt flew from Hatston in severe wintry conditions to deliver an urgent consignment to HMS *Victorious* off the Faroes. In the heavy seas, the landing deck was heaving more than forty feet and the pilot, Sub.Lt. Snowdon, with no experience of deck-landing a Sea Otter, which had no arrester hook fitted anyway, wisely chose the landing strip on Faroese soil. A more experienced Swordfish pilot from *Victorious* flew in to collect the vital box.

700 Squadron was based initially at Hatston where, when runways were busy, aircraft had the initial advantage of being able to land in Kirkwall Bay and taxi up the slipway. This was, after all, one of the main reasons why Hatston was chosen as the Royal Navy's first airfield. Circumstances change quickly in wartime and, it was decided that 700 Squadron should join the other non-combatant squadron, 771 squadron at its new base at Twatt and the move was made. But 700 Squadron had barely settled in when front-line pilots preparing for *Operation Torch*, the North African landings, spilled over to Twatt for, once again, Hatston was unable to cope. As a result, in September 1942, 700 Squadron was required to move yet again - temporarily, to RAF Grimsetter and 820 and 822 Squadrons took up residence at Twatt. By December 1942, 700 Squadron had returned to Twatt where, for 18 months, they had a busy programme. By this time the Squadron had 63 Walrus aircraft on capital ships, cruisers and shore stations. 18 of these are recorded at Twatt on one occasion. A contributor to *Flight Deck* in December 1945 recalls his time there in 1942 when '8 Walrus did a *balbo* across Twatt airfield at nought feet' which he goes on to describe as a 'weird and wonderful sight' as I am sure it was. Any Air Show Committee would pay handsomely to repeat such a performance today!

In addition to its Air Sea Rescue, Anti-Submarine Patrol and Communications roles, 700 Squadron now assumed responsibility for training newly formed catapult flights. For pilots and observers, a ten week course, parts of which took place at Donibristle, Dundee and on HMS *Pegasus*, culminated in final training with 'A' Flight at Twatt before joining their ship. More space was required for these developments and, in time, the squadron had its own hangars, accommodation blocks, messes and wardroom built at Quoys on the Twatt airfield.

As time went by and more sophisticated radar was fitted to ships, there was less need for spotter aircraft. The advent of escort carriers and MAC-Ships (merchant aircraft carriers) hastened the demise of the catapult flights. Headquarters Flight of 700 Squadron, Twatt, continued to perform its roles for a time but finally, on 24 March 1944, the squadron was disbanded and merged with 771 Squadron on the same airfield, a real marriage of convenience. To the variety of aircraft already operated by 771 was added the Walrus and Sea Otter, the latter remaining with that squadron until the end of the war. Former 700 pilots could now gain experience on fighters such as the Hurricane or Corsair or opt for a twin-engined conversion course on Blenheims or Bostons.

The first Royal Air Force squadron to be based in Orkney was No.254 Squadron equipped with Blenheim IV bombers. This squadron had, in fact, been posted to the new airfield at Sumburgh in Shetland to undertake patrols over coastal shipping, a duty for which, according to its Norse motto, *Fluga, vakta ok ljosta*, to fly, to watch and to strike, it was well equipped to do in this northern setting. However the Squadron had to await the establishment of a Station Headquarters at Sumburgh and had therefore to move in to the RN Air Station at Hatston since RAF Grimsetter was still far from completion. Hatston itself was extremely busy at this time with seven squadrons on station but, with the departure of five squadrons on 21 April 1940, the Blenheims of No.254 Squadron were able to move in next day. As well as shipping protection patrols the squadron assisted in diverting unidentified and neutral shipping into the large Contraband Base which had been established in Kirkwall Bay, just off Hatston. Here, up to 100 merchant vessels would lie impatiently at anchor while Britain considered it had the right to search them for strategic materials bound for Germany. The squadron also undertook reconnaissance duties from Hatston in its brief time there. On 16 May 1940, it finally took up station at Sumburgh but returned briefly to Orkney three years later, on this occasion equipped with Beauforts. From Skeabrae they conducted an anti-shipping strike off the Norwegian coast.

One whole year after the war with Germany started there was still no permanent RAF presence in Orkney. A small beginning was made however on 15 September 1940 when the first aircraft, a small ex-civil Miles Whitney Straight flown by the Commanding Officer, Wing Commander C F H Grace arrived at Skeabrae. Though they now had an airfield, such were the demands for the defence of the south of England, that the RAF had, unfortunately, not one squadron to spare. 804 Squadron of the Royal Navy, Hatston, newly equipped with Grumman Martlets originally intended for the French Air Force, moved in on 10 October 1940. Here they remained until 6 January 1941 when No.3 Squadron of the Royal Air Force took over.

Altogether 19 RAF squadrons were in residence in Orkney during World War II. It is not desirable to give details of every one of these squadrons for there was little variation in their duties during the war years. Indeed it is not possible to give more than a skeletal outline of the activities of some of these squadrons. It is well known fact that some RAF squadrons active during the war on the British mainland and indeed beyond disappeared without leaving one photographic record behind them. Skeabrae was no exception. Only a handful of photographs of RAF aircraft at Skeabrae is known to exist. Apart from a very fine Operational Record in the Public Records Office little is known about the Station apart from what has been gleaned from the memories of servicemen and women who spent some time there. With the help of these notes it is possible, by concentrating on several squadrons to give an idea of the role of Skeabrae in the war years. No.3 Squadron was one of the oldest RAF squadrons, being formed as early as May 1912. Equipped with Hurricanes, it was based at Croydon at the outbreak of the war. It had been severely hammered in France and by 23 May 1940 it found itself in the North of Scotland where it remained for almost a year. It arrived at Skeabrae on 7 January 1941. Desmond Scott, a New Zealander, had just joined No.3 Squadron as a pilot. His brief impression of Orkney was not favourable. In his book, *One More Hour,* he writes:-

I was so exhausted by the time we reached our destination, I still can't remember where we disembarked at Scapa Flow - Lyness or Kirkwall. All I remember was that it was bitterly cold and snow lay everywhere. Skeabrae was one hell of a place. The two asphalt runways were a luxury for our Hurricanes but everything else was either half finished or surrounded by a sea of mud and slush. Gale force winds would sweep down from the North Sea almost every day, driving the snow into deep drifts and filling the ditches that had been excavated in preparation for the laying of pipes for the station's drainage system . . .

There were no trees on the Orkneys and most of the civilians who were working on the station's complex were from Ireland. The war didn't seem to mean a thing to them and it was not uncommon to see a bunch of them huddled around a coal-fired brazier playing cards. The defence forces guarding the huts were the very opposite. If they couldn't find any Huns to shoot at, they gave us their full attention. The Navy at Scapa flow was the worst offender - their motto being to shoot first and to ask questions afterwards.

At any rate No.3 Squadron was in no doubt from the start what its duty was when the pilots were taken to see an almost perfect example of a Ju88 in a Skeabrae hangar. It had been shot down on Christmas Day 1940 by a Royal Naval Grumman Martlet of 804 Squadron which had been based at Skeabrae pending the arrival of the RAF Squadron. After a very short tour of duty, No.3 Squadron left on 8 February, the shortest stay of any of the RAF fighter squadrons, indeed much shorter than many of the disembarked Royal Naval squadrons. It was necessary to rotate squadrons between the very active and the quieter stations but it is difficult to understand this short stay when the station was just getting itself going as a fighter base.

The primary function of the RAF fighters at Skeabrae and, later, Grimsetter, was to intercept enemy aircraft intruding into British airspace in the North of Scotland. More particularly, its role was to protect Scapa Flow not only from enemy bombers but also from the apparently innocuous reconnaissance aircraft which appeared over the islands with increasing frequency. Other duties included providing escorts for convoys which passed regularly through the Pentland Firth. The Hurricane fighter had a limited endurance and, if the weather was favourable, operated in endless relays from before dawn till after sunset. On clear moonlight nights single patrols would continue and the throaty sound of the solitary Hurricane could be heard in the still Orcadian air. The ships of the Home Fleet had also to be escorted to the limit of the fighter's endurance when they left Scapa and on their return. The cruisers of the Northern Patrols, for example the *Suffolk, Norfolk, Birmingham, Edinburgh* and *Euryalus* were kept particularly busy. RAF Skeabrae was regularly used as a training centre for pilots who had recently qualified. The policy of using the remoter stations for training was introduced by Air Chief Marshal Hugh Dowding at the height of the Battle of Britain to give pilots further flying experience. Orkney squadrons would sometimes have as many as ten new pilots! Later on in the war, pilots were trained for overseas postings. The training these pilots received in the defence of Orkney was put to good use defending another island community - Malta. By contrast Orkney was also, as we shall see later, a staging post for pilots who were able to unwind from some of the fiercest air battles of the war.

After the German invasion of Norway in April 1940, the possibility of an invasion of Britain from the north became very real and the possession of Scapa Flow, the base of the Home Fleet, would have been a severe blow to British morale. Experience had taught the British that in the blitzkriegs which had characterised German progress on the continent of Europe, the destruction of airfields was the first priority. There were four fully operational Air Stations in Orkney by July 1941 and they would be the first to be destroyed: this would be followed by an invasion of the east coast of Orkney supported possibly by airborne troops. The stations themselves were well defended and to test the defences there were several large scale mock invasions of Orkney. By far the largest was *Operation Leapfrog* which took place between 9th. and 11th. August 1941, doubtless to impress King George VI who was in Orkney at the time. An invasion force of 18,000 troops supported by tanks landed on the south-east of the Orkney Mainland, the main objectives being the

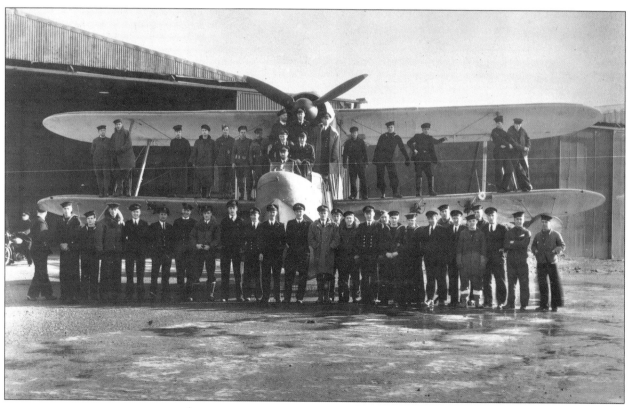

Sea Otter of 700 Sqdn. outside 700 Sqdn. hangars in March 1944, just prior to the disbandment of the squadron.. Officers standing in front of engine and cockpit: Sub. Lts. James, Astley, Snowdon, Weaver, Cyril Davison, Lt. Bottomley. Standing in front of aircraft: Sub. Lt. Vallely, Lt. 'Happy' Day, Lt. Cdr. Hyde (CO), Sub. Lt. Green, Sub. Lt. Brown. Others: On the starboard mainplane, Corp. RAF Bill Mattick, first from the engine on the starboard mainplane, Air Fitter Frank Kendrick, first from the engine on the port mainplane, Air Fitter George Thain, on Sub. Lt. Brown's right is Senior TAG Steve Lock, in front of A/C's port float, A.B. Tim???, New Zealander and next to him, A.B. 'Joe' Brain – REMMINGTON

seizure of Skeabrae and Twatt aerodromes. Air support was given to the invaders from all aircraft on the islands and also from the Scottish mainland. Hurricanes of No. 253 Squadron carried out attacks on the defending troops and provided escort for Blenheims which bombed the aerodromes. Both Air Stations were overwhelmed on the second day. For the Commanding Officer of Twatt it must have been a baptism of fire in more senses than one: his station had been operational for only three weeks! Valuable lessons were learned from such manoeuvres.

By December 1940, the Luftwaffe had called off its daylight offensive in southern England and switched its tactics to the bombing of London by night. The Spitfire squadrons were powerless to intervene and were gradually dispersed throughout Britain to give more general cover. No.253 Squadron Hurricanes took over the defence of Scapa Flow from No.3 Squadron on 10 January 1941 and it must have been reassuring for the Station Commander, Wing Commander Lea Cox, to count among the new squadron, veterans of the Battle of Britain. Strange new tongues and twangs gave Orcadians a taste of what was to come for practically the only thing these pilots had in common was their Hurricane!

One of the continued unpleasant tasks of the Hurricane pilots was the shepherding of neutral North Atlantic merchantmen into Orkney waters for contraband clearance. General cargo vessels were directed to Kirkwall Bay and oil tankers because of the risk of explosion were required to anchor in Inganess Bay further to the east. The frustration felt by the crews of these vessels as they waited in the long queue was heightened by the danger of being identified in British waters as a British vessel and the consequent risk of U-boat attack for there was no boom protection for them. Such a fate had already befallen the 10000 ton Danish tanker *Danmark*. The interference and delay was too much for one neutral merchantman who opened fire on a patrolling Skeabrae Hurricane of No.253 Sqdn. The merchantman was never identified or perhaps the British government chose to let the matter rest because of widespread disquiet about the impounding of neutral vessels on the high seas.

The most serious challenge facing the Hurricane pilots and the most frustrating was the appearance, at regular intervals, of high altitude German reconnaissance aircraft which, on fine days, would leave their vapour trails thirty to forty thousand feet above Scapa Flow. The croaking ring of the field telephone, 'the Bandit', scramble call and the ensuing futile chase left pilots dispirited. There was no way in which a Hurricane could make a successful interception at that altitude. As one officer remarked, 'By the time we got up there, Jerry

was back home looking at the prints!' It was perhaps a little comforting for the pilots to know that British reconnaissance aircraft cruised equally contemptuously over German territory.

By this time the Battle of the Atlantic, to the west of Orkney was in full swing. To provide intelligence for the U-Boat commanders, FW200 Condors, capable of a range of 2,200 miles would begin their flight in Bergen or Stavanger and sweep in a broad arc round the west coast of Britain well into the Atlantic. After the fall of France they landed at Bordeaux. Long range Ju88's also operated reconnaissance patrols from Bergen. All Atlantic reconnaissance aircraft generally flew to the north of Shetland, well out of harm's way but, with some cloud cover, pilots would risk the short cut through the Fair Isle Channel. On 4 March three Hurricanes of No.253 Squadron intercepted one such Ju88 and after a brief engagement it crashed into the sea east of Westray Sound. Royal Naval as well as Royal Air Force patrols would come across these aircraft sometimes quite unexpectedly and some regrettably did not return to tell of their unexpected encounter. The invaders were rarely picked up by Orkney radars though the radio monitoring services sometimes had a brief forewarning. A typical incident is described by Air Commodore Brown former pilot of No. 253 Squadron at the time:-

On 11 September 1941, my last day in Orkney and on my last patrol, I was flying a Hurricane on my own to the east of Fair Isle when I was suddenly confronted with a Ju88 which popped out of the cloud immediately ahead and only a few hundred yards away. Closing in on its port quarter with guns firing I swung round on to its stern. It was a good prolonged burst but, apparently unscathed, the '88 pulled up into the cloud and disappeared. Its presence was reported to sector operations by radio but neither the radars nor the listening service had any trace of it. Back on the ground at Skeabrae I was told there was no doubt I had attacked a twin-engined aircraft but did I know that an RAF Blenheim had been badly shot up and had landed at Sumburgh in Shetland with two of its crew wounded? I was certain that the aircraft had been a Ju88: I had been so close to it, within a few hundred yards, that the German markings were unmistakable. For about an hour there was strained silence in the crew caravan. Then the Squadron Commander appeared. In hospital the Blenheim pilot had been told that the Hurricane pilot was very sorry for his error. "What error?" he exclaimed, "what Hurricane squadron? We were shot up by a bloody Ju88!" No doubt the same one. But what if the Blenheim had crashed into the sea and all the crew had been killed?

In common with practically all the squadrons who were resident in Orkney, No.253 Squadron had its share of accidents and fatalities. On 31 May 1941, Orcadian farmer Robbie Taylor was working in one of his fields at Cumlaquoy in Marwick when a Hurricane aircraft began to make a series of power dives off Marwick Head. Robbie formed the impression that the pilot would have difficulty getting out of one power dive. The aircraft disappeared behind the cliffs. There was an explosion, followed by a huge pall of black smoke

The cruiser HMS Bermuda catapulting her Walrus, Scapa Flow, 1943 – EDWARDS

Walrus returning to the cruiser HMS Bermuda, Scapa Flow, 1943 – EDWARDS

Defiant DR933 of 771 Sqdn. hits a barrage balloon cable in Scapa Flow and crash lands: pilot unknown – HAMILTON

which, after some time, drifted over his field. Hurricane V2735 crashed at Crustan near Birsay village. This was to be Skeabrae's first fatality. Two weeks later a fellow pilot was seriously injured when his aircraft crashed near Wasbister in Rousay. The pilots of No.253 Squadron and indeed of all squadrons had to see Orkney, its weather and sea in all their moods. At times battered by wind and rain or blinded by the thickest of Scotch mists and all the attendant anxiety about getting back to base, there were times when the air was crystal clear with unbelievable visibility. The exhilaration felt by some of these young pilots for whom at times war must have seemed a million miles away is expressed beautifully by Brown in his vignette of Orkney *Changing Skies*:-

The most abiding impression of Orkney was a sense of freedom, both in the air and on the ground. Apart from the gun defended area of the Flow the islands presented an extensive, uncluttered and unrestricted aerial playground. Long range aircraft and modern fighters see little of the air and countryside around their bases except fleetingly, when taking off and landing, but Hurricanes, with their limited range and the sea all around Orkney stretching into the distance, were confined to the islands and their adjacent waters except when on operational patrol. For the sole benefit of young fighter pilots, this exclusive flying arena provided, from time to time, huge white cumulus clouds with sharply defined edges and deep caverns through and around which to tailchase, twist, turn, dive vertically down the blossoming faces and climb steeply to loop over their burgeoning tops. It was one of the rare occasions when a pilot could get a perception of height and depth and a surprising

realisation that some of the cumulo-nimbus clouds would boil up faster than a Hurricane could climb! At the other end of the aerial scale, at low level, there was the sea rolling in from the Atlantic and offering its broad curling waves with their foaming crests to be skimmed and the breakers to be chased along the deserted curving beaches. There were uninhabited islands over which to practise low level aerobatics with no one to complain and, hopefully, a Squadron Commander blissfully unaware of just how low they were. And if an appreciative audience was required, the lighthouse keepers always seemed to enjoy the show and the unexpected company.

Is it any wonder that, at the beginning of the war, some volunteer pilots thought they had to pay to join the RAF!

On 20 September 1941, No.253 Squadron moved out to be replaced by No.331 Hurricane Squadron. With its motto *For Norge*, this squadron was made up completely of Norwegians - 35 officers and 178 airmen - 213 personnel altogether, under the command of Major Bull. Many of them had had something of the experience of war already, escaping from occupied Norway at the risk of their lives. Among them was pilot Leif Lyssand who writes:-

Along with a party of other Norwegians we escaped by boat from occupied Norway. Sailing westwards, just as other harassed Norwegians had done a thousand years before, we made landfall on the island of Sanday in Orkney. Here we received a great welcome. It was my ambition to join the Royal Air Force and become a pilot. In this I was successful. I was even lucky enough after many tests, to qualify as a fighter pilot. I joined 331 Sqdn. which was made up entirely of Norwegians. Imagine my surprise and delight when I was eventually posted back to the Orkneys. We were stationed at Skeabrae. When my first flight took me over the North Isles of Orkney I saw Sanday far below. When I had arrived there, some months before, exhausted from my journey and anxious about the future, little did I know that, so soon, my burning ambition would be realised.

The Squadron felt very much at home here on old Norwegian soil and, less than three weeks after their arrival, there were emotional scenes at Skeabrae when His Royal Highness, Crown Prince Olaf of Norway and Admiral Reiser Larsen, Officer Commanding the Norwegian Air Force, visited them. Sergeant Pilot Ulf Wormdal, 'Worm' as he was known, was artistically inclined and the visit inspired him to design a Squadron Crest, a winged Viking ship floating on clouds, all on a shield of the Norwegian flag. This crest can be seen today on the memorial to this squadron at North Weald in Essex. To the usual operations carried out by the Skeabrae squadrons, No.331 added air to air firing. A glider was towed up several times to about 4,000 feet and then released over the aerodrome. It came down twisting and turning whilst attacks were made on it. The Squadron were disappointed in their time there to have only two encounters with enemy aircraft despite having frequent scrambles especially at dawn. Lt. Birkstead suggested a permanent state of readiness by flying dawn and dusk patrols and this became a feature of operations on the station until

Hurricane minus wing tip after striking barrage balloon cable – Twatt, 18.05.44 – BURKE

10 May 1945 when they were discontinued. In operational flying, No.331 had two fatal accidents. On 16 March 1941, Sgt. Pilot Ulf Wormdal crashed into the sea, unable to pull out of a practice dive on a Swordfish. The other fatality occurred mysteriously during one of the many scrambles to the north of Orkney. 2nd. Lt. James Endresen flying in line astern at 25,000 feet with Lt. Henning Leifseth disappeared without trace although visibility was good. Despite an extensive search no trace was ever found.

With so few opportunities for real action, the Norwegians became restless. To while away the time they planned invasions of their homeland and listened eagerly to news from any source. 801 Squadron with Sea Hurricanes spent the period 8 November 1941 until 14 February 1942 at Skeabrae and made great friends with the Norwegians. Some of the pilots had taken part in operations off Norway in HMS *Ark Royal* in April 1940 when equipped with torpedo bombing Skuas. Harald Meltzer tells of George, a pilot in 801 Squadron of the Royal Navy who caused great amusement by relating the following story:-

George had led a Flight of four torpedo carrying planes up some fjord in the north of Norway during the campaign there. Visibility was not too good and he found that the mountains on each side of the fjord gradually closed in on him so that he had not enough room in which to turn nor could he go upwards to make a turn: in front of

him were mountains at the end of the fjord. The three aircraft that were with him crashed on the mountain sides and the pilots were killed but somehow or other he himself managed to make a safe landing. Eventually he got back to England on a destroyer and made his way to London. In his own leisurely time he rang up the Admiralty to say he was back but he was not perfectly understood by them and he was told, "Oh yes, George, he was killed in Norway." Well George said no more. Here, he thought, was a wonderful opportunity for some free leave. So he rang up his wife who said, "Who is that speaking?" "George," he replied. "George who?" she asked. "Why George," he answered. "Yes, but which George, there are so many Georges?" George said he then hung up the telephone and thought "By Jove, here is another chance!" He told us he spent a month in London having a wonderful time and, finally, getting a bit bored, he went along and reported to the Admiralty for further duties. He had this story well worked up with all the skill of a great raconteur!

The Norwegians enjoyed their seven months stay in the islands where they had trained hard and learned a lot but the pilots wanted more action and could not disguise their joy when, on 28 April they learned that they were to be posted to North Weald in Essex where they were likely to get all the excitement they wanted. On 3 May 1942 the Squadron moved out and their place was taken by No.164 Spitfire Squadron.

The constant flying duties of the solitary Skeabrae squadrons placed a considerable strain on them and, during the period when the Norwegians were resident, an additional RAF squadron was brought

700 Sqdn. Maintenance Crews with Walrus and Petrol Bowser outside squadron hangars, Quoys, Twatt, 1943.
Left to Right: Air Artificer Joseph (HMS Belfast), Air Fitter C Gilbert, Air Fitter Wilson (HMS Belfast), Ldg. Air Mechanic G. Edwards, Ldg. Air Mechanic Simmonds, Air Fitter Frank Kendrick, Radio Mechanic Harry Stephens, Air Mechanic White?, Air Fitter L... (uncertain), Air Mech. Slater, Air Fitter Gupwell, (in front kneeling) Air Fitter J. Hannah – EDWARDS

in to reinforce the RAF presence. No.132 Squadron with 16 Spitfire IIb's arrived from Peterhead on 15 February 1942 and began to share duties with No.331. After four months at Skeabrae it transferred to RAF Grimsetter in the East Mainland of Orkney and converted to Vb's. Grimsetter had in fact been open since October 1940 as a satellite of Skeabrae and had been in regular use since then. Though a small station it was, as Fighter Sector Station in 14 Group, operationally very important. Sited at a suitably strategic distance from the airfield (and still standing) was the massive RAF Operations Room which controlled fighter movements from the Faroes to Caithness and which provided a listening service for bombers operating off Norway. Tactically the positioning of the second squadron in the east of Orkney made sense. It was from this direction where the enemy generally came and the five minutes gained by positioning a squadron here could make all the difference between a successful and an unsuccessful interception. Despite the positional advantage, No.132 Squadron recorded no interceptions. Records of their activities are meagre. On a training flight off Deerness on 22 August 1942 Sgt.Pilot Renyard was killed when his Spitfire Vb, BL667 crashed. No.132 Squadron left Grimsetter on 22 September 1942.

The arrival of No.164 Spitfire Squadron at Skeabrae on 4 May 1942 brought yet more strange tongues to the islands. The Squadron had at least one Argentinian pilot and bore the Spanish motto *Firmes Volamos*, firmly we fly, since the money for the squadron had been collected by the Argentine-British. No.164 had been formed at Peterhead only a few weeks previously and got off to a bad start by losing two aircraft on landing at Skeabrae, Spitfire X4328 landing too close to R7220 and chopping off the tail. Fortunately no casualties were recorded. A similar incident occurred at nearby RNAS Twatt some months later but in severe weather conditions. No.164 squadron is remembered in official records for the number of accidents in which it was involved all of which can be probably attributed to inexperience. One pilot, by breaking to the left instead of the right after a mock attack on the Fleet in Scapa Flow went straight between the masts of one of the capital ships and removed all the aerials. Remarkably, he got back to base. The same pilot, coming in low from the Atlantic over the cliffs of Yesnaby shortened his propeller blades by a few inches yet lived to tell the tale! There were other accidents and one casualty. Pilot Officer D B Bridger, the Argentinian, was killed when his Spitfire Va P9563 hit a workman's hut in a low pass over the station. In the many patrols carried out by this squadron it had only one partially successful contact with the enemy when a Ju88 was attacked

Norman Brown, Observer, Twatt, in front of a Walrus, August 1943 – BROWN

and damaged to the east of Orkney. The squadron left Orkney on 10 September 1942.

In September, No.132 Squadron at Grimsetter was replaced by No.129 and, on the departure of No.164 for Peterhead, No.602 Squadron took over duties at Skeabrae. For No.602 Squadron this was the first of two periods of residence at Skeabrae. For both squadrons, their stays were uneventful. By early 1943 they had left the islands.

To give the squadrons much needed air to air firing practice No.1494 Fighter Gunnery Flight moved to Skeabrae in early 1943 with target towing Lysanders. In March a most unfortunate incident occurred. To prevent the tail of an aircraft rising when the pilot brought the engine to full power it was normal practice for two aircraftmen to lie on the tail. This was invariably the case with Lysanders for, in the Orkney winds, the Lysander had a tendency to become airborne before the engine started! The pilot of Lysander T1580 mistook a signal and took off with an aircraftman still on the tail. He climbed to 200 feet at which point the rigger fell off, the aircraft went out of control and crashed. L/AC A C Lane was killed and two of the flying crew were injured. This resulted in one of several courts-martial held at Skeabrae during the war in two of which pilots had to stand trial. It is difficult to understand why this accident had to happen at all for an identical incident, fortunately not fatal, had occurred with a Seafire aircraft of 894 Squadron of the Royal Navy at Hatston barely three weeks earlier. The fantastic adventure of this member of the ground crew made the national newspapers and is described under the chapter *The Carrier Men*. The same Gunnery Flight devised a new method of releasing a drogue but due to a misunderstanding between the pilot and the winch operator, the plane flew very low over the station dragging behind it some 1,500 feet of cable. Unfortunately, on the end of this cable was a 5lb. lead weight which passed through the Station at 120 mph., almost demolishing the Armourers' Section. Hitherto, only seaplanes had been known to cast anchor. One wonders what would have happened had the lead weight hooked on anything! Incidents like this were rarely isolated. Although the Royal Navy at nearby Twatt were experts in drogue towing, on one occasion a drogue broke away and the winch which reeled in the cable jammed. Before the TAG could clear the blockage the drogue cable had sped over the Orkney countryside to the great alarm of a farmer when it passed between his horse and his plough.

Because of the peculiar requirements of the Orkney Stations, there was close liaison between the RAF and the Royal Navy. 801 and 880 Seafire Squadrons disembarked from *Furious* and using lodger facilities at RAF Skeabrae took advantage of the presence of No.601 Spitfire Squadron of the RAF to get in some valuable dog-fighting practice in early 1944. RAF personnel fitted ground installations into cruisers such as the *Suffolk* and *Norfolk* to enable the fighter pilots to communicate directly with the Fleet. Also No.1476 Ship Recognition Flight, equipped with Ansons was moved to Skeabrae where it remained for more than a year. There was enormous scope in Orkney to give pilots much needed experience in identifying British, Commonwealth and Allied warships. Among the other twin engined aircraft to visit Skeabrae were the torpedo carrying Beaufighters of No.254 Squadron based at North Coates in Lincolnshire. They spent a week on the Station at the beginning of April 1943 engaged in anti-shipping strikes off the Norwegian coast.

Is it a mere coincidence that all the RAF squadrons based at Grimsetter appeared to have been funded from Indian sources? No.132 Squadron had the name *Bombay*: No.129 was called *Mysore* and had as its badge the *Gunda Bherunda of Mysore*: No.234 was

Sea Otter over Orkney, March 1944 – BROWN

known as *Madras Presidency*. Signals Officer, Mike Walker who was based at Skeabrae from 1942 until 1943 writes that because of problems with the Control Tower at Grimsetter he had to drive a signals truck from Skeabrae to Grimsetter in time for the arrival of No.132 *Bombay* Squadron. An Eastern Potentate was going to give some money for aircraft but wanted to see a static firing display before he did so and Grimsetter had the only runway that could be used to fire out to sea. No.234 Squadron was the last RAF squadron to be resident at Grimsetter. In the interests of economy and efficiency the RAF moved out and based both squadrons at Skeabrae. It will be recalled that the RAF required only one station in Orkney in the first place, but, by default, ended up with two. The Royal Navy desperately wanted its own original air station, Skeabrae, back but a compromise was reached with the RAF when the Royal Navy assumed control of Grimsetter on 6 July 1943, becoming an independent command on 15 August 1943 when it was commissioned as HMS *Robin*. Altogether eleven RAF squadrons were based in Orkney during the remainder of the war. In keeping with the cosmopolitan nature of the pilots responsible for the aerial defence of Scapa Flow, these included No.312 and No.313 (Czech.), No.441 (Royal Canadian Air Force), No.329 (Free French) and No.451 and No.453 (Royal Australian Air

Force). Operations were routine and differed little from what has already been described but there were, nevertheless several highlights.

All pilots speak of the fickle nature of the Orkney weather and a good, though sad, illustration of this can be given from a No.66 Squadron patrol. The Station Diary of Skeabrae records that on 12 March 1943, two Spitfires took off at 10.53 on a sector recce counter clockwise round Orkney. The weather was fine with occasional heavy showers. The last fix on Pilot Officer Donald's aircraft was south of Westray at 11.33. At 11.41 the patrol ran into a severe blizzard and Pilot Officer Donald radioed "My screen is covered, I can see nothing" and required an immediate fix but because of interference from another transmitter the Control Tower could not give the aircraft its position. Control successfully brought in the other patrolling aircraft the pilot of which reported that, off Birsay, visibility dropped to ten yards. Despite extensive searches by four Walruses, two Lysanders and a Dominie, no trace of Pilot Officer Donald's aircraft was found.

German reconnaissance over Scapa Flow stepped up in early 1943 for the course of the war was turning and Germany feared a renewed attempt at invading Norway from the north. The Station Diary records that, on 22 March 1943 at 17.10 a Ju88 on reconnaissance flew over Scapa Flow at 34000 feet. On this occasion visibility was perfect and vapour trails could easily be seen. Guns were fired from the Kirkwall area but the aircraft was travelling at great speed. Warrant Officer Lawson of No.66 Squadron intercepted this aircraft at 17.15, 20 miles east of Scapa Flow and gave a half second burst at 1200 yards but the enemy dived into cloud. This is a fairly normal entry to be found in the Operational Record Books of all the northern Fighter Stations. What makes this entry of particular interest is that, much later, the pilot of that German aircraft was interrogated when he crash landed in Britain. Under interrogation he spoke of his operations, including this:-

On 22 March 1943 I took off from Ålborg (in northern Denmark) for a photographic reconnaissance of Scapa Flow and I returned with film which, in view of the anxiety about the invasion of Norway, was developed and taken immediately to Oberst Rowell and shown to Hitler personally. Thirty six ships were identified. I flew at 36000 feet above cloudbase and encountered extraordinarily accurate fire. I took evasive action but was followed by the AA fire. Fortunately they slightly underestimated my speed or I could easily have been shot down. When leaving Orkney I was chased for twenty minutes by three fighters and I went into a steep dive but I was followed all the way by the fighters. At 3500 feet I ran into cloud base and escaped.

The menace of high flying reconnaissance aircraft remained - and they were getting faster. To counter this menace, a specially modified High Flying Spitfire was introduced: only a few were ever made and sent to strategic parts of Britain. These were

700 Squadron Christmas card sent from Twatt: the aircraft is a Walrus and appears to be W2741 – EDWARDS

Spitfire VI's and VII's with Rolls-Royce two stage supercharged engines, pressurised cockpit and increased wing-span to cope with the rarified air at 50000 feet. Two of these truly magnificent flying machines were based at Skeabrae. No.312 Czech Spitfire seems to have been the first squadron at Skeabrae to be equipped with these Spitfires though there is no record of these aircraft in use by them. The only clue we have is a photograph taken sometime between mid-January and mid-February 1944 of a Mk.VII with the markings DU-G and a note to the effect that the Spitfire 'belonged to a previous squadron'. Czech No.312 Squadron had aircraft in the DU series and there seems little doubt that the Czechs were the first to experiment with these aircraft.

No.602 Squadron was based at Skeabrae from 18 January 1944 until 13 March 1944. This squadron was known as the *City of Glasgow* Squadron, the money to equip the squadron having been raised in that city and it was appropriate that Glaswegian Ian Blair, pilot of Spitfire Mk. VII, MD144, DU-G should distinguish himself in the short time the squadron was based in Orkney. On 20 February 1944 he intercepted and shot down a long-range Messerschmitt Bf 109 20 miles to the east of Orkney. A fellow pilot in the Squadron was Pierre

Clostermann who later in the war became one of France's flying aces and a well-known writer and politician. In his book *The Big Show*, Clostermann, using rather too much writer's licence, gives a graphic account of this incident. He claims he took part in the action and did everything apart from shooting the enemy aircraft down. Squadron pilots know better. At the time of the incident he was actually on the ground! Clostermann does however give an excellent description of a scramble at Skeabrae:-

Jacques and Kelly were on readiness from 1030 hours to 1400 hours. Superb weather but bitterly cold. Not having anything much to do, Ian Blair and I were playing a game of chess. At 12 o'clock everybody went off to lunch but we decided to finish our game. Kelly enviously watched the others going - this cold sharpened the appetite and, as usual, he was famishing. We ended up by taking pity on him and offered to take their place. They accepted joyfully for it must be admitted that this high altitude readiness was rather a bind. They went. We slipped on our Mae Wests, put our parachutes and helmets ready in the two Spitfires. 1222 hours.

"Your queen's had it," said Ian.

My queen certainly was cornered but just as he stretched out his hand to take it, the air-raid siren went. In the ensuing turmoil, queens, pawns, rooks, everything, went for six. The fitters rushed into the corridor with a clatter of boots. I dived for the door shouting Scramble, scramble! Ian leapt out of the window. In less than 50 seconds I was installed, strapped in, oxygen switched on and with the engine ticking over.

Cannon shells being loaded at Skeabrae – HORNE

Skeabrae: inserting ciné gun cassettes in a Spitfire in place of belts of bullets: petrol bowser in background –
HORNE

RAF Skeabrae – operating the trolley accumulator used for starting aircraft engines – HORNE

Three white rockets from Control showed that the runway was clear. The ground was frozen so hard that we could safely cut across the grass to get on the runway. At 1223 hours 35 seconds exactly we took off at full throttle and already Control was giving us our first instructions.

"Hallo Dalmat Red One, Pandor calling, bandit approaching, B for Baker at Z for Zebra, climb flat out on vector zero, nine, five. Out!" I fumbled inside my boot for my code card which had become mixed up with my maps. I was so clumsy about it that I had to ask Pandor to repeat.

O.K. a Jerry was approaching Scapa Flow at altitude Z - I looked it up on the card. Phew! Z meant 40,000 feet! I set my course, still climbing at full boost. Ian's Spit hovered a few yards away and I could feel his amused eyes on me under the sun goggles. It was a wonderful winter's day - not a trace of cloud in the sky -and the Arctic sun pierced my eyes. I switched on the heating and set the pressure in my cabin.

"Hallo Dalmat Red One. Pandor calling, bandit now over B for Baker. Hurry up!"

"Hallo, Pandor, Dalmat answering, I'm climbing flat out on vector 095, I'm angels R for Roberts.

"What did the controller take us for - rockets? In five minutes we had got to 23,000 feet; not bad going. In the meantime I had been thinking: this Jerry must be a reconnaissance aircraft. In this weather he must be able to get perfect photographs. The Fleet's ack-ack couldn't shoot because of us, naturally, and the navy must be cursing. At all costs we had to get that Hun. If we didn't, the Admirals would get us!

Pilot Officer (later Squadron Leader) Blair takes up the story:-

There were always pilots ready for action should any unidentified aircraft be picked up by radar. It was 20 February 1944 and Fl/Lt. Bennett and I were on stand by at readiness in the Flight Dispersal Hut. In my experience nothing much ever happened but this day a hurried message came over the Tannoy. 'Scramble: enemy aircraft approaching coast'. We took off and climbed full out. I was about 38000 feet and levelling out when I received the signal Dalmat I, bandit ahead. Sure enough, right ahead were vapour trails. He must have seen me just at that time for he dived to starboard on a southerly course going all out. I opened up everything I had and went into a power-dive after him. We were now at about 4000 feet diving hell for leather seaward. My speed was so terrific that I was forced to throttle back to avoid passing what I could clearly see was a long range Bf 109. I took careful aim and gave him a two second burst with both cannon and .303 machine gun. His starboard wing broke off and flew in the air. There was a crash and a shudder as I collided with some of the falling debris. The Messerschmitt turned over and over and plunged seawards. I saw it burning with a cloud of black oil smoke on the water as I turned to head for base.

But my fortune was soon to change. The debris had hit my radiator and my engine was failing. I was still 50 miles off the coast of Orkney and further still from Skeabrae. I thought I might have to bale out but I kept heading westwards. Land appeared to starboard and I reckoned it was Stronsay. I thought I could save the aircraft and myself if I did a belly landing there. I picked a spot and came down. It turned out to be less than ideal for I ploughed through a couple of fences and ended up against a turf wall. I was lucky to get away with a nasty bang in the face - I was certain that I must have at least broken my nose. Climbing out of the cockpit I saw at a short distance away a farmhouse which turned out be the farm of The Hill. There was no one around so I went up to the farmhouse door and knocked. It was opened by someone whom I found out later to be Miss Reid. I told her "I've pancaked in your backyard: I need a doctor." Miss Reid was very suspicious: she thought I was a spy. To convince her I wasn't a Messerschmitt pilot I asked her to come and see the plane and its RAF markings! From then on, all was well. A Dr. Pyle arrived and did a stitching job on site: he told me my nose didn't appear to be broken and apart from the cut I would, at worst, get away with two good black eyes.

Three months later, on 30 May 1944, there was another successful interception from Skeabrae when three enemy aircraft appeared on the Orkney radar screens. No.118 Squadron were scrambled and identified them as Ju88's. At 25000 feet Flight Officer J J Parker, an Australian, and Warrant Officer Taylor isolated one and, after a short exchange, the aircraft crashed into the sea. There were no survivors. This was the last successful engagement over Orkney.

With the focus of the war now in Central Europe intrusions into Orkney airspace became fewer and fewer. One type of German aircraft appeared from time to time but, to the great frustration of RAF pilots, was allowed to pass. This was the German meteorological flight, known to the RAF as *Weather Willie*. After the cracking of the Enigma Codes the British made use of the valuable meteorological information which was transmitted regularly back to base from these long Atlantic sorties. To prevent arousing the suspicion of the Germans, squadron pilots were instructed to make mock attacks on them with short bursts of fire which, of course, invariably missed. At least this did give the Spitfire pilots some degree of satisfaction but one wonders how this bizarre instruction was explained away to the pilots for it must have been evident to them that receiving of meteorological data by the enemy was as important to them as reports on the location of allied merchantmen.

No.331 Norwegian Spitfire Crest designed by Ulf Wormdal when he was stationed at Skeabrae − LYSSAND

With the change in the direction of the war, the operational work of the RAF diminished. In fact when No.66 Squadron and No.234 left Orkney in June 1943, only one squadron, No.312 replaced them. The remaining squadrons posted at Skeabrae were at times very stretched to cover convoy and patrol work but they remained vigilant - it was all too easy to be jumped on without warning. On 10 March 1945 Fl.Lt. E W Martin of No.441 vanished without trace while on patrol to the south of Scapa. But it was possible to be too vigilant. On 11 June 1944 two Spitfires of No.118 Squadron on patrol to the east of Orkney came across an unidentified aircraft which did not respond. The pilot of BL718 opened fire and the aircraft crashed into Auskerry Sound. Unfortunately the aircraft was a Mosquito of No.33 Squadron Leuchars on passage to Sumburgh. One of the crew members was killed. In the subsequent court-martial, the Spitfire pilot was cleared of blame. There were several incidents like this during the war - particularly when the war was in its early stages and nervous fingers were on the trigger. The Royal Navy almost brought down one of its own Skuas coming in to Hatston after a report had been received of enemy aircraft approaching. On 31 March 1940 a day when many enemy reconnaissance patrols passed over Orkney, a warship fired at a Hurricane of No.605 Squadron from Wick passing over Scapa Flow even though it was flying at a height of only 1200 feet! A month later the cruisers *Arethusa* and *Galatea* out of Scapa opened fire on Red Section Hurricanes of No.43 Squadron also based at Wick. On 25 November 1940 Hurricanes of No.3 Squadron, by this time based at Castletown just before their move to

Skeabrae were on Scapa patrol and intercepted what they believed to be a captured Whitley and shot it down. The aircraft crash landed at Wick and none of the crew was injured. This was fortunate as the aircraft was a genuine RAF Whitley from Kinloss.

With more experienced pilots, better aircraft and communications, there were few fatalities among the RAF squadrons at Skeabrae towards the end of the war but the Orkney weather and topography sometimes proved master. On 6 April 1945 Capitaine Sassard of No.329 Squadron Free French Air Force failed to clear the top of mist covered Skelday Hill in Birsay as he took off on dawn patrol. The Squadron Diary solemnly records his funeral ceremony in Kirkwall on 10 April.

By contrast there were great celebrations at Skeabrae on 8 May: even the WAAFs had a free pint of beer with their mid-day meal. There was no work in the afternoon so that everyone could have an opportunity to hear the Premier's speech which was relayed over the Tannoy at 3pm. In the evening a dance for all ranks was held. Celebrations went on next day: there was a free film show in camp in the evening and more entertainment for, by coincidence, the Gordon Highlanders' concert party was visiting the Station that night. On 10 May dawn and dusk patrols were discontinued, presumably because none of No.451 Australian Squadron was fit to get up! One week later, on 17 May, readiness state came to an end. By 24 July, at nearby Twatt, the whole of 771 Squadron with its 51 aircraft had moved out but it was September before the Aussies had sufficiently recovered to get themselves airborne. 15 Spitfires headed south to the sun.

Harrow Transport of No.271 Squadron flies out after bringing in No.132 Squadron to Skeabrae on 15 February 1942. Village of Dounby under tail wing. Photograph taken by Roc of 771 Sqdn. Twatt – FAAM

Spitfires of No.164 Squadron on dispersal at Skeabrae, sometime between May and September 1942 (R E G Sherward via C H Thomas) in David Smith's 'Action Stations' – SHERWARD

Equipment Store Personnel, Skeabrae 1943: of the WAAFS in the middle row, the second on the left is L.A.C.W. E M Dunnett, first WAAF at Skeabrae: to the left of the WAAFS is ???? Ball and to the right, Smalley: WAAF Officer Southern in front row – DUNNETT

High Flying Spitfire MD114 in pen at Skeabrae,, January, 1944: notice modified wings – BLAIR

Battle of Britain pilot F/Lt. Ken Souter RAF, relaxes at the Bay of Skaill, May 1945: F/Lt. Souter was finally based at RNAS Twatt, one of a number of RAF personnel attached to RNAS stations in Orkney – PEMBERTON

Vicky Luker with Roger Bush, Pilot Officer 611 Sqdn. Skeabrae, Christmas, 1943 – HORNE

"That's the fourth time this week he's done that, he used to be a Spitfire pilot" – HOLDEN

Drama rehearsal at Skeabrae for Gaslight by Patrick Hamilton; Frederick Peisley, later a very famous actor with WAAF Vivian Marwood – HORNE

WAAFS and WRENS at Skeabrae, March 1944, before the Twatt Wrens were accommodated at Skogar, Twatt; these Wrens were R/T operators and worked at the Fighter Direction Centre at Hesta Geo, Birsay – TAYLOR

Chapter Five

The Carrier Men

On 27 August 1939, the aircraft carrier HMS *Ark Royal* entered Orkney waters and disembarked the Skuas of 800 Squadron of the Royal Navy, the first front-line squadron to touch down at the new Royal Naval Air Station at Hatston. During Hatston's short but busy life another 71 squadrons of the Royal Navy and six squadrons of the United States Navy were to disembark here. The squadrons came and went according to the movements of their parent carrier; on average the accumulative total for each Royal Naval squadron was ten weeks but this varied from the 4 days spent at Hatston by 1842 Squadron in August 1944 to the 80 weeks spent by 804 Squadron between November 1939 and May 1944. 804 Squadron was not however initially a disembarked squadron: it was formed at Hatston in September 1940 as a front-line squadron with the specific task of defending Scapa Flow until this role was taken over by the Royal Air Force.

In the beginning all carrier squadrons disembarked at Hatston airfield but as the war progressed and Scapa Flow became busier Hatston was unable to cater for the needs of all carriers. There were, on occasions, ten carriers in Scapa, all with different requirements, and other air stations as they became available, on the Mainland of Orkney coped with the overflow from Hatston. Between June and September 1940, there were, at times, no less than 8 squadrons based at Hatston, far beyond the capacity of the station. By 10 October RAF Skeabrae was operational and 804 Squadron with its Sea Gladiators moved there from Hatston. Altogether 10 squadrons or detachments of squadrons of Royal Navy aircraft had lodger facilities at Skeabrae during the war. By June 1941, Twatt was able to accommodate front line fighters: the first visitors were 812 Squadron with Swordfish which also moved in from Hatston. The large numbers of aircraft in 700 and 771 Squadrons meant that Twatt was rarely in a position to offer facilities to disembarked carrier planes but, despite this, Twatt handled 15 front line squadron disembarkations. In October 1942 RAF Grimsetter had to accept 700 Squadron of the Royal Navy while Hatston, Twatt and Skeabrae stations trained front line squadrons

for the *Torch* landings in North Africa. As explained elsewhere, Grimsetter was eventually transferred to the Royal Navy to ease pressure on Hatston and, before the war was over, 21 front line squadrons had used the airfield.

After the sinking of HMS *Royal Oak* on 14 October 1939, most of the Home Fleet dispersed and after 16 October when HMS *Ark Royal* disembarked 816 Squadron for one day at Hatston, aircraft carriers did not use Scapa Flow for six months until the defences had been reinforced. After the German invasion of Norway on 9 April, the strategic importance of Scapa Flow assumed a new significance. In April and May, as explained in the chapter *In the Front Line*, shore based aircraft attacked enemy positions but with the arrival of the carriers HMS *Glorious* and HMS *Ark Royal* in April, a pattern of combat was established which continued intermittently until the end of the war. Fighter support was badly needed over Norway where the flush-deck carrier *Furious* had taken up position. Initially equipped with two Swordfish squadrons, 816 and 818, but no fighters, *Furious* had been damaged by enemy bombing and now, with only eight serviceable aircraft left, had to return to Britain for urgent repairs.

Arriving off Scapa on 22 April 1940, *Glorious* disembarked her 823 Swordfish Squadron, taking on board 803 Squadron Skuas and 804 Squadron Sea Gladiators from Hatston. The carrier already had on board 18 Gladiators of No.263 Squadron RAF which were being ferried to Norway. Meanwhile 800 Squadron and 801 Squadron Skuas, also from Hatston joined *Ark Royal*. On 23 April, with cruiser and destroyer support, *Glorious* and *Ark Royal* sailed from Scapa, heading east to Norway on *Operation D.X.*, which had several aims, most importantly to give aerial support to the ground troops between Trondheim and Åndalsnes. Even before they left, the crews had a good idea of what was in store for them. Five days earlier, Hatston Skua pilots had found themselves powerless to stop the persistent bombing of the cruiser HMS *Suffolk* on passage from Norway to Orkney. Now, for all to see, it lay beached and severely battered at Longhope in Scapa Flow, having struggled across the North Sea, latterly with no steering gear.

Altogether *Ark Royal* and *Furious* had on board 21 Swordfish, 29 Skuas, 5 Rocs and 18 Sea Gladiators of the Royal Navy and 18 Gladiators of the Royal Air Force. On paper, it was quite a formidable aerial armament. But things did not go well on the Norwegian operations. The RAF Gladiators were destroyed by the Luftwaffe shortly after they landed in Norway: *Glorious* lost five Skuas and eventually only four were operational. These transferred to *Ark Royal* and on 27 April, only four days after leaving Scapa, she set sail again for Orkney to embark more aircraft. The carrier was held up in Orkney because of bad weather which prevented the aircraft flying on but by 1 May she had rejoined the Task Force. *Glorious* arrived to find that central Norway, around Namsos, was being evacuated and the carriers were immediately caught up in determined Luftwaffe action. Despite heavy bombing of the British warships no vessels suffered a direct hit and only one Skua was lost in intensive aerial combat. Some surprise was expressed at this by the British pilots because the naval gunners, with so little experience, had great difficulty in distinguishing between friend and foe and fortunately their fire was highly inaccurate!

At the end of the day, it was considered that the risk to the warships was too great in relation to what they were able to do to support the ground troops and the carrier force withdrew, heading back once more for Scapa Flow.

Ark Royal returned on 6 May and covered the naval bombardment of Narvik. Miraculously she escaped the heavy bombing encountered by the British support vessels but Bill Lucy, CO of 803 Squadron who had planned the *Königsberg* raid from Hatston was killed along with his Observer Hanson when driving off attacks by Heinkel 111's. *Glorious* sailed from Greenock on 14 May to ferry No.46 Squadron Hurricanes of the RAF to Norway and *Furious* joined her with No. 263 Gladiator Squadron which had just been brought up to strength. All three carriers met off the Norwegian coast on 18 May, the first time they had been together. The weather was so bad that it wasn't until 21 May that *Furious* was able to land her Gladiators, even so, two of the Gladiators and the guiding Swordfish crashed into a mountain on the approach to Bardufoss, to the north of Narvik. It was decided not to land the Hurricanes in these circumstances and the three carriers set off for Scapa once more. On the return trip to Norway, the Hurricanes were finally flown off *Glorious* to Bardufoss, on 26 May, two weeks after being embarked. On that very same day, the British suffered an enormous blow when the cruiser HMS *Curlew* equipped with sophisticated radar for anti-aircraft defence, was sunk near Narvik. All did not go well for *Glorious* either: a disagreement between the Captain and the Commander (Flying) about the wisdom of mounting a particular operation led to the return of *Glorious* to Scapa Flow and the transference of the Commander (Flying) to the *Dunluce Castle* on his way to a court-martial.

On 31 May, *Glorious* and *Ark Royal* left Scapa, turned west into the Pentland Firth bound for the last time for Norway from where all 25,000 allied

Swordfish being loaded with 100 lb anti-submarine bombs at Hatston 1941: centre left probably V4631 – FANCOURT

troops were to be finally evacuated. *Ark Royal* re-embarked 800 and 803 Squadrons from Hatston to provide fighter cover for the troops: *Glorious* already had 802 Squadron Gladiators and six Swordfish of 823 Squadron aboard but primarily for her own protection since it was to be her duty to ferry back to Scapa the remaining aircraft of No.263 Gladiator Squadrons of the Royal Air Force which had done such outstanding work after they had been landed at Bardufoss. As for the Hurricanes, it was considered impossible to land them on a carrier: they would have to be abandoned. However when *Glorious* was off Norway the bold plan was devised of attempting to bring back the Hurricanes too. In a brilliant display of flying both Gladiator and Hurricane squadrons were successfully embarked. The evacuation of Norway went perfectly to plan and by midnight on 9/10 June, the flotilla was on the move westwards, some to Scapa, some to the Clyde. The story of the fate of HMS *Glorious* is well known. Accompanied by only two destroyers, the *Ardent* and *Acasta* she detached herself from the rest of the Fleet and headed for Scapa. On the way she was intercepted by the German battleships *Scharnhorst* and *Gneisenau* and, along with her accompanying destroyers, *Glorious* was sunk with the loss in total of more than 1,500 lives. Sadly the RAF Gladiators and Hurricanes which had been so skilfully flown on in the evacuation were lost too. The *Scharnhorst* had been damaged in the encounter and sailed south to Keil for repairs. As *Scharnhorst* was on her way south on 21 June, 821 and 823 Squadrons from Hatston made a revenge torpedo attack on her but to no avail: one squadron aircraft was lost. Three days later another torpedo attack was made by 823 Squadron against destroyers and transports off the Norwegian coast but again with limited success.

As for *Glorious'* Commander (Flying), he was still awaiting his fate in Scapa Flow. With the Captain of *Glorious* lost, there was no prosecution and, in fact no court-martial ever took place. This was nevertheless a most unsatisfactory state of affairs and the Commander spent many of the post war years setting the record straight and successfully clearing his name. Thus ended the Norwegian campaign. For six weeks there had been intensive carrier activity in Scapa Flow: now the focus of the war in Europe was to shift south and for a time there was only sporadic carrier activity in Scapa Flow. HMS *Furious* appeared in Scapa in July and 825 Swordfish Squadron flew to Hatston for several days, returning again in September when both 825 and 816 Squadrons were disembarked after an attack on shipping in Trondheim harbour in which five of 816 Squadron Swordfish were lost. After participation in the North African landings in October, *Furious* returned to the base of the Home

Swordfish pilot, Hatston: name unknown –
HAMILTON

Fleet at Scapa and 801 Squadron disembarked on several occasions at Hatston after taking part in convoy patrols. Another quiet six months passed at Scapa until the Norwegian offensives began again in July 1941 and the big carriers returned once more.

In May 1941, the new Vickers-Armstrong carrier, the *Victorious* entered Scapa. She was not yet fully worked up, carrying only a few fighters and torpedo bombers for her own protection and had on board crated Hurricanes bound for the Middle East. With the danger of *Bismarck* and *Prinz Eugen* breaking out into the Atlantic her sailing plans were shelved and from Hatston she embarked 825 Squadron Swordfish recently arrived from Campbeltown. The Squadron Leader was Lieutenant Commander (A) Eugene Esmonde, who was later (12 February 1942) to win a posthumous Victoria Cross for his Squadron's attempt at preventing the German warships passing through the English Channel. *Victorious* sailed from Scapa on 22 May when it was learned that *Bismarck* had escaped into the Atlantic. Her own fighter squadrons, Fulmars of 809 Squadron from St. Merryn in Cornwall attempted to join her but were forced to return because of bad weather. On 24 May Swordfish of 825 Squadron launched a torpedo attack on *Bismarck* scoring one hit and forcing the

HMS Victorious steaming off Orkney in 1941 when the squadrons were working up: note the black wind baffle up front: the aircraft on deck are Albacores with a solitary Fairey Fulmar of 809 Squadron on the stern – COOPER

An Albacore leaves the flight deck of HMS Victorious in Scapa Flow – IWM

vessel to reduce her speed. Running short of fuel, *Victorious* had to withdraw and leave the chase to *Ark Royal* which moved up from Gibraltar. The outcome of *Ark Royal's* intervention is well known. The *Bismarck* was crippled by a torpedo attack by 818 and 810 Squadron Swordfish which damaged her rudder and she was eventually sunk by battleships of the Royal Navy.

The new Norway offensives began with the arrival at Hatston from Donibristle on 24 March 1941 of 828 Albacore Squadron. Its local role was anti-submarine patrol work but extensive torpedo training also took place in preparation for an attack on enemy shipping in Norway. One Albacore was lost in a dummy torpedo attack when it plunged into the sea near Sanday on 2 May 1941 killing the Observer and, a few days later another was written off after it made an emergency landing at Hatston. The Squadron's first break came on 23 May when, after a month's training it flew to Sumburgh to strike at *Bismarck* near Bergen. The operation was cancelled (fortunately in the opinion of the Station Commander) when it was learned that the enemy battleship had left her anchorage and was heading for the Atlantic. Finally, on 2 July, after 13 weeks' training, the squadron flew on to *Victorious* which,

after the *Bismarck* operation, had entered Scapa triumphantly. Meanwhile 809 Fulmar Squadron, fresh from St.Merryn, had spent three weeks at Hatston. They too joined *Victorious* along with 827 Squadron Albacores which had just arrived from Machrihanish. *Victorious* was joined by *Furious* in Scapa Flow and, from the new airfield at Twatt 812 Squadron Swordfish flew on. Clearly, a big operation was underway.

The aim of the operation was to offer some help to the Soviet Union which had been invaded in June 1941 and the plan was to attack the German forces in Northern Norway and Northern Russia. The strike took place on 30 July, 812 Squadron Swordfish and 817 Squadron Albacores from *Furious* were to attack Petsamo while 827 and 828 Squadron Albacores from *Victorious* headed for Kirkenes. The whole operation which, almost unbelievably, took place in broad daylight, was a disaster. John Cooper was a young pilot with 809 Squadron Fulmars whose duty it was to provide CAP (Combat Air Patrol) for the Albacore Squadrons from *Victorious*. He had spent a very pleasant three weeks at Hatston before he flew on. His personal account gives some idea of the shortcomings of the mission:-

'Tex' Van Epps, 809 Sqdn. pilot of Fulmar N4026 makes his first landing on an air craft carrier – HMS Victorious off Scapa: his radio transmitter was on and his comments were noted! – COOPER

The Home Fleet, under the command of Admiral Wake-Walker flying his flag in the cruiser *Devonshire* arrived at Scapa after working up in the North Atlantic and Icelandic waters. 809 Squadron landed on *Victorious* off Orkney. For most of us it was a hair-raising event because we had received very little Dummy Deck Landing Training at Yeovilton. We hadn't even seen an aircraft carrier let alone land on one! Fortunately we all managed with the exception of American fellow pilot 'Tex' Van Epps. He had left his radio on in error and we all heard, first hand, his feelings as his aircraft swung to port and ended up half over the side!

The next shock came on our first take off. To enable the pilots to take off at 20 second intervals the engines were all started at once. Pilots who took off last had to make their way through the whirling and dangerous confusion of propellers and slipstream to reach their aircraft - at least such pilots had the consolation that they had the longest deck run! Fine judgement was required if the ship was rolling and pitching. The few Dummy Deck Landings we had done could not convey to us how, in a gale, a carrier's deck could rise and fall 70 feet!

Our first engagement with the enemy was on the borders of Northern Russia. The Kirkenes/Petsamo operation has been well documented: I think that if I were to say anything, it would be so derogatory of those who planned the operation that it might cause embarrassment, mainly because the orders to attack Petsamo and Kirkenes were directed to be carried out in broad daylight, about 50 miles to the north of the two northern ports, with German spotter aircraft in sight above the Fleet. These aircraft were, of course reporting our every move and I know of nobody who took part in the attack on Kirkenes, the target allocated to *Victorious*, who did not think that the order to fly off and attack, invited heavy resistance and casualties.

For 809 Squadron, it was the first operation since our formation and most of us were very young and inexperienced. We flew south towards Kirkenes in line abreast and the first I knew of anything amiss was when I saw someone to our right bale out of a burning plane and descend towards the sea by parachute. We were in fact being attacked by Messerschmitt 109's and 110's which had been sitting up sun awaiting our arrival - and they had had plenty of notice! I broke away from the formation and dived with a vague idea of giving some protection to the Albacores. Through the Gosport tube, a voice said, "Don't let's be over enthusiastic sir". It was L/A Frank Gilder, my Telegraphic Air Gunner. Poor Frank, he had no gun and was not a navigator - I'm not quite sure what his role was but he soon found one and proved an invaluable help as a spotter of enemy fighters. I had a rear view mirror but Frank had a wider view of aircraft attacking us from the rear and kept up a running commentary and countdown until the optimum moment to turn. The Fulmar, though large and not very fast, was a manoeuvrable aeroplane and could out-turn the 109's and 110's. When Frank called out "Zero!", I would slam down the wheels and flaps and turn as tightly as possible. The German fighter would whizz past at speed in a wider turning circle.

Being on the receiving end of these attacks, made it almost impossible to protect the Albacores below us which, laden with torpedoes and labouring into a strong head wind were making slow progress towards Kirkenes from which, incidentally, most ships had already fled! The Albacores were sitting ducks for the 109's and 110's; it was distressing to see the Germans running their bullets or cannon shells through the water behind them, passing forward through the body and kicking up the sea in front of them. After a confused period of dogfighting with glimpses of friendly and enemy aircraft, sea and coastline during which I fired my guns if and when I could, we found ourselves alone and undamaged.

Land-based German pilots never liked flying far out to sea and, after we had flown north for a while, we were lucky enough to spot a solitary Albacore below us, lucky because we knew it would be carrying a navigator and we had a good chance of getting back to *Victorious*. This we did and, dispensing with an approach circuit as we had used so much fuel in the dogfighting, we landed on but only just; our engine cut out after we had taxied over the crash barrier. When I reported to the Flying Bridge, Commander Flying asked how many of our aircraft were flying out behind me. He was in tears when I said, "None, sir". No fewer than 11 of our 20 Albacores had been lost together with 2 Fulmars: some of those who made it back to the ship contained dead or wounded crewmen.

On the evening of the attack, or maybe a little later when the Fleet had withdrawn to Spitzbergen, Admiral Wake-Walker came on board and addressed the aircrews in the Wardroom. His intention was to boost morale by pointing out that, in spite of losses, the operation had succeeded in showing the Russians (who had just entered the war) that we were supporting them. However the pilots and observers were so angry about the mishandling of the operation that they received what he had to say in stony silence. The atmosphere was both eerie and embarrassing and he had no course but to withdraw.

I was awarded a DSC for my part in the operation. This was, of course, an honour, but, to be candid, any one of the 809 Squadron pilots would have merited it.

A dispirited Fleet sailed back again to Scapa where the carriers disembarked what remained of their squadrons. While *Furious* took part in a Malta convoy, *Victorious* continued to use Scapa Flow to mount attacks on shipping off the Norwegian coast and, from time to time military targets ashore. In August *Victorious* took part in operations in the Barents Sea and in October attacks were made on the Bodø area of Norway. At other times she escorted North Russian convoys, intermittently landing her squadrons at Hatston or Twatt. John Cooper again gives a vivid description of life aboard a carrier in a convoy:-

The squadron stayed in *Victorious* for many months, often escorting Atlantic and Russian convoys. This involved flying endless patrols and attacking any German long-distance aircraft shadowing and reporting our position to U-boats. Among these aircraft were the BV138's which were so big we called them Odeon Cinemas! Some hundreds of ships of all sizes would form convoys which would, of course, travel at the speed of the slowest. If any small ship started making smoke and falling further and further behind, we in our fighters would go back to say 'Goodbye', flying past the bridge at sea-level to give them a wave. Such stragglers were easy prey for U-boats.

Flying from a carrier in convoy was extremely tiring, both physically and mentally. Naval pilots and other aircrew have generally agreed that, in the war-time Fleet Air Arm, one was either very bored or very frightened. Life for us as fighter pilots was certainly tiring because of the limited number of aircraft; on *Victorious* there was only one fighter squadron consisting of 12 Fairey Fulmars. We were seldom given more than five minutes notice to get into an aeroplane and fly it off the deck - and that was in all kinds of weather. When there was no actual operation going on, we had a minimum of two pilots sitting in an aircraft on deck ready to fly off within 60 seconds of any alarm or emergency. If the sea was very rough, the aircraft would be mounted on a catapult with the other waiting to take its place. In addition to this, four pilots would be in the Ready Room, fully clothed in their flying gear ready to man their aircraft if required. The squadron's remaining pilots would be resting down below or in the Wardroom and would be expected to be ready to fly in less than five minutes. We used to think that our lot in carriers was worse than that of our fellow pilots in the RAF because when they landed, they could relax, or go to the local pub with their wives or sweethearts whereas we returned to a bouncy ship, couldn't sleep in our cabins if they were below the waterline and didn't see a girl for months!

In *Victorious* and no doubt in all warships, one of the major strains was the Tannoy communications system through which all orders were transmitted and announcements made. Although 99% of these concerned only ship routine, the other 1% would be an alarm call to 'Action Stations'. Then aircrews among others would drop everything they were doing, wherever they were, and join in a mad rush to man their aircraft. When the Tannoy was switched on therefore, we would all get very tense until our minds and muscles were relaxed by some innocuous announcement such as 'Fatigue party fall in on the foc'sle'. For some odd reason, after fifty years I remember 'Open Royal Marines bathroom' which always seem to occur at night, I don't know why! Over very long periods, with the system operating night and day, nerves could become frayed. I know of some pilots, observers and gunners in *Victorious* who were 'shovelled ashore with twitch' as we termed it because of this continuous strain which had nothing to do at all with enemy action but rather with this ceaseless, frustrated anticipation. The actual one in a hundred Action Stations alarm was very noisy. I think it consisted of intermittent blasts on a klaxon followed by an announcement by the Captain.

Victorious could stay at sea for a very long period of time and it was seldom that we got any shore leave at home or went ashore in New York when we escorted convoys westward to the United States. On arrival we would swing around a buoy or steam round the Hudson Light or perhaps head directly to an Icelandic fjord to join a convoy going back to Britain. This endless movement could be very disorientating especially for the hundreds of crew who lived for most of the time below the water line. It used to be amusing for us to see a deck hatch open, an old string vest pop out, the bearer have a sniff of the Arctic air and disappear. That was possibly the first time he had surfaced for months and probably would have no idea whether he was off New York, Murmansk or Spitzbergen. The perpetual daylight in the Arctic summer - and indeed in Orkney to some extent - often confused us tired pilots too. I have experienced the peculiar feeling of looking at my watch while playing poker in the Ready Room and not knowing whether it was one o'clock in the morning or in the afternoon.

When we were at sea for very long periods we often ran out of fresh fruit and vegetables and made do with rice balls instead of potatoes. Once our supply of alcohol almost ran out. I recall one tragic period when an evil looking purple liqueur was the only drink available in the Wardroom bar. Of course the majority of pilots drank very little or not at all because they were never off duty in operational waters and could be called upon to fly at short notice. Alcohol combined with carrier take-offs and landings made a very bad cocktail as some tragically found out.

Living for long periods in such conditions, it is little wonder that the front line crews let their hair down when they disembarked to Orkney airfields. After a series of such convoy operations, 809 Squadron was disembarked to Twatt on 26 October 1941. The officers' mess at that time was a Nissen hut and officers have memories of having to lift their feet to get to the bar - their first target - because the wind was blowing so strongly that it was lifting the linoleum off the floor! The Station Commander ended up in a circular static water tank that

night and high spirits were still not defused by Christmas. In this pastoral scene the Station Commander had been able to fatten some geese, no doubt for Christmas Wardroom festivities, but on 23 December a messenger reported that his geese had flown. Indeed they had: with his revolver, a New Zealand pilot of 809 Squadron had brought their lives to a premature end and fellow pilots were all required to carry a goose on their laps when they flew off to *Victorious* on 23 December! One might infer that the Station Commander was not very popular but this isn't true: a correspondent describes him as a good sort but he must have found it difficult to forgive the final prank.

Immersion in a circular static water tank seemed to have been the culmination of the night's festivities on a number of occasions, the victim usually being a high ranking officer who entered into the spirit of things or, sometimes, a more risky adventure, a superior officer who had not respected the norms of the Wardroom. An Army officer who commanded a local brigade and who had appeared more than once in the Wardroom in full peace-time mess kit did not endear himself to the carrier men, especially when he made advances to a Senior Officer's very attractive daughter. He was given a naval experience when he was deposited in the static water tank which happened to be conveniently placed just outside the Officers' Mess. When he returned to his transport, he found that his tyres had been deflated. This was too much for the Commanding Officer who immediately closed the bar for two weeks. Imagine the anguish of front-line pilots newly arrived only to find the bar was closed! Fortunately the Commanding Officer was a humane man and invited them up in groups to his cabin for drinks!

Squadrons disembarked at Hatston had their moments too. Duncan Hamilton, the celebrated Jaguar racing driver of the '50's, was Senior Aero Engineer at Hatston and saw many squadrons come and go. In his book *Touch Wood* which deals for the most part with his racing career, he devotes a chapter to his experiences at Hatston. Here he describes getting caught up with high spirited young pilots and observers:-

We lived at a tremendous pace: it is impossible to explain some of the crazy things we did. They just seemed natural at the time. We loved to compete against one another. One visiting officer was able to lick the red hot side of a mess stove without burning his tongue. Another who attempted the feat was unable to eat or drink for several days. The unfortunate officer, trying to explain to the Captain why he could not speak properly, or appealing to the M.O. for assistance, was thought to be funny. The inability of one side to understand why it was necessary to lick a red hot stove and the inability of the other to explain why it appeared to be a good idea at the time, created just the situation we enjoyed.

On 23 February 1942 *Victorious* disembarked 817 and 832 torpedo squadrons at Hatston for a little

Two Fairey Fulmars from Hatston flying in formation – HAMILTON

809 Sqdn. pilots in the Wardroom of Victorious after flying from Twatt on Chrstmas Eve, 1941: they stole the Commander's geese before they left and brought them back on board! – COOPER

over a week and they had a busy training programme which was just as well for they were soon to be put to the test. *Victorious* sailed again from Scapa Flow on 4 March and rendezvoused with convoy PQ12 which had sailed from Reykjavik three days earlier. On 7 March it was learned that the German battlecruiser *Tirpitz*, based at Trondheim, was in the Atlantic and, having failed to intercept the convoy, was returning to Vestfjord. On 9 March 832 Squadron Albacores sighted the enemy and the squadron diary records the subsequent engagement:-

Visibility was anything up to 30 miles. Cloud base was at 4000 feet. The squadron started to climb and soon we were above the clouds with the *Tirpitz* about 15 miles away. We were guided on to the target by ASV but at 09.20hrs the first sub-flight 4A, 4B and 4C dived to the attack with the enemy on its starboard bow below. As soon as the first sub-flight came out of the clouds, the enemy opened fire and they encountered heavy flak during the dive. They dropped on the port bow at approximately 1000yd with the *Tirpitz* turning towards them. The second third and fourth sub-flights then dived to the attack just after the first sub-flight had successfully turned away . . . the enemy put the wheel hard over to starboard and appeared to avoid all torpedoes. The target was thickly obscured by smoke and it is doubtful that a hit would have been seen. During the attack 4P was hit and crashed into the sea. One aircraft of 817 Squadron was also hit, set on fire and likewise crashed. We set course for the carrier and landed on at 10.30hrs.

The torpedoes missed the target and *Tirpitz* escaped to the safety of Vestfjord. The last opportunity for the Fleet Air Arm to confront this battlecruiser on the open sea had been lost. She did not venture out again when carriers were in the convoy in case she suffered the same fate as the *Bismarck*. Damaged by heavy seas, *Victorious* had to be withdrawn at the end of March for a short refit. Disembarking her 809 Squadron Fulmars at Twatt she sailed south, her place being taken by the carrier USS *Wasp*.

Wasp sailed for Britain on 26 March 1942 with Task Force 39 in the company of the battleship *Washington*, two heavy cruisers and six destroyers, to reinforce the Home Fleet of the Royal Navy. Commanded by Rear Admiral John W Wilcox in *Washington*, the Task Force got off to an inauspicious start when, during a severe Atlantic storm, Admiral Wilcox was swept overboard and drowned. Rear Admiral Robert C Giffen assumed command in USS *Wichita*. The Task Force was met off Orkney on 3 April by a force based around the light cruiser HMS *Edinburgh*. No sooner had *Wasp* arrived in Scapa Flow than the Captain received orders to take part in a most unusual mission. Although attached to the Home Fleet, *Wasp's* first assignment was to go to Malta which was being hammered by enemy bombing and on the point of submission. Air Vice-Marshal Lloyd wrote: "Malta's need is for Spitfires, Spitfires and more Spitfires". He sent a distinguished pilot, Wing Commander Gracie, back to Britain to tell the authorities at first hand what the situation was like. As a result,

Winston Churchill sent a message to President Roosevelt. Spitfires were indeed available in Britain, but there were no British carriers seaworthy at that time with the capability of carrying and flying them off. Churchill wrote:

Air attack on Malta is very heavy. There are now in Sicily about 400 German and 200 Italian fighters and bombers. ....would you be willing to allow your carrier *Wasp* to do one of these [air ferry] trips, provided details are satisfactorily agreed between the Naval Staffs? With her broad lifts, capacity and length, we estimate that *Wasp* could take fifty or more Spitfires. . .

Roosevelt signalled back: 'Admiral King will advise Admiral Poland that *Wasp* is at your disposal as you request'. This operation involving *Wasp* meant that British planes would be flying off a US aircraft carrier and the *Wasp* herself would be the first American warship to enter the European theatre of war on what amounted to a combat mission. The first piece of history was in fact made by Capt. H. St.John Fancourt, CO of Hatston who flew aboard *Wasp* in his Gloster Gladiator, the first British serviceman to land on an American carrier.

To make room for the Spitfires which were to be embarked on the Clyde, *Wasp* disembarked part of her well-trained Air Group 7 at Hatston. Three squadrons of aircraft flew to Hatston - Douglas Devastator torpedo planes and Vought Vindicator dive bombers as well as a Grumman Duck, a single float biplane. She retained a squadron of 11 Grumman F4F-4 Wildcat fighters to cover the Malta operation. Duncan Hamilton recalls the arrival of the Americans at Hatston:-

. . . we were summoned to the Captain's quarters where we were given the exciting and unexpected news that the American fleet would be arriving the following day. We had a tremendous rush getting the hangars, squadron offices and so on ready for them and had to work through the night. However when their first aircraft from the great carrier *Wasp* flew in, we were ready to receive them. They flew in close formation, a most impressive sight. No sooner had they landed than their wings folded up and they parked themselves in tightly packed groups. It was a fine technical exercise, perfectly performed; yet we knew to our cost that such limited dispersal of aircraft was no longer feasible. One or two well placed bombs and a whole squadron could be wiped out. I had seen aircraft burn in rows like that when the Luftwaffe had bombed Lee-on-Solent.

These American pilots were very experienced airmen; I believe I am right in saying that none of them had less than twelve hundred hours flying to his credit. That night I had my first introduction to the great American game of crap and played on until the early hours. The American fleet is a dry fleet and some of these fellows had not had a drink for weeks. As a result there were many casualties. When Shea and I went down to the landing stage - where launches waited to take them back to their ships - to see them off, their departure looked like an evacuation after defeat. The unsteady walk and green face was much in evidence and the choppy sea was a formidable obstacle to be crossed before their friendly bunks could be reached. Watching the launches as they approached the ships, it appeared that many officers were leaning over the side as if looking for fish. If the local fish had any sense they gave those launches a wide berth that morning.

The *Wasp* stayed in the Flow for six days during

USS Wasp at anchor, 1942,: she joined the British Home Fleet at Scapa in May 1942 and disembarked all her aircraft at Hatston for five weeks – FANCOURT

First British aircraft to land on an American carrier: Capt. H. St. J. Fancourt of RNAS Hatston in a Gloster Gladiator – FANCOURT

which time her aircraft did a mock attack on Hatston aerodrome for Admiral Giffen. Ken Baylis, Air Fitter at Hatston at that time writes:-

Whilst the USS *Wasp* was in Scapa Flow, they put on a show of attacking the aerodrome for Admiral Giffen. I was detailed that afternoon to start up and see off an RAF Spitfire flown in from Skeabrae by a Sergeant Pilot [No.132 Squadron G.L.]. I had a grandstand view as I was on the apron with the RAF Spitfire and saw the Wildcats come in just over the hangars with the Devastators a little higher coming from another direction. At the same time the Vindicators came screaming down with wheels and diving brakes lowered. When the American show was over the RAF pilot took off and I returned the trolley accumulator. By this time the Yankee ground crews were starting to go for tea. Suddenly the Spitfire came over our heads at hangar top level and proceeded to give a superb display of aerobatics, finishing with victory rolls all along the runway. One Yank asked me what the aircraft was and I was delighted to say - just casually - "Oh it's an RAF Spitfire, nothing unusual," but inside I was really proud of that Sergeant. I swear he was there on purpose just to show the flag. The fact was that we rarely saw RAF planes so I feel it was more than a coincidence that he was there that afternoon.

The American Squadron Commanders at Hatston were Lieutenant Commanders Eldridge and Turner and Lieutenants Rooney and Romberg.The squadrons trained intensively while based at Hatston. On 26 April the Devastators took part in an exercise with No.86 Squadron RAF based at Skitten in Caithness and some landed there. The American squadrons worked closely with the Royal Navy though not always successfully. Duncan Hamilton describes his experiences when flying with one of the American squadrons:-

The Americans were always training and we flew with them whenever we could. They had many casualties: some flew into high ground, others out to sea on the wrong compass reciprocal and on to Norway where the German fighters got them or they ran out of fuel trying to get back when they realised their mistake. They found flying in and around Scotland a new experience and took some time to adapt themselves. One day Galley and I were flying with their 54th. Pursuit Squadron commanded by Lieutenant Commander Turner. In the exercise the Squadron was to dive-bomb an imaginary submarine.

We took off and flew in close formation for about an hour. Both Galley and I knew how hazardous flying could be in this part of the world and hoped that we would not dive-bomb through cloud. We hoped in vain for suddenly Turner fired his guns - the signal that he was about to dive - wheeled over and dived through the cloud below him, followed by some thirty-five to forty aircraft. A microphone attached to a gun ring in front of me no longer hung down but stayed suspended at right angles. In other words the rate of our descent was equal to the gravitational pull of the earth. I became alarmed; not only was there another plane no more than thirty feet behind us but cloud as thick as this might end on top of a mountain. Suddenly we broke cloud and my fears were confirmed for over on our starboard side was an ominous looking mountain. Fortunately the sea was on our port side and we had some two thousand feet in which to come out of our dive. As we skimmed along over the water, everyone realised that if Turner had been a little starboard of where he was when we broke cloud, the whole squadron would have gone into that mountain. As the pilot of my plane put it, "This is not like flying in Arizona." Incidentally we never saw anything of the submarine we were supposed to dive-bomb though apparently it waited for us all afternoon. The Americans were quick to realise that flying conditions around Britain were not to be trifled with.

The five weeks' hard training in Orcadian skies no doubt paid dividends. In mid-May *Wasp* was withdrawn from the Home Fleet and sailed for the South Pacific. On 7 August 1942, USS *Wasp* took up station off Guadalcanal and Eldridge and Romberg's Squadrons lifted off to lead the American invasion.

On right Capt. Reeves commanding USS Wasp with Capt. Fancourt, CO, RNAS Hatston – FANCOURT

After her short refit, *Victorious* returned to the Home Fleet and to Scapa where she continued for the most part on North Atlantic convoy duty but, at the end of July she was required to join *Operation Pedestal*, a Malta convoy and on 4 August 1942 a new class of carrier, HMS *Avenger* appeared in Scapa Flow to take over the North Atlantic convoy patrols. *Avenger* was the first of the so-called Escort Carriers to enter service with the Royal Navy: they were all simple conversions of merchant hulls, had wooden decks and one hangar. She had on board 802 and 883 Sea Hurricane Squadrons and a Flight of 825 Swordfish. *Avenger's* aircraft spent a month working up in Scapa and the carrier finally set sail on 3 September to join convoy PQ18 off Iceland. Nine days later the carrier pilots were involved in fierce air battles with enemy aircraft in a series of massed torpedo attacks on the merchant ships. Five enemy aircraft were destroyed and 21 damaged. Unfortunately four Sea Hurricanes were also lost, three brought down in error by fire from the merchant ships. After this brilliant intervention in the North Atlantic *Avenger* was joined in Scapa by HMS *Furious* in preparation for the invasion of North Africa in November 1942. In addition to her 823 and 824 Albacore Squadrons, *Furious* had on

board 807 Squadron recently equipped with 12 Seafire IIc's, the first time these aircraft had been seen in Orkney. The Orkney skies were to see many more of them in the months to come.

Operation Torch, the code name for the North African landings, caused a considerable stir in and around Scapa Flow for it was here where the huge carrier Task Force was assembled. In September fourteen different squadrons (including the RAF) could be counted at airfields in Orkney. Eight Royal Naval squadrons used Hatston during this month, two Royal Naval squadrons had to use lodger facilities at RAF Skeabrae and to enable 820 and 822 Squadrons to disembark, the Headquarters Flight of resident 700 Squadron of the Royal Navy was required to move to RAF Grimsetter. Extensive training went on in the skies over Scapa. In one such exercise to the west of the island of Hoy, 807 Squadron lost its first Seafire when, in a fighter attack, the pilot over-corrected a spin.

By October *Victorious* joined the Task Force at Scapa having miraculously survived fierce enemy action in the Malta convoy, *Operation Pedestal*, during which the carrier HMS *Eagle* was sunk. The carriers HMS *Biter* and HMS *Formidable* completed this impressive armada which altogether had on board

US Naval Airmen and planes at HMS Sparrowhawk, Hatston: US crews with Devastator dive bombers fallen in for inspection in front of their machines: April 1942: in background, Vindicator bombers – IWM

US pilots at Hatston watching some of their machines in flight: April 1942 – IWM

103 fighters and 50 strike aircraft, many of these being airborne at the same time. By 21 October the Task Force had sailed and Scapa Flow was empty. On the way south, the carriers HMS *Argus* and HMS *Dasher* joined the Fleet and as it approached the Moroccan coast it was met by five aircraft carriers of the American Atlantic Fleet, the *Ranger*, *Sangamon*, *Chenango*, *Suwanee*, and *Santee* with, in all, another 136 aircraft embarked. The largest of these carriers, USS *Ranger* was later to become a familiar sight in Orkney waters. *Operation Torch* was a huge success, giving the allies a foothold in North Africa, the only tragedy to mar the mission being the loss of the carrier *Avenger* to torpedoes from U-115 near the end of the operation on 15 November. There were only 17 survivors.

After *Operation Torch*, *Victorious* arrived in Scapa and discharged some of her damaged 884 Squadron Seafires to Hatston for repair. She then left for a short refit, after which she sailed westwards to join the United States Navy for operations in the South Pacific and *Furious* joined the Home Fleet in January 1943 to replace her. In the same month extensive training began in Orkney for the next operation, the landings in Italy, exercises for which were to go on for six months. Royal Naval squadrons flew in from all parts of Britain for training in the wide open

Orkney skies; 880 and 899 Squadron Seafires and 817 Squadron Albacores due to see action in HMS *Indomitable* and the 878 and 890 Martlets and 894 Seafires bound ultimately for HMS *Illustrious*. Meanwhile Russian convoy patrol work continued. On 26 February the carrier *Dasher* entered Scapa Flow badly damaged after running into a severe Atlantic storm on her way to join up with JW 53 convoy en route from Iceland: many of her aircraft had also been rendered unserviceable. She disembarked 816 Squadron and a detachment of 837 Swordfish and 804 Sea Hurricane squadrons. Mike Crosley was one of the 804 Squadron pilots. He describes the hectic scene at Hatston on his arrival:-

[We] . . . flew north to Hatston which was crowded with fighters [there were 7 squadrons there at the time G.L.] including some new Seafire squadrons working up for *Illustrious* and *Formidable**. We watched them taxying round the narrow perimeter track, unable to see ahead without swinging their long noses from side to side. Sometimes they overdid it, running onto the grass and up-ending in a drainage hole. They were doing their decklanding practice somewhere in the North Sea. They were very impatient when we on the runway kept them waiting. They suffered badly from overheating particularly when taxying downwind - and they would start waving frantically from their cockpits at Flying Control to let them take off before they boiled. We had already seen one of them take off in a cloud of steam. * more probably *Indomitable* [G.L.]

The Seafires were in fact doing deck landing practice on *Furious* probably somewhere off Deerness. During these exercises an air mechanic of 894 Squadron had a most terrifying experience. It was customary for ratings to lie over the tail of an aircraft to keep it down while the pilot revved up to full power. It was also normal practice for them to remove themselves before the aircraft started moving! A very strong wind was blowing down *Furious'* deck and a snowstorm had just begun as she turned into the wind. The pilot came to full revs and one of the ratings jumped off: the pilot assumed that both men had left the tailplane and so he took off. The wind strength, the slipstream and the noise of the engine combined to make the aircraft movement imperceptible to the tail-borne rating. There was no means by which the deck party could communicate with the pilot and the aircraft set course for Hatston. Leading Air Mechanic James Overed takes up the story:-

I had my eyes closed but on opening them I saw to my horror that the carrier was below and astern and that we were just passing over the top of a cruiser underneath. I hung on like glue . . . I thought of my wife and daughter . . . I thought my number was up. I was tempted to let go when I saw the cruiser for he might rescue me if he was watching but decided to hang on. After about 15 minutes or so I heard a reduction in engine revs and I prepared for a crash landing, not knowing where I was. The runway (at Hatston) was white with snow so I thought he was crashing in a field so I pulled my legs up in order not to have them trapped under the fuselage. After landing I did not remember anything more until I came to inside the ambulance. I was told afterwards that the pilot removed me and placed me upon the snow and covered me with his flying coat and put his Mae West under my head for a pillow.... Next morning the pilot visited me in hospital and though I was too full of admiration for his skill to speak, he said, "Good show, jolly good show!"

When mechanic James Overed joined the Squadron he probably hadn't thought too deeply about its motto *Capable of anything anywhere!* It was said that the fitter was so cold that all the way to hospital he had to be kept in the same shape without bending him! Both the pilot and air mechanic had done a magnificent job, bringing themselves and their aircraft down safely. Less fortunate was the pilot of a RAF Lysander who, at Skeabrae only three weeks later, took off with an aircraftman on the tail. At 200 feet the aircraftman fell off, the aircraft went out of control and crashed, injuring two of the crew.

In the busy training period leading up to the invasion of Italy, four Seafires were lost in Orkney, two in a mid-air collision. Two Grumman Martlets also crashed in the islands, running out of fuel after they had lost their way in low cloud. As far as the Italian landings was concerned, from the point of view of the Fleet Air Arm, it was a qualified success. The *Indomitable* was crippled by one torpedo dropped by a lone Ju88 which escaped unharmed. With the capitulation of the Italian Navy in September 1943, there was little need for a carrier force in the Mediterranean. *Formidable* returned to the Home Fleet at the end of 1943 and *Illustrious* headed for the Indian Ocean: it was to be late summer 1944 before carriers reappeared in the Mediterranean.

On 13 July 1943, a new bird arrived at Hatston. 12

Grumman Avenger I's of 845 Squadron flew in from HMS *Chaser* after their journey across the Atlantic. They were joined soon after by 846 Squadron Avengers and both squadrons became familiar sights in Orkney skies when they embarked on extensive training and evaluation exercises which, in the case of 845 Squadron, went on for six months. The intensity of the programme can be seen from the Log Book of Sub.Lieutenant Burrenston in November 1943.

Extract from Log Book of Sub.Lieutenant Burrenston, November 1943

Date	Duration	
1		
2		
3		
4	0.45	bombing, Bogue method from 5000 ft.
	2.00	A/S bombing followed by A.L.T. on HM ships
	0.35	A/S bombing, Woodwick range
5		
6	0.50	homed by DF method from Stack Skerry area
7		1.15 attack on HM cruiser: dropped torpedo runner
8	1.45	attacks on HMS Duke of York,
	1.55	homed by W/T to Wick and back by R/T
	2.00	night exercise 100 miles out to sea: good W/T contact
9	0.40	A/S bombing, Bogue method
	0.45	A/S bombing from 5000 ft. two direct hits
10	0.50	air firing: cross overhead exercise: 180 rounds: zero hits
11	1.55	torpedo and dive bomb attacks on Stack Skerry
	1.00	attack on HM ships by formation of 16 aircraft
12	0.35	bombing, Bogue method at Woodwick Range
	0.35	air firing: cross overhead exercise: 200 rounds: zero hits
13	1.25	A.L.T. formation of 17 aircraft attacking enemy ships
14		
15	0.55	bombing from 3500 feet: dropping sticks of two
16	0.55	radar exercise: homed on submarine and small drifter
	1.30	night exercise: attempted attack on HMS Gambia: got lost in snow storm: homed on D/F
17	0.50	astern defence exercise: range 400 yds.: 4 hits
	0.35	dropped four sticks of two bombs
18		
19	1.05	homed on submarine: range approx. 5 miles
20		
21		
22	0.35	A/S bombing of towed water target
	1.45	Naval Exercise: W/T OK: returned early: rough weather
23	1.00	air firing: fired turret into sea: R/T OK
24		
25	0.25	A/S bombing: putrid weather
	0.25	A/S bombing down to 100 feet
26	1.10	14 aircraft attack on HMS Duke of York
27	1.15	night flying: attempted attack on HMS King George V and HMS Howe with 8 aircraft
28		
29	0.30	A/S bombing on Woodwick Range
	0.20	A/S bombing; stick of two moving water target
30		

Making allowances for Orkney weather and the short hours of daylight in November, this is a good record. The pilots of these Avengers (or Tarpons as they were known then) were not to know that another six months were to pass before they were to fire their guns in anger - not in the European theatre of war but in the far Pacific when, operating from *Illustrious* and in conjunction with Navy units from USS *Saratoga*, they attacked the Japanese naval base at Surabaja on 19 May 1944.

Meanwhile, in Norwegian waters, there had been little Fleet Air Arm activity. Only *Furious* had been available and, with her limited endurance, only restricted operations had been possible. However, in August 1943 the Americans returned once more to Scapa Flow. USS *Ranger* of the American Atlantic Fleet, had been loaned to the Home Fleet while the *Illustrious* was engaged in supporting the landings in Italy. *Ranger* entered Scapa Flow on 19 August 1943. The oldest purpose built carrier in the American Navy, launched in 1933, she was still a formidable fighting force and set out to prove it. Her 71 aircraft of Air Group 41 consisting of Dauntless dive bombers, Avengers and Wildcats, disembarked to airfields in Orkney - Hatston, as before and also Twatt where 15 TBF-1 Avengers landed. Exercises were conducted within and outwith Orkney culminating in a surprise strike on Bodø in Norway on 4 October 1943 when a harbour full of shipping came under attack. American Dauntless bombers and Avenger torpedo bombers sank or damaged ten enemy ships for the loss of three aircraft. *Ranger* returned to Scapa Flow on 6 October and patrolled with the British Navy in waters reaching to Iceland. She sailed from Hvalfjord in Iceland on 26 November 1943 to rejoin the American Navy.

At the beginning of 1944, the Royal Navy began to step up activity in Norwegian waters. While attempting to intercept a convoy, the *Scharnhorst* had been sunk by the *Duke of York* on Boxing Day 1943 and now the continued presence of the battlecruiser *Tirpitz* in Kaafjord and the prospect of yet another break out into the Atlantic led to a Fleet Air Arm plan to destroy this warship in her base. Preparations had been made in early 1943 to do this when *Tirpitz* was in Altenfjord. A planned torpedo attack on the warship at night by Swordfish squadrons was abandoned however when the carrier *Dasher*, which was scheduled to take part in the operation, blew up in the Firth of Clyde on 27 March 1943.

Scapa Flow was assembly point for *Operation Tungsten* which comprised six aircraft carriers with 153 aircraft embarked and with supporting warships. All the preparatory work for this operation was done in the north of Scotland. Loch Eriboll in Sutherlandshire was chosen as a dummy

Members of the US groundstaff loading ammunition in a Devastator dive-bomber: in the background a Wildcat is being refuelled from a petrol bowser – IWM

range because of its resemblance to Kaafjord and here a mock battleship was marked out on an island in the sea loch. *Furious* disembarked her 827 and 830 Barracuda Squadrons and 801 Seafire Squadron to Hatston in December 1943 for initial training and, the following month, 831 Barracuda Squadron arrived. 880 Squadron Seafires arrived in February at Skeabrae and in March, 1834 Squadron Corsairs flew in to Grimsetter. It was the first time Corsairs had been seen in the islands. The squadrons had to fly from Hatston to Loch Eriboll for training and on 23 March a most unfortunate incident occurred when 827 and 830 Squadron Barracudas, flying in misty conditions, ran into shellfire from a battleship firing at a drogue towed by 771 Squadron from Twatt. By some miracle there were no casualties and the crews were given a foretaste of what they were to experience in Norway.

Operation Tungsten on 3 April 1944 was the most successful of the Fleet Air Arm attacks on the Tirpitz. The battlecruiser was badly damaged and put out of action for three months and the Arctic convoys were able to have a brief respite. When the Fleet returned to Scapa on 6 April no less than seven squadrons disembarked, mainly from the Escort Carriers *Emperor*, *Striker*, *Fencer*, *Pursuer* and *Searcher*. *Emperor's* Hellcats landed at Hatston: these aircraft had not been seen in Orkney before.

Training continued and, in one exercise on 20 April Barracuda DP983 crashed into Scapa Flow after striking a barrage balloon cable. These raids on Norway were, partly, the contribution of the Royal Navy to *Operation Fortitude North*, a deception sustained mainly by false radio signals to delude the enemy into thinking that the invasion of Europe was to come from Norway.

On 19 April *Activity* and *Fencer* accompanied by twenty one other vessels left Scapa Flow for the Soviet Union, this escort force being required to bring back 45 merchant ships of convoy RA59 from Kola Inlet. The ships were nominally empty but advantage was taken to transport back to Scapa Flow over 2000 Soviet sailors who were to crew the battleship *Royal Sovereign* after its transfer to the Soviet Union: on board *Fencer* were Admiral Levchenko and his staff. The return convoy was constantly harassed by enemy submarines and during one encounter a merchant ship with a large complement of Soviet sailors on board was sunk. *Fencer's* 842 Wildcat and Swordfish squadron were nevertheless credited with the destruction of three enemy submarines. There was no rest for *Fencer*: she was immediately ordered south to cover *Operation Overlord*, the Normandy landings.

In May *Victorious* arrived in Scapa Flow and when bad weather restricted operations off the Norwegian coast King George VI took the opportunity to visit the Fleet in Scapa Flow. He went aboard many of the ships including the carriers *Searcher* and *Victorious*. The latter put to sea flying the Royal Standard and the King watched with interest as 28 Corsairs of 1834 and 1836 Squadrons and 21 Barracudas of 827 and 829 squadrons took off from her flight deck and landed on.

In June 1944 an extraordinary thing happened at RNAS Hatston. This busy station which had been packed with fighters since the outbreak of war found itself abandoned. The answer was simple. With the Normandy landings in progress many Royal Naval squadrons were moved to RAF bases on the south coast of England and Orkney based squadrons created diversionary attacks on Norwegian shipping. From 10 June until 13 June there were no aircraft at Hatston: for the Station Commander, these must have been blissful days! The relief was short lived: by 8 July 1944 there were seven squadrons on the station - that meant over 90 aircraft and the Fireflies of 1770 Squadron which had earlier experienced three months hard training at Hatston were required to move out to nearby Grimsetter. The reason for this concentration of aircraft was another planned attack on *Tirpitz*. *Operation Mascot* as it was called brought the new carrier *Indefatigable* into Scapa as well as *Formidable* and *Furious*. By 14 July the carriers had embarked all their aircraft including 1770 Squadron Fireflies which were to see action for the first time. On the way to *Formidable* from Hatston, Corsair pilot Lt. Hewetson of 1841 Squadron crashed on the Hoy Hills and a whole week passed before the wreckage was found. For the second time in a month, Hatston was left empty, on this occasion for four days! *Operation Mascot* took place on 17 July: unfortunately the attacking aircraft found their quarry enveloped in a smoke screen and the mission was abortive. But the Fleet Air Arm was persistent. The carriers returned to Scapa and training went on. In August there were five squadrons of Barracuda Torpedo bombers based in Orkney and the Seafire and Wildcat squadrons there were joined by 18 Corsairs of 1842 Squadron. The British Escort Carrier *Trumpeter* and the Canadian manned *Nabob* joined the Carrier Fleet *Furious*, *Formidable* and *Indefatigable* in Scapa Flow for *Operation Goodwood* which was to take place at the end of August 1944. These five carriers had altogether 167 aircraft embarked! When we consider that there were five shore based squadrons in Orkney at that time (including 771 Squadron which alone could muster 35 aircraft) there would have been well over 300 aircraft in the Scapa area. *Operation Goodwood* had only limited success. Eleven aircraft were lost and on 26 August *Nabob*, after 1,100 miles of steaming, limped into Scapa after being hit by a torpedo which had torn a hole fifty feet by forty feet in her thin hull. The US built frigate *Bickerton* was less fortunate: she too was torpedoed and had to be scuttled off Norway. It fell to RAF Lancasters of Nos. 9 and 617 Squadrons with 12000 lb. Tallboy bombs finally to dispose of the *Tirpitz* at Tromsø on 12 November 1944.

The aged *Furious* took part in only one more operation - minelaying in the Leads off the coast of Norway in mid September. She was then withdrawn from service with the Home Fleet and placed in reserve. Her place was taken by the new

Hurricane II landing on board a carrier off Orkney: possibly HMS Avenger – HAMILTON

One of Nicolas Horne's photographs – not taken in Orkney but a common occurrence in Orkney nevertheless – holding down the tailplane while the pilot warms up for take-off: see page 96 for a special reference to this – HORNE

Avenger, 845 Sqdn. at Hatston – FAAM

Aircrew of 846 Sqdn., Hatston, Orkney –
FAAM

carrier HMS *Implacable*: although her keel had been laid down in 1939 she had had so many modifications on the basis of carrier performance in action that she was only now operational. Arriving in Scapa in October she immediately embarked further squadrons for some highly successful strikes off the Norwegian coast accompanied by *Fencer*, *Pursuer* and *Trumpeter*. Lieutenant Commander (A) Mike Crosley was by this time commanding 880 Seafire Squadron. They flew on to *Implacable* from Skeabrae on 8 November 1944. In his book *They gave me a Seafire*, he describes this experience:-

Implacable had originally been designed to take only a little more than half the 78 aircraft that she would shortly have to accommodate in her two hangars. No guns or other impedimenta had been removed to compensate for the extra space now taken up to be the extra hangar. With 500 extra crew, she was grossly overcrowded. When 880 and 801 with 828 (18 Barracudas) and 1771 (12 Fireflies) arrived, the squadron's ratings had to take pot luck with the left over messdecks. The initial result was that most of our squadron were having to sling their hammocks in the passageways. These were in use day and night and our men were being bumped by people trying to get by and were losing their sleep. Many of the more junior officers in the ship had to treble up. As all of us (A) RNVR boys were most junior of all, we got a particularly poor choice. I had the deepest, noisiest and least ventilated cabin the builders could have devised. It was three decks down and out over

the starboard outer screw. Still it was at least mine own and there was plenty of room to spread out.

Another mission on 21 November was abandoned after the carrier was caught in severe gales. 880 squadron was happy to get back to Skeabrae where Christmas preparations were already underway:-

We now had to be allowed some time for Christmas leave. In order to make our unexpected arrival home more welcome, we decided that we would each take a turkey with us on the journey south. Dougy Yate, whose father ran a chain of East London butcher shops, knew all about turkeys and he came round on the squadron BSA motorbike and side-car to visit the crofters on the islands. The crofters would then parade their turkeys, either in the farmyard or in the kitchen, depending on the weather. Dougy would pick the ones he liked, diving on the poor birds before they knew what was coming. Our cabins at Skeabrae were full of feathers for the next few days as Dougy organised a squadron plucking party.

It is comforting to learn that their Christmas birds were obtained legitimately in contrast to the 809 Squadron Fulmar pilots who had left Twatt two years earlier with the Commander (Flying)'s geese on their laps!

In January at the smaller and normally quiet RNAS Grimsetter, there were two Seafire squadrons based, 801 and 880, both of which had 24 aircraft. In addition 881 Squadron with 20 Wildcats were based there. Fortunately for much of the time some of the

Wildcats were detached to *Premier* and *Trumpeter* since the station could not have coped with 68 aircraft! Both 801 and 880 Squadrons were bound for the Pacific and though the war in Europe was near a close, there was no respite for these squadrons. Mike Crosley again:-

Norman, Dougy and I had had much experience in 804 in manoeuvring fighter formations easily in the air. All that was necessary for us now was to use this formation and method of manoeuvre to position our Seafires for a simultaneous dive on ground targets so that the strafing attack could be completed in 20 seconds and before the enemy gunners could remove their fingers. Up to 16 of our Seafires would dive simultaneously from three different directions and the enemy would not know which to aim at. After careful thought we worked it out that 16 Seafires diving at once would have only one sixteenth of the gunners firing at each Seafire for one sixteenth of the time! In theory we would therefore have about 60 - 100 times less chance of being shot down. Our formation dive from at least three different directions would also reduce the time taken to reform afterwards and so save fuel.

We practised these coordinated attacks - with radio silence - on every target we could find, islands in the middle of Scottish lochs, various ships with prior permission - and our own airfields and dispersals. At times our aircraft crossed over each other in the pullout of the dives. Of course there was bound to be danger from our own shells when we used our guns instead of the camera guns. However we reckoned that the risks from this were slight compared with the risks of coming down singly to zero feet on an airfield well alerted and defended by 200 guns or more.

With *Implacable* capable of flying off at least 50 aircraft in one strike - more than two British carriers worth heretofore - constant decklanding practice was essential. We aimed at 20 second decklanding intervals. While we were at Grimsetter we had all 48 Seafires in the air at once.

The standard of flying of these two large squadrons was extremely high: during their nine weeks training in Orkney there was only one fatality and that was caused through a freak accident. Midshipman Ian Penfold's glove caught in the cockpit hood as he slid it forward on take off. His vision was obstructed at a vital moment and he lost control of his aircraft. On 15 March *Implacable*, left her moorings at Scapa: on board were 1771 Firefly Squadron and 828 Squadron Avengers, both squadrons having earlier spent over a month in training at Hatston. Off Orkney 801 and 880 Seafire squadrons flew on: they were bound for the Pacific Ocean and another war.

For the remaining months of 1945 it was the Escort Carriers *Campania*, *Nairana*, *Puncher*, *Premier*, *Trumpeter*, *Queen*, *Vindex* and *Searcher* which frequented Scapa Flow. Their aircraft were engaged in minelaying and bombing operations on the Norwegian coast to hold up the German convoys but, as the months passed, targets were getting fewer and fewer. The last raid and one of the most successful took place on 4 May 1945, only four days before VE day when 44 aircraft from three Escort carriers attacked Kilbotn U-boat supply base, destroying the depot ship and sinking a U-boat. The last war-time carrier to enter Scapa Flow was the Escort Carrier HMS *Premier* which arrived two days after VE Day and disembarked 856 Squadron Wildcats. The last of the carrier men, nine Avengers of 846 Squadron left Twatt on 31 July for Crail in Fife.

846 Sqdn. Hatston Avengers at rest at the end of the day: 1944 – HOWES

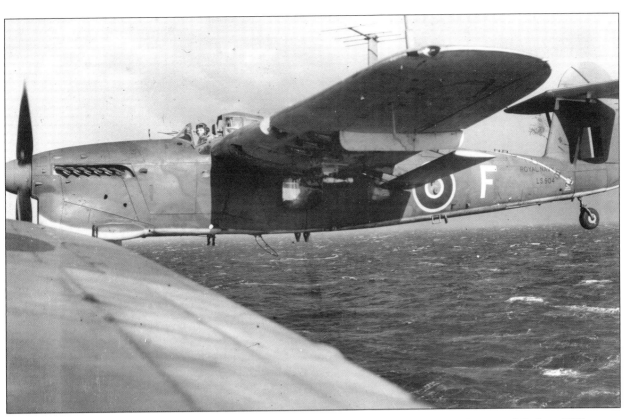

Barracuda II, LS904 off Orkney, 5 October, 1944; note aerial – standard ASV (Air to Surface Vessel) Radar – HILL

HMS Searcher, based at Scapa with 882 Sqdn. Martlets embarked – COOPER

Barracuda pilot at Hatston, 830 or 831 Sqdn. 1943: name unknown –
HAMILTON

822 Sqdn. Martlets taking off from HMS Searcher off Orkney: the smoke is coming from Searcher's exhausts which are located on the side of the vessel
– COOPER

*Captain Davies,
HMS Searcher,
with Commander
Flying, Scapa Flow
– COOPER*

King George VI arrives on board HMS Victorious at Scapa, May 1944 – COOPER

King George VI talks to John Cooper, CO 822 Sqdn., on HMS Searcher in Scapa – COOPER

HMS Tracker in convoy off Orkney with Avengers embarked: August 1944 – HILL

The cruiser HMS Kent and HMS Implacable in Scapa Flow, July 1944 – FAAM

Seafire pilot, 801 Sqdn. Skeabrae, ashore from HMS Implacable, December 1944 – HORNE

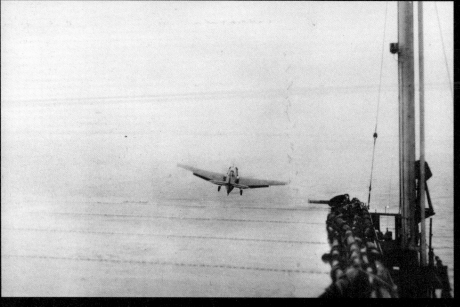

Avenger YZ155 of 846 Sqdn. takes off for Hatston from HMS Trumpeter in Scapa Flow on 24 August, 1944, for compass swinging. Pilot Sub.Lt. Thomas, Observer unknown, David Heath Air-Gunner, Air Mechanic Arthur Jacobs. The wind is too light and the aircraft fails to gain height – HOWES

The Avenger pancakes in Scapa Flow – HOWES

Remarkably, the Avenger floats: bow of HMS Trumpeter in the foreground – HOWES

The crew scramble out as the aircraft drifts towards the stern of the carrier – HOWES

Air Mechanic Jacobs can be seen grasping the hatchway near the roundel and the turret housing: Air Gunner David Heath on the wing – HOWES

Air Gunner Heath standing on the port wing, Pilot, Observer and Air Mechanic on the starboard side – HOWES

Seafires of 801 Sqdn. at Skeabrae, ashore from HMS Implacable, December 1944 – HORNE

801 Sqdn. or 880 Sqdn. aboard HMS Implacable, Scapa Flow – HORNE

Fleet Air Arm pilots, 801 or 880 Sqdn. Skeabrae, disembarked from HMS Implacable, December 1944 – HORNE

882 Sqdn. pilots in Ready Room of HMS Searcher: John Cooper, CO of the squadron is briefing his men before an operation in Norway: during this operation, the officer on the extreme right, 'Gladys' Pearson, was shot down and captured: 'Ned Kelly' Edney, the pilot whose head only appears, was shot down and killed – COOPER

Divisions at Scapa Flow: march past on HMS Vindex to Rear Admiral Cunningham Graham, March, 1945 – FAAM

Landing accidents on aircraft carriers were common: barrier crashes were frequently caused by gremlins which held down the arrester wires! HMS Vindex, Scapa Flow, 1944 – FAAM

898 Sqdn. with CO Dickie Henderson on board HMS Searcher off Scapa Flow – COOPER

HMS Premier in Scapa Flow, 26 September 1944 with 856 Squadron embarked: it consisted of 9 Grumman Avenger torpedo bombers, 3 Grumman Avenger torpedo bombers and 3 Grumman Martlet (Wildcat) Fighters: they were engaged in anti-submarine patrols, Norwegian coastal bombing, minelaying and Murmansk convoy support: arrived in Scapa two days after VE day and the squadron was disbanded – FAULKNER

846 Squadron leaving Hatston for Twatt, 1 August 1945 – HOWES

Chapter Six

A Posting to Orkney

For servicemen and women there were many ways to arrive in Orkney during the war. None emulated the arrival of the German balloonists Distler and Joerdens who, as early as 1910, made the epic flight from Munich to Kirkwall. It would be wrong to assume that all those attached to the flying services arrived by air. Perhaps the strangest wartime arrival was Leif Lyssand, a Norwegian airman who escaped from occupied Norway and, after a 200 mile journey, made landfall with other compatriots on the island of Sanday in a small boat. Leif became a Spitfire pilot in No.331 Squadron and, by sheer concidence, was posted back to Orkney! The majority of servicemen and women generally made a less hazardous though much longer journey to the islands, a posting from St.Merryn in Cornwall taking two days for a distance of over 800 miles.

Pilots, Naval Observers and TAG's usually flew in with their squadron from shore stations or from carriers. It was normal practice to fly off the carrier before it entered Scapa Flow since the ship had to head into the wind to assist take-off. Ratings attached to the squadron were usually transferred to a lighter in Scapa Flow and from thence to the pier at St.Mary's in the parish of Holm or to Scapa Pier which was nearer Hatston. The official chronicler of RNAS Hatston writes:-

Scapa Pier is a venue that will linger for long in the memories of squadron personnel embarking or disembarking with stores and personal baggage at short notice at all hours of the day and night - usually in the rain.

When aircrew were joining a new squadron at any of the military airfields in Orkney, they were required, like anyone else, to make the long journey by train usually to Thurso. Lieutenant Keith Remmington, 771 Squadron pilot was posted from Freetown in Sierra Leone to Twatt! He writes:-

I can well remember the journey north - anything but comfortable - I travelled on the daily troop train which left Euston at 10 o'clock - it was very full and the only refreshment on board was a canteen car run by the Salvation Army. The train was due in at Perth at 20.30 and fortunately it arrived on time which allowed us to have a meal in the Station Hotel. If you arrived after 21.00 you were unlucky. From Perth there were two trains, one leaving at 22.30 with the Army, Air Force and Women's Services, the latter were locked in their carriages, no doubt to protect the poor men. The Naval train

departed at 23.00 and we arrived at Thurso at 7 o'clock the next morning and transport took us to the Royal Hotel for breakfast and then on to Scrabster where the *Earl of Zetland* was waiting for us. An uneventful crossing to Stromness followed and I subsequently realised how lucky I had been after some more lively crossings on later occasions. Transport then conveyed us to Twatt having been travelling then for a full 24 hours.

The train described by Keith Remmington is the famous *Jellicoe*, a train run specially for the services. This troop train had its origin in World War I and the nickname *Jellicoe* had stuck. On 16 April 1940 this service was re-inaugurated, the longest train journey in Britain. Normally this journey was long enough and bad enough but, in February 1941, in a severe snowstorm, the Inverness - Thurso leg of the journey took four days to cover 120 miles! Even after a reasonable rail journey north there was still the prospect of being delayed for a day or more at Thurso if the weather was too bad for the ferry to cross to Orkney. Sometimes the ferry was held up for other reasons. Twatt Wren Mary Treby remembers arriving at Thurso in May 1944 and getting no further for some time:-

In my instructions I was told to report to the Wrennery in Thurso for breakfast before crossing the Pentland Firth to Stromness where I would be met with transport. I duly made my way to the Wrennery which I discovered was opposite the small station. I promptly reported to the regulating Petty Officer only to be told that after breakfast I wouldn't be allowed to make the crossing for some time. The reason given was the King and many important people were having a conference on board the Flagship in Scapa Flow. I was told to remain in the Wrennery in case a signal came to say that I could cross. I was confined indoors until just before 4 p.m. and I was standing by the window looking out when suddenly there appeared an old fashioned Rolls Royce with the Royal Standard flying in the breeze. It drew to a halt outside the railway station and out smartly stepped our beloved King dressed in Naval uniform. Within a very short time a signal came through to say that I could now make the crossing to Orkney. I quickly gathered my belongings and made my way to the quayside where I boarded the *St. Ola*. I cannot remember exactly the time we sailed but I do remember that it was a very rough crossing; there were only a few civilians on board and I was the only representative of the services.

Muriel Wears, another Twatt Wren describes her arrival at Stromness:-

I arrived as an urgent replacement and of course, as usual, in the Services, nobody knew I was coming! I looked a very sorry sight sitting on a box of kippers at Stromness, absolutely dejected. I had been sick all the way over, my hair which was very long at the time had all come straggling out of my little round hat and I was rather like a pea-green colour. Eventually a three ton truck arrived to take me up to Twatt. It was driven by a sergeant in the Marines. He told me to get in the front with him and put my luggage in the back which I did and when I settled down in the front, he started patting my knee and saying "How about coming to the camp dance with me tonight?" My first thought was, "Gosh they must be short of women up here because I was looking the most miserable little wreck you've ever seen!"

On 18 January 1944 No.602 Squadron arrived at Skeabrae from Detling in Kent. It appears that the pilots were taking over aircraft left by a previous squadron and so the whole squadron was to be moved directly by Transport Command. England was enveloped in fog and a decision was made to move the squadron by rail instead to Aberdeen. From there trucks would take them to RAF Peterhead from where huge Harrow transports would take them to Skeabrae. In the Station Diary of Skeabrae, is a copy of the note sent to No.217 Squadron Transport Command, Doncaster requesting '8000 lbs. lift at am 18 January to emplane No.602 Squadron Peterhead to Skeabrae'. Pierre Clostermann was a No.602 Squadron pilot and in his book, *The Big Show*, he gives an account of the journey north:-

We piled our luggage into the lorries and went and had lunch at the Star in Maidstone where we found Jimmy Rankin and Yule. A few last rounds of drinks, promises . . . As usual I was cluttered up with a mass of belongings - mandoline, Irvin jacket, etc. Luckily Jacques was there to help.

On the way through London we dropped in, in a body, - 24 pilots - at the C——, a very swanky and exclusive club in Soho. After half an hour, the manager, fearing for his interior decoration and seeing the alarm of his immaculately dressed clientele, came and asked us to move on. A few well chosen arguments, including the transfer of his magnificent white carnation to Ken's buttonhole and a threat of public debagging, were enough to calm him down. From 6 to 9.30 (our train was at 10.20) we drank hard - whisky, beer, whisky. By 9.30 we were bottled and singing our squadron ditties. I belong to Glasgow followed Pistol Packing Momma and Gentille Alouette and gradually we embarked on the more lurid terms of our repertoire. Our fellow guests began to feel embarrassed, to blush, and some of them even discreetly made themselves scarce. Robson climbed up on a table, upset a few bottles and we began to intone in chorus 602's war cry:

One, two, three, four, five!

Six, hoooo! Twooooo!

At that point the captain very nicely reminded us that we had a train to catch. It was just as well he did, for, as we were getting up, the proprietor burst in escorted by two policemen and half a dozen MP's. After a few minutes of confused explanations we succeeded in getting rid of them and surged down the Piccadilly Circus underground. A civilian permitted himself an out-of-place remark about those good-for-nothing RAF blokes. Robson and Bob Courly inserted his umbrella into the moving staircase which jammed with a terrifying din. We took a compartment by storm, the passengers regarding us with a mixture of incredulity and horror and finally we found ourselves at King's Cross.

We piled our luggage on the electric trolleys. Carpenter took over the controls and embarked on an epic dash along the platforms crowded with travellers, the warning bell going full-blast. It was such a riot that the stationmaster took a hand in person, followed by an imposing escort of military police. An unwise move on his part for, within a minute or two, his beautiful cap, covered with gold braid, had mysteriously found its way into Tommy's suitcase. This cap now figures among the Flight's most valued trophies, together with a London policeman's helmet, a Canadian general's beret and a Panzer Grenadier colonel's forage cap, brought back from Dieppe by Bill Loud.

The platforms were swarming with people and, what with the blackout, it was hard to find our way about. However we did eventually succeed in finding our reserved compartment at the door of which, an MP and a railway official were mounting guard. Our Pullman was divided in two, with a communicating door. The other half was occupied by 129 Squadron from Hornchurch, also going on rest. We soon made friends. A terrific racket again, everyone singing, bottles flying. Round about 2 am, we organised a rugger match, but it fizzled out for lack of players. By 3 o'clock, everyone was asleep, on the seats, under the tables, on the carpet in the gangway, even in the luggage racks.

18th. January 1944 It was a pitiful squadron which emerged from the train at Aberdeen at about 5 o'clock in the morning. Dishevelled, unshaven, covered with soot, our mouths like the bottom of a parrot's cage, we first had to unload our luggage and manhandle it over to the lorries and buses taking us to Peterhead. Then we embarked in two gigantic Harrow transports, piling our luggage in the fuselages. I noticed that each one of us unobtrusively sat down on his parachute bag. Some clot began repeating the story of how a Harrow had been shot down on this trip by a Junkers 88 a few weeks earlier.

During the take-off we all clenched our teeth but when we were airborne, we heaved a sigh of relief and began to crack a few jokes. Not for long! The air was far from calm and the machine began to pitch and toss, shaken by air pockets. The laughs soon gave way to a mood of profound gloom. This pathological state was not unconnected with the state of our stomachs which had not yet recovered from the corrosive mixture of beer and whisky. Every pilot held his head in his hands, his elbows on his knees and nobody thought of admiring the beautiful snow covered country over which we were passing.

We reeled out of the Harrow at Skeabrae in Orkney with dry throats and asleep on our feet. We wished the Station Commander would go to hell as he did his utmost to make us welcome in a charming little speech which we had to listen to standing in the open under the piercing blasts of the wind.

Skeabrae in winter might just as well be the North Pole. God knows what maniac at Air Ministry had the bright idea of setting up a fighter base in those god-forsaken islands. A few hours' daylight in the twenty-four: occasionally a gleam of sun pierces the wan clouds, disperses the Arctic mist and reveals a desolate countryside, windswept rock emerging from the thick snow.

It was mid January after all! Although Orkney is normally fortunate in getting very little snow, during the war years, there were some very heavy falls which created considerable problems on the airfields. During one of these snowfalls there was sent from Hatston a Naval Message which must surely rank as one of the funniest wartime Naval communications. It read, "Snow clearing equipment has been found under snowdrift!" A very touching winter story is told by Norman Mills, attached to 823 Squadron at Hatston. The squadron was moving south but first he had to dig his Swordfish out of a snowdrift. To his great surprise he found a sheep buried but still alive. Trying to extricate the sheep he was astounded to come across a little kitten tucked up cosily in its fleece! The sheep ran away and there was little time to solve the problem of the kitten which had to take flight with the squadron. It was adopted as the family cat and lived to the age of twelve but to the last remained as wild as the Orkney winter!

No matter what season they experienced in Orkney, many servicemen expressed sentiments similar to Pierre Clostermann. This is typified in that well known poem:-

The Bloody Orkneys

This bloody town's a bloody cuss -
No bloody trains, no bloody bus,
And no one cares for bloody us -
In bloody Orkney.

The bloody roads are bloody bad,
The bloody folks are bloody mad,
They'd make the brightest bloody sad,
In bloody Orkney.

All bloody clouds and bloody rains,
No bloody kerbs, no bloody drains,
The Council's got no bloody brains,
In bloody Orkney.

Everything's so bloody dear
A bloody bob for bloody beer
And is it good? - no bloody fear,
In bloody Orkney.

The bloody flicks are bloody old,
The bloody seats are bloody cold,
You can't get in for bloody gold
In bloody Orkney.

The bloody dances make you smile,
The bloody band is bloody vile,
It only cramps your bloody style,
In bloody Orkney

No bloody sport, no bloody games,
No bloody fun, the bloody dames
Won't even give their bloody names
In bloody Orkney.

Best bloody place is bloody bed
With bloody ice on bloody head
You might as well be bloody dead
In bloody Orkney.

Captain Hamish Blair

An unknown serviceman rose to defend Orkney against this scurrilous attack :-

The Blessed Orkneys

I read a most distressing verse,
In accents bloody and so terse
That I produce one the reverse
Of this, our Orkney.

It is a shame - I do not know 'im,
The author of that vile poem,
For I would dearly love to show 'im,
A lovely Orkney.

Blossoms with their edges creaming,
Daffodils in thousands teeming,
Caused all through the Gulf Stream streaming,
To fair Orkney.

We came up here with naught to lose,
For pleasure there is much to choose,
Especially if you want to booze,
In Flowing Orkney.

The Royal Hotel - a perfect bar,
If you ever want a jar,
On Saturdays, remote, afar,
In silent Orkney.

I watch the Walrus and the Skua,
Over Scapa Flow so sure,
If they flew low they would be fewer,
In well-armed Orkney.

If you are on dancing bent,
The ATS and WRENS and WAAFS are lent,
Sometimes no chaperons are sent,
In trusting Orkney.

We came up here we understood,
To fight, to die, to shed our blood,
Even if it's mixed with mud,
In driest Orkney.

The troops on Burray, Hoy and Flotta,
Go to Kirkwall for a spott'er,
Recreation and what not'er,
In gayest Orkney.

My seven days' leave I almost spurn,
With all those wasted hours to burn,
Before the moment of return,
To blessed Orkney.

Anon

This was probably a minority view! To the pilots, the weather meant everything and pilots' logs for the winter seasons are sprinkled with diabolical, putrid, foul, in reference to the weather. In *About Tern*, the magazine of HMS *Tern*, Twatt, the writer asked, 'What have Orkney and the opera Madame Butterfly in common?' Answer - 'One fine day!' It would be true to say that everyone found it difficult to adjust to the high winds so frequently experienced in Orkney. Harald Meltzer, pilot with No.331 Norwegian Squadron describes the weather of March 1942:-

. . . there were at least twenty days in March on which the wind blew hard. There were periods of five, six or seven days when the wind blew a gale without stopping. The draughts would come tearing in through every crack and crevice but we had learned the art of keeping warm by putting on enough clothes and keeping fires going well in our rooms. The wind would make a roaring noise in the chimney pipe day and night: still we could sleep all right in spite of it. A 100 m.p.h gale would often shake our little hut so much that we would lie in bed and almost believe we should be airborne any moment!

And airborne they did become on some occasions. The official historian of Hatston writes of conditions in the autumn of 1939:-

Accommodation, during what turned out to be a windy autumn, continued to be a major problem. Huts were slow to arrive and tents were still in use until about the end of November; mud was everywhere and, despite precautions, tents, partially completed huts and hangars suffered damage from the most severe winter experienced in Orkney for the past 25 years. It was a matter of

departmental pride that the Meteorological Hydrogen Balloon Filling Tent was the last to become airborne.

John Cooper, 809 Squadron Fulmar pilot, was intrigued by the most unusual natural phenomenon he observed in the officers' mess at RNAS Twatt. When the wind blew strongly it would sweep under the hut and lift the linoleum right off the floor! The strong winds would create such a powerful draught in the chimney of the cast iron heating stoves that they would become red hot! Is it little wonder then that we find recorded in the official history of Lyness the sober fact that Royal Naval establishments in Orkney consumed three quarters of a million tons of coal in the five years, May 1940 - May 1945!

But there were others who loved what they saw and wrote very movingly of their impressions of Orkney. Cyclops Brown, Hurricane pilot with No.253 Squadron moved from a round of:-

. . . weekend and evening tennis parties, cricket, golf, country clubs, ice-skating at Purley and Streatham and at the Queen's Club, a wide choice of good restaurants and pubs, and, for the more adventurous, some of the London clubs and shows were still open, and only a taxi ride back home. And then, suddenly, the squadron found itself on an apparently bare, windswept island. What on earth had Orkney to offer compared with all that?

. . . there were some people who took to the place almost from the start and for many men with an urban background it began to grow on them as an acquired taste, to be explored, experienced and then savoured. A Czechoslovak sergeant pilot of No. 253 Squadron was overheard to remark to a Norwegian pilot officer "It certainly beats

Officers' accommodation at Bryameadow, Twatt – HILL

Prague!" The pilots were the most privileged. In the first instance they had probably flown in to Orkney and then, from the air, were soon familiar with the islands and their surrounding seas as a complete entity and, if they so wished, were able to take an intimate look at the wilder, deserted places and otherwise inaccessible bird and marine life. Many among the transitory population came to enjoy this new scene, at least in retrospect and even those who never took to Orkney and regarded Skeabrae as yet another dreadful hutted RAF camp would have acknowledged that at least it was different.

Jack Holden was a Leading Stoker in the Royal Navy. But, as he said, he 'joined the Navy and never went to sea' - the whole of his service life was spent at RNAS Twatt. His first impression of Orkney was not good but gradually he saw the islands in a new light:-

I can't find a word suitable for the winter of 1942 - 1943. It rained and it blew and when it got fed up of that it blew and it rained. I hated with all my heart this bleak island and its flaying wind. The Spring of 1943 was one of these rare years when winter departs as if cut off with a knife. The island, so it seemed to me, was transformed overnight. The land was carpeted with wild flowers, trout leaped in the lochs, birds were everywhere. I looked at it all, "Well it's not such a bad place after all," I said to myself. Hatred had turned to a cautious liking and as the year progressed, that liking turned to love, a love so deep that it embraced every stick, stone and sprig of heather and went into every fibre of my being and has remained with me to this day. I have never been outside the British Isles but I know there is nowhere else on earth for me. This is the land for which I was born and here, one day, I will be buried. I can ask for no more than that. Much of the transition from hatred to love of Orkney was due to the Moars of Howe, a family with whom I had become very friendly. Every off-duty day I was never in the camp, I was with them, working in the fields, shooting, trout fishing or sea fishing. The fishing in Orkney in war time was superb. Many a time we rowed home in the endless daylight of summer with a boatload of cod or haddock under the magnificent cliffs of Marwick Head. The air above us was filled with thousands of wheeling seabirds, razorbills, guillemots, puffins, kittiwakes. I would walk back to camp in the early hours and it seemed that the corncrake rasped in every meadow and the corn buntings jingled on every fence. As I write this it all comes back so vividly. Orkney was, to me, a land of endless wonder. Long winter nights (I had an all-night pass) were spent yarning indoors under the light of the Tilley lamp. It became my home and my family and so it has remained to this day. The old folk have, alas, gone now as old folk must, Mother, Father, Grandad, Auntie Jessie, Uncle Bill, all gone now. They lie at rest in a lovely little cemetery near the sea in Birsay. When I am that way, I go in and look at the headstones. My mind goes back to the years when we were all together. I have a feeling, it can be no more than a feeling, that they know I am here and are as happy as I am. We are, in a sense, all together again.

After the war Jack moved from Kent and took up residence in Orkney. His last wish, to be buried in Orkney, became reality in 1988.

The accommodation and facilities at the stations improved enormously as the war progressed so what the service personnel found when they arrived depended on when they came to Orkney. Despite the fact that Hatston was the Royal Navy's first purpose built station, conditions were rather grim at the beginning as the official history of Hatston points out:-

When war was declared, the runways were nearly complete but only two hangars had been erected; suitable accommodation for aircrews, maintenance ratings and personnel operating the ancillary services were non- existent; the only house in the vicinity, Grainayre and Scott's House being already earmarked for offices and stores. Billets were found nearby in houses, hotels, the Drill Hall and Kirkwall Public Library as well as a few even in the prison! The overflow lived under canvas, the weather at this time being, providentially, warm and dry . . . Kirkwall Bay was busier with traffic than it had ever been: the piers were totally inadequate to receive the hundreds of tons of goods to be unloaded; ships had sometimes to sail without discharging their full cargoes with the result that while Orkney was in despair for roofing material to complete their huts, Lerwick had a superabundance of roofs but no floors or windows or vice versa . . . In the spring and summer of 1940, work on the station continued at top pressure and conditions steadily improved although lack of fresh fruit and vegetables resulted in a case considered to be due to lack of Vitamin C; the patient who had been on the station for nine months, was treated for scurvy with large doses of orange juice and made a rapid recovery. This incident resulted in fresh fruit and vegetables being flown up from Donibristle and there was no recurrence of the trouble. The Wardroom was ready for occupation in October, thus releasing other hut accommodation for ratings but the quarters for Wrens [who arrived at the beginning of 1940 G.L] were not completed until about a year later.

Very wet weather prevailed in Orkney in early 1940 and the construction sites became seas of mud. Ashes from the ubiquitous cast iron heating stoves were used to make paths and keep the quarters reasonably tidy. Station staff had a difficult job creating reasonable conditions for the new arrivals. In his book, *"It's Really Quite Safe"*, Hank Rotherham explains how some of these problems were overcome at Hatston:-

Our Paymaster-Commander was a Welshman by the name of Ivor Dummer. He was a superb scrounger and had managed to acquire from liners being converted to troopships, pictures and furniture which would otherwise have been thrown out. These were used to fit our otherwise stark Mess and cabins. The dentist doubled as wine secretary and he kept us well supplied even when London was tightly rationed. He did this by bartering such things as eggs and lobster which were readily available in the Orkneys but very hard to come by on the mainland. Wine merchants seemed to be most obliging in finding stock in the furthest recesses of their cellars when offered either of these commodities. By common consent, a small bomb shelter was dedicated to the safety of the wine - it being thought it was well worth running some personal risk in the event of an air raid rather than face the greater perils of drought.

When the first party of Royal Naval personnel arrived at Twatt in March 1941, they had similar problems to face. A small croft served as a galley and dining hall while the Administration Block housed the Wardroom, officers' sleeping quarters, general offices, Naval stores, SPO office and sickbay! By June 1941 when Lt.Cdr. Rotherham assumed command a ratings' dining hall had been built which doubled up as sleeping accommodation. As for Skeabrae, it was in such a state when the first RAF party arrived in September 1940 that 50% had to be sent on leave! In October the Officers' Mess was still at Holodyke House,

Can this really be Orkney? On a beautiful summer's day Twatt Wrens Celia Green and Mary Kiddie gather wild lupins on Yonbell, the hill above RNAS Twatt – PEMBERTON

about two miles away! The Station Diary records:-
officers have to be billeted out: the men however do their best to settle in in a very sporting and cheerful manner with little grousing and make the best of a somewhat uncomfortable situation.

New arrivals at Twatt were highly amused by the name which has vulgar associations in English. Some ratings used the address T.W.A.T.T. to avoid embarrassment hoping that their families would see this as merely another Royal Naval abbreviation! The station actually lay in the district of Isbister and should have been given this name but it apparently took its name from the nearest Post Office. The Orkney placename Twatt stems from the perfectly innocent Old Norse word *thveit*, meaning a clearing. When slit trenches were dug round the camp perimeter, these were referred to amusingly as the Chastity Belt. The first Station Commander, Lieutenant Commander Hank Rotherham capitalised on the name of his station and visiting dignitaries were presented with a fine scroll which gave them the *Freedom of Twatt*. Designed by rhymster Lieutenant Commander Archie Fleming and artist Royal Marine Major Bertie Bass, it caused much hilarity. It is not on record whether this freedom was bestowed on His Majesty, King George VI, when he visited the station in March 1943!

Royal Naval personnel were particularly pleased to find Wrens well represented in Orkney. When, at the outbreak of war, the Queen Wren, Vera Laughton-Mathews proposed that Wrens be immediately despatched to Orkney to release men for other duties, the suggestion was scoffed at. She protested, "My girls have it up here you know". "It doesn't matter where your girls have it", said an Admiral, "my boys will find it!" So the story is told by ex-Fleet Air Arm officers! But the Admiralty came very quickly round to thinking along the lines of the Queen Wren. Before 1939 was out, there were already Wrens at Lyness, the Headquarters of the Home Fleet and, at its peak, that Station could boast 615 Wrens. RNAS Hatston received its first Wrens in early 1940 and eventually had a complement of 265. On 13 April 1943 WAAFs arrived at Skeabrae: Wrens did not appear at Twatt until late 1943. There were only six initially and they had to share accommodation with the WAAFs at Skeabrae. At Grimsetter there was also a small complement of WAAFs towards the end of the war. The location of the camps for the Wrens and WAAFs produced considerable debate. Lady Cholmondeley arrived from London and insisted that the Wrennery be a mile or two away from RNAS Hatston but, fortunately, her visit coincided with a snowstorm and she immediately saw that, with little transport available, the plan was impracticable. The Wrennery was built directly opposite RNAS Hatston - though with a main road between them

and, eventually, the fences were breached so that a station gate faced the Wrennery gate! At Skeabrae the WAAF camp was situated in a small enclosure some miles away from the station and as Mike Walker, a Signals Officer there at the time says: "Security there was considerably tighter than round Scapa Flow". By 1944 very fine Wrens quarters had been built *within* the perimeter of RNAS Twatt providing accommodation for 7 officers and over 350 other ranks. Despite this progressive move they were very closely chaperoned on station.

Wrens and WAAFs were not the only women to be found on the Orkney airfields. Keith Remmington, 771 Squadron pilot describes the excitement of a new arrival at Twatt:-
. . . the Corsair was a bit of a brute. It was especially difficult on the ground because of its long nose and taxying was always a problem. I shall always remember the first one being delivered to us. When it taxied in to dispersal, we all gathered round full of interest and some apprehension. The cockpit hood slid back and, to our astonishment, out got a petite American lady pilot. We were amazed that someone so small and so attractive could handle such an ugly looking brute of an aircraft. When asked what it was like to fly she replied "It sure is a hot ship. You fan her in at 95 knots and when you cut the throttle, she sure does stop flying." I think that was a pretty fair description of the aeroplane!

The woman was of course a member of Air Transport Auxiliary which employed a number of American women pilots. This is the only record of an American woman pilot in Orkney but, considering the vast numbers of new aircraft which arrived, she was probably one of many.

Experienced pilots found these young ladies intriguing and there was a sneaking admiration for them and their skill in handling powerful military aircraft. Mike Crosley speaks of quite a bit of banter among the pilots of 801 Squadron when the new Seafire LIII's were delivered to Skeabrae in December 1944 by the ladies of ATA:-
Dougy (Yate) was wondering how they managed at 5 g. He reckoned their bra straps would part. He invented a new type with a cantilever system of weights and pulleys which was self compensating. The Mark II version used more sophistication still - solenoids and rheostats to arrange constant uplift at all g loadings from minus -2 to +8!

As far as women on the stations are concerned we must not forget the ubiquitous NAAFI girls. Catherine Mair was in the NAAFI at Twatt:-
I was met at Stromness by a Mrs. Lindsay, a very formidable lady who later was very nice to a homesick Scot. As mobile canteen driver, I was pretty much my own boss. I also became a very popular girl if only for my 'cup of char and a wad'. I was Jock or Lofty to them being 4' 11"! It was my duty to supply Stand Easy (tea breaks) morning and afternoon and even through the night sometimes. A cup of tea was 2d. and that was for any size of cup! One day a bright spark brought along a 2lb. tomato tin as a cup! When a matelot was broke I sometimes let them write his name on the slate which I had fixed to the roof of the van. I was only let down once as far as payment was concerned and by a fellow Scot too! He ran up a bill a bit higher than most (the boys knew I had to clear the money out of my own pocket). Unfortunately the Scot

boasted in the bar that I could whistle for my money. The upshot of that was, a sailor with a very black eye came to the van with an apology and cleared his debt. I never knew who gave him the black eye but he got no more credit.

I got to know the area very well and when a sailor was going home I was often asked to get something to take with them so I became very well known at the surrounding steadings and farms as I always managed to find butter, cheese and eggs and sometimes even a chicken for them. There was also a NAAFI at the RAF station at Skeabrae nearby and there was great rivalry between the Skeabrae NAAFI driver and myself. We always tried to see who could reach the NAAFI bakery in Stromness first in the morning to get the best cakes for our boys. Most of the matelots at Twatt were English and Eccles cakes were in great demand. I always made sure I had a good supply of them!

By 1944, new arrivals found large and busy stations. There were over 400 permanent staff at Hatston. When seven squadrons and their ground crews were disembarked, there were certainly times when there were more than 1000 men on the Station assisted by more than 200 Wrens. The station had a very fine cinema-cum-theatre and a very active theatrical group. Originally run by Hatston test pilot, Lieutenant Shea Simmonds, this role was later assumed by Donald Hewlett who was later to become well known on stage and on television. Twatt and Skeabrae also had fine cinemas. From the Twatt magazine *About Tern* (the station was known

as HMS *Tern*) we learn something of the large part played by the cinema in the lives of the men and women on station:-

There are so many different things which go to make *The Orcadia* one of the best cinemas in the islands. Naturally, most of our patrons consider only the 3d. 4d. or 6d. that they pay for some kind of seat and then if the film comes up to their expectations, they go away feeling very pleased about the whole thing. While on the subject of seats, it may surprise you to know that well over 100,000 people have paid cash to see the 317 big performances that have been exhibited in the last twelve months. This does not include such performances as special instructional films, ENSA's dances or the three special children's matinées.

The box-office record in *The Orcadia* is held by *This is the Army* which drew a crowd of 1171, closely followed by *Mutiny on the Bounty* with 1167. *Song of Bernadette* came third with 1133. It may interest the officers to know that more of them attended the *Song of Bernadette* than any other show. The average weekly takings for a film show is between £20 and £25 out of which 15gns. is deducted to pay for the lease of the films. Films are supplied by the Royal Naval Film Corporation.

As these figures show, Twatt, by this time was a very large establishment. Living quarters offered accommodation for 173 officers and 965 other ranks. The new Wrens camp on station had accommodation for 7 officers and 357 ratings. It is doubtful whether the Station ever reached its full complement: the official Station history talks of 150

Skogar Wardroom party, Twatt, December 1944: Graham Peacock, Freddy Watts, side view of Peter Cornish, Lt. Cdr. Dobson, back of Joe Mence, side view of Alan Moore, 'Crem', Cdr. Jackson, W D Bundy, Elizabeth Wright – PEMBERTON

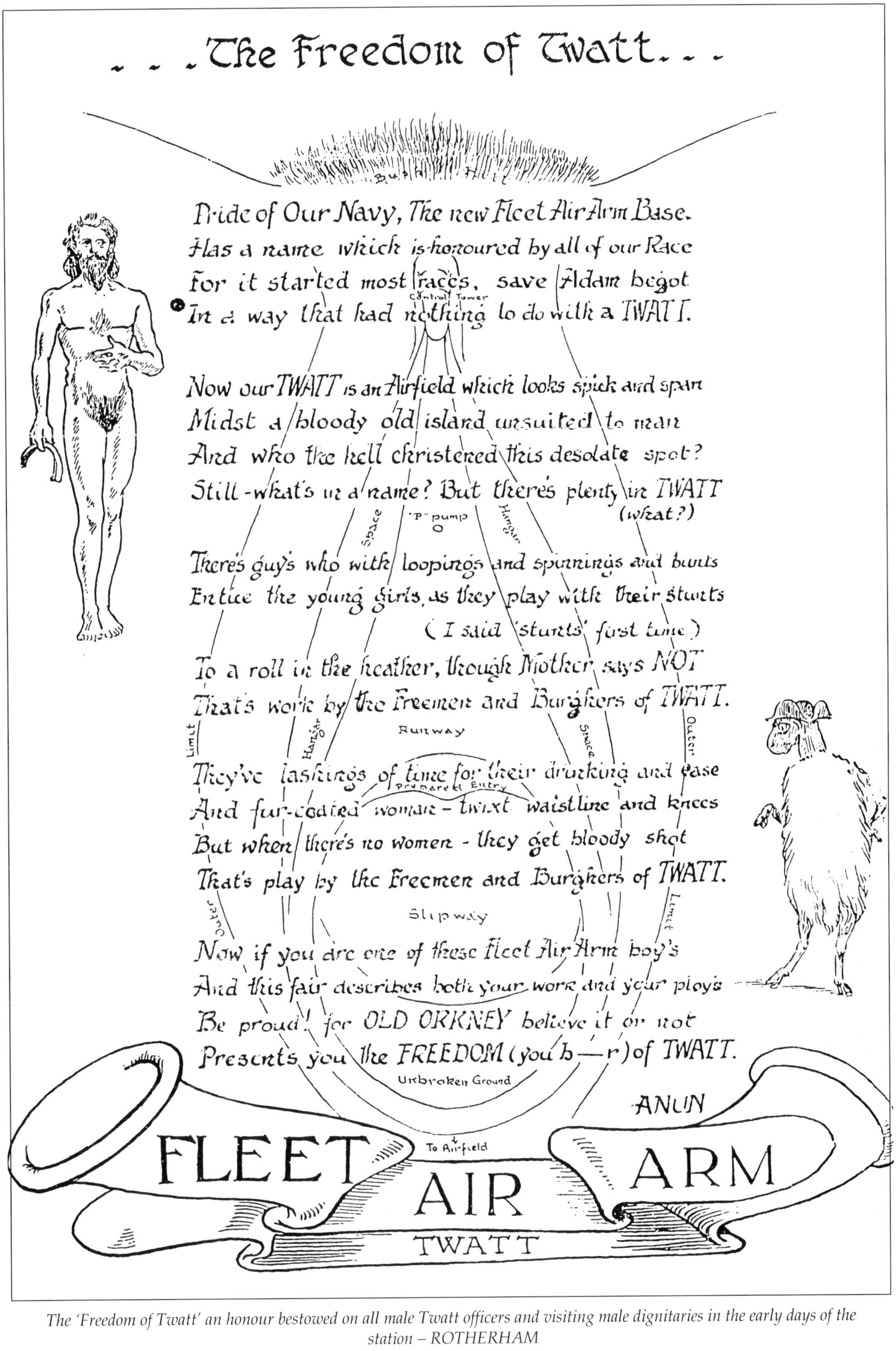

. . . The Freedom of Twatt . . .
Bush Hill
Pride of Our Navy, The new Fleet Air Arm Base.
Has a name which is honoured by all of our Race
For it started most races, save Adam begot
In a way that had nothing to do with a TWATT.
Control Tower
Now our TWATT is an Airfield which looks spick and span
Midst a bloody old island unsuited to man
And who the hell christened this desolate spot?
Still - what's in a name? But there's plenty in TWATT
(what?)
Space
"P" pump
Hangar
There's guys who with loopings and spinnings and bunts
Entice the young girls, as they play with their stunts
(I said 'stunts' first time)
To a roll in the heather, though Mother says NOT
That's work by the Freemen and Burghers of TWATT.
Limit
Hangar
Runway
Space
Outer
They've lashings of time for their drinking and ease
Prepared Entry
And fur-coated woman - twixt waistline and knees
But when there's no women - they get bloody shot
That's play by the Freemen and Burghers of TWATT.
Outer
Slipway
Limit
Now if you are one of these Fleet Air Arm boy's
And this fair describes both your work and your ploys
Be proud! for OLD ORKNEY believe it or not
Presents you the FREEDOM (you b—r) of TWATT.
Unbroken Ground
ANUN
To Airfield
FLEET
AIR
ARM
TWATT

The 'Freedom of Twatt' an honour bestowed on all male Twatt officers and visiting male dignitaries in the early days of the station – ROTHERHAM

At Hatston: on the occasion of the visit of King George VI: the C/O with his WREN officer staff: third from the left, Mrs Rumbelow-Pierce: third from the right, Miss Pride, second from the right, Mrs 'Puckiz' Finch Noyes, extreme right, Margaret Baikie, Hall of Tankerness: Captain H. St. John (Fanny) Fancourt: Albacore aircraft in background – BODEN

Twatt officers and Wrens picnic among the sand dunes at Aikerness in Evie: note the gramophone! Left to right – Len Page, Rachel Murray-Bissett, Keith Remmington, Muriel Wears, Helen Wilson – REMMINGTON

Wrens on site. Towards the end of the war a fully equipped hospital offering X-Ray facilities and catering for the whole Station was built adjacent to the Wrens' quarters. The story is told that the only operation in the theatre was conducted on the Commander's dog. Found chasing sheep, an irate farmer had discharged his shotgun at it but the pellets were skilfully removed by a naval surgeon! Talking of medical matters, perhaps the most extraordinary thing to happen in the history of the Royal Navy occurred at RNAS Twatt. A child was born on the ship! A Wren Petty Officer who had just been drafted in became very ill one night and caused great consternation among the younger Wrens. Twatt Wren Muriel Wears gives the inside story:-

In the middle of the night the Petty Officer started moaning and some of the girls went in to see what was wrong with her. She complained of terrible pains in her stomach so they got her an extra hot water bottle, some more blankets and gave her a good stiff dose of Andrews Liver Salts. Despite this she kept on making an awful lot of noise and moaning so two of the girls decided they would have to go and get the Duty Wren Officer because, by this time the whole hut was not only awake but very concerned. The officer arrived quickly, took one look at the patient and exclaimed "My God, she's having a baby!" That really shows how young and innocent we all were. The girls in the cabin were quite shocked! The Petty Officer was transported to the Sick Bay where a young doctor safely delivered a bouncing baby boy. The birth was duly entered in the ship's log! Later in the day some of us were going to Stromness and begged a lift from the Station ambulance. The girls spoke of their adventure during the night. "I know all about it", said Dr. McCaskey - "I was there!. Frankly", he went on, "I was a bit apprehensive - I'd never delivered a baby before and I didn't expect that to be one of my duties on a Naval Air Station!"

On 4 April 1941, the Skeabrae Literary and Debating Society discussed the motion *It is possible to be happy though in Skeabrae!* The motion was carried by 24 votes to 12! By any standards Skeabrae was a large and busy Station. Even at the time the motion was discussed there were 550 service personnel on site plus one Hurricane Squadron and its servicing echelon which could have counted for at least another 150. The WAAFs were still to arrive and by 1944 there were occasions when four squadrons of aircraft were based here. As the outcome of the debate suggested, Skeabrae does seem to have been a happy station. It featured a well organised social life. The camp had its own cinema in 1942 and later a well equipped gymnasium was added: the Commanding Officer was proud to record in the Station Diary that there were classes in German and French, choral and dramatic societies, music club and facilities for every sport including squash.

Arrival of the Queen Wren, Dame Vera Laughton-Matthews at Twatt, 10.06.45: Captain Jackson, Dame Vera, her secretary and I/O Foster-Barham: Dame Vera was the author of Blue Tapestry, the story of the Wrens – PEMBERTON

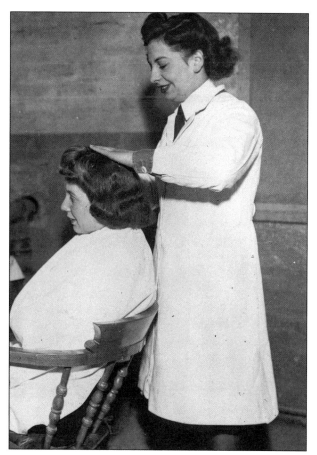

Lily ???, Wren Hairdresser, Twatt, 1945: Wren Mary Treby
(née Rogers seated) – TREBY

In common with all the larger military camps in Britain, the Fleet Air Arm and Royal Navy were entertained regularly by ENSA concert parties. The huge garrisons stationed in Orkney attracted the very best in the world of entertainment and a veritable galaxy of stars came and went to Orkney during the war years. Tommy Handley recorded one of his ITMA shows from Twatt, Gracie Fields visited twice: other stars included John Mills, Bernard Miles, Gertrude Lawrence, George Formby and Terry Thomas. Leslie Henson the comedian was a popular entertainer and when he appeared in the Garrison Theatre on the island of Flotta, King George VI was in the audience. Yehudi Menuhin accompanied by Marcel Gazelle, the Belgian pianist, played at both Hatston and Twatt and made a tour of the warships in Scapa Flow, staying overnight in HMS *Duke of York*. He writes:-

It was most exciting to be among those wonderful men and feel that very British amalgam of men, sea and ships. On my trip back to the Orkney Mainland, I had to board a destroyer in dense fog and I was landed on an abandoned shore at the northern-most tip of Scapa where I boarded a waiting car on the slope behind the beach. I shall never forget that: it was almost unreal.

All kinds of activities were encouraged by the Station Commanders. Hatston counted an experienced pigman among the staff and what began as a small hobby soon grew into a commercial undertaking! There were 100 pigs on

Station at one point fed on swill from the kitchens! Commander (Flying) at Twatt kept geese and a Squadron Commander happily cared for his plot of radishes on the same station. A garden competition was held annually at Skeabrae. Lieutenant Shea Simmonds kept at Hatston a pet Shetland pony which developed a great liking for beer and would wander into the Junior Officers' Mess for a noggin. On one occasion, it inadvertently got itself into the Senior Wardroom much to the alarm of a visiting Admiral who registered a very strong complaint to the Station Commander when the pony stood on his foot apparently because no beer was forthcoming! The owner of the beast and his totally innocent fellow officer had their mess bills stopped for a month. All ranks were allowed to keep dogs at Skeabrae. 2nd. Lieutenant James Endresen, pilot with No.331 Squadron Norwegians at Skeabrae kept his dog in his room. Fellow pilot Harald Meltzer wasn't amused at first:-

(James) moved in with a dog - a damned dog I called it at first because it had long shaggy hair (front and back looked alike!) and smelled terribly. Mud, hairs and smell were spread all over the room and I complained bitterly - but only at first. In a few days, James washed the dog and, after I had recovered from the first shaking of water over my bed, the hair, mud and smell problem was resolved. The dog was called *Fury* but I never saw him show any. He seemed to get some of James' spirit for he was always pattering about quite happily.

At Hatston there were even sufficient dogs on station at one time to permit a Dog Show! Lieutenant Duncan Hamilton had a small spaniel there which he called *Lucky*. He had returned from leave to Hatston sitting in the nose of an unheated Boston bomber with *Lucky* on his knee wrapped in an Irvin jacket. *Lucky* sat happily in the corner of his office until, one day when left alone for a short time, he started, out of boredom, to chew up some papers. Unfortunately the papers were the assembly instructions for crated American fighters about to be built and transferred to a waiting convoy in Scapa Flow. The story goes that the Fleet, unaware of this act of canine sabotage, waited until further copies were flown in via Iceland!

Sometimes airmen, especially pilots, were able to enjoy themselves during the course of their duties too! There was no Air Traffic Control in Orkney and, when on non-operational flying and out of sight of the station, the powerful engine of the fighter and the freedom of the Orkney skies often tempted the pilot to test not only his own skill but the capabilities of the machine. Passing between the Old Man of Hoy and the cliff face was something of an initiation test for young pilots. Shortly after arriving in Orkney, Skeabrae pilot Cyclops Brown of No.253 Squadron made a fast pass through the gap in his Hurricane and congratulating himself on his achievement banked his aircraft sharply round only to see to his great surprise three Royal Navy

Skuas follow him through! Less fortunate was an Albacore pilot ferrying an aircraft from Ayr. Apparently caught in violent unpredictable turbulence and updraughts along the cliff face, the aircraft struck the Old Man of Hoy and crashed on the Hoy Hills. Only recently some of this Albacore has been salvaged and used to complete the only surviving example of this aircraft which is held in the Fleet Air Arm Museum at Yeovilton in Somerset.

It was one thing for a pilot flying solo to attempt this feat but it was another thing for the pilot to subject his Observer or TAG to such an experience. Even a lumbering Walrus of 700 Squadron with Sub.Lieutenant Lawrence at the helm and Norman Brown as Observer completed this dangerous manoeuvre. Dick Stark, 771 TAG at Twatt had similar experiences. He writes:-

Some pilots made you feel very confident in their ability to fly the aircraft, others were jittery. At the other extreme were wild fellows who at the end of an exercise would do all kinds of tricks probably just for a Wardroom boast. Once we came back from an exercise in the Pentland Firth so close to the cliffs of Hoy that the aircraft was getting thrown around with the turbulence and I was violently sick. It was the only time I was ever airsick. Twice I made the journey home between the Old Man of Hoy and the cliff. That was a dangerous manoeuvre but many pilots tested their skill in that narrow gap. Everyone knows that part of the main road between Kirkwall and Stromness was closed to traffic to become the main runway at Hatston. On one occasion we actually landed on a main road which was still in use! I think the pilot probably did it for a dare. We were flying parallel to the Evie road, the pilot had a good look to see that there was no traffic and down we went! Of course we didn't stop - we just carried on and took off again.

Tom Halhead was a TAG with 771 Squadron based at Hatston. On 21 February 1941 he was detailed to fly in a Hawker Henley with Midshipman Peter Twiss as pilot. He wasn't to know at that time that Midshipman Twiss had the makings of a test pilot. Tom describes the experience:-

The wind was such on that day that we took off over Kirkwall Harbour. We got to the end of the runway at a terrific rate of knots, wheels up at a height of a few feet and the next thing I remember seeing were the seagulls leaving the tops of the masts of the fishing vessels, I would say - hastily. I suppose this was to be expected, the trouble was that I, instead of observing this from above, happened to be looking up at them!

Pilot Twiss pulled the stick back and vertically upwards we shot to about 3,000 feet where we did a sort of roll off the top and headed overland to a RAF station which was nearing completion at Skeabrae. Here we did every sort of show-off manoeuvre in the book and clewed up making all sorts of passes at the Control Tower. There was some RAF bod out on top shaking his fist at us in anger: he looked really annoyed. I reminded the pilot we were supposed to be doing a height finding exercise for the Army Ack-Ack units. His reply was some kind of mumbo-jumbo and up into the sky we went to about 20,000 feet. It was a bit cold up there so down we came in rolls, dives, twists and turns - you name it, we did it!

I had not done any aerobatics ever before and, after an hour of it, I

Watchkeepers Cabin off duty, Twatt: Back Row: Paula Edwards, Janet Renton, L/Wren Helen Wilson, Nan Chisholm, unknown, Hilda Smith. Front Row: Doreen Campbell, Margaret Mitchell, unknown, unknown – REMMINGTON

Cathy Mair (née McKenzie) and Elizabeth Sinclair, two NAAFI girls at Twatt – MAIR

'Stand-easy', coffee break on the squadron: Air Mechanics of 771 Sqdn. Twatt, at the main camp, 1944: L/A Mechanic John Shedden: Wren Jean Wenham: Wren Ruby Heymans: Air Mechanic Cyril ?? – HEYMANS

The auditorium: the ex-cinema seats were specially flown up by the Nuffield Services organisation – HORNE

Hatston Show, The Importance of Being Ernest by Oscar Wilde – HEWLETT

was beginning to feel really groggy. I told the pilot this but got no let-up. I recall sending a message to the Army that our height was 8,000 feet and then I was violently sick somewhere over Scapa Flow and away went my teeth! I felt so rotten, I didn't care a hoot! However our time was up not long after this and we came back to Hatston where, of course, everyone considered it to be a huge joke, including the CO who was very decent about it and got me fixed up with a new set of false teeth in no time at all. Initiation? I was never airsick again.

Wing Commander Lea Cox, Station Commander at Skeabrae, did show his anger at this brash intrusion from RNAS Hatston but he let it pass. Captain 'Fanny' Fancourt, Commanding Officer of Hatston was most displeased when the RAF hit back with its own Hurricane shortly afterwards:-

Flying a Hurricane to the north of Kirkwall one day led, inadvertently, to my only direct contact with Hatston and its commander. I was minding my own business when, suddenly, out of the clouds, pounced a stubby little Martlet naval fighter. Clearly its pilot wanted to play. Then followed a hectic dog-fight, screaming tight turns, vapour streaming from the wing tip vortices in ribbons, flick half rolls and the dangerous, therefore forbidden head-on attacks. As always in such affairs the tourney got lower and lower and both pilots were oblivious that it had shifted to the centre of Captain Fancourt's airfield and around his hangars. The Martlet pulled up, waggled its wings, lowered its wheels and went in to land. I returned to Skeabrae but I found to my surprise that, awaiting me, was the Squadron Commander. "The Captain of

Hatston wishes to see you tomorrow," he said. "At what time?" I asked. "He will see you when you get there. You are going to walk - all eighteen miles - and no lifts." I was dismissed. To get there at a reasonable time the following day I decided to set off at midnight. About eleven hours later I dusted off my battered shoes, straightened out my crumpled best blue jacket and entered the Captain's office. As an introduction I was told that, in normal circumstances, I would have been interviewed with the other offender but he had turned out to be a distinguished naval officer much senior to me and the Captain was not going to let the Air Force see and hear him receive an old fashioned dressing down which he, assuredly, was about to be given. I was then informed that neither the Fleet Air Arm, nor the Royal Air Force nor the Luftwaffe was going to be allowed to create mayhem over Captain Fancourt's Royal Naval Air Station. If I, as a Royal Air Force fighter pilot, was so fond of violent manoeuvres at low level I would be sent to sea for a month in a destroyer. I was wished good-day and told to have a pleasant walk back to Skeabrae.

[Cyclops Brown was the Hurricane pilot: the distinguished Senior Naval Officer could only have been Lieutenant Commander J M Wintour, CO of the ill-fated 802 Squadron, at that time based at Hatston. The original 802 Squadron went down with HMS *Glorious* on 8 June 1940: it was reformed at Hatston on 21 November 1940 with 12 Martlets. In September 1941, the squadron embarked in HMS *Audacity* on a Gibraltar convoy and in an engagement on this trip the CO was shot down. Subsequently HMS *Audacity* was torpedoed and the whole squadron lost again. G.L.]

On 22 March 1943 German photographic intelligence identified 36 ships in Scapa Flow and

Kirkwall Arts Club, Club Room, 1944: this club was founded by Lt. Donald Hewlett, a Royal Naval Met. Officer at Hatston in October 1943 – HEWLETT

HATSTON EMPIRE

DONALD HEWLETT

PRESENTS

"Robinson Crusoe"

"ORKNEY HERALD" OFFICE

The Hatston Pantomime was a great success! – HORNE

they feared an imminent invasion of Norway. John Cooper, was First Lieutenant of 881 Squadron Martlets based at Hatston between March and August 1943. The Squadron trained hard for this mock invasion of Norway codenamed *Tindall*. Mock enemy counter moves were also rehearsed. John Cooper volunteered for one of these defence exercises as a respite from aerial combat and became overnight one of several German saboteurs dropped by parachute over the Mainland of Orkney with a brief 'to enter Hatston Air Station and blow up aircraft, vehicles and military installations'. They were permitted to commandeer any military vehicle and any piece of military equipment to achieve their aim and blowing up was defined as 'placing a sabotage sticker on' an aircraft or piece of equipment. Volunteers were dressed in plain blue sweaters and trousers and allowed nothing in their pockets except one coin to telephone for help if necessary. Three days were allowed for the task during which time the saboteurs were not permitted to speak English.

What appeared initially to be a lot of fun transpired to be rather a dangerous assignment. It wasn't possible to tell the civilian population about the exercise and anyone not in military dress, unable to

speak English and snooping about an Orkney farmyard was extremely likely to have both barrels of a shotgun discharged in his direction. (Orcadians would not assume he was a spy or even if he was they would be more concerned that he was stealing eggs!) If he did succeed in walking unobtrusively over the open Orkney countryside (a difficult exercise since the only cover offered for the most part would be fencing posts) he was still likely to be torn apart by the guard dogs at Hatston or dispatched by a nervous Marine guarding the perimeter fence. John Cooper describes what really happened:-

On my first exercise I found myself alone beside a road at two o'clock in the morning somewhere on the Mainland of Orkney while the Naval van which had dropped me off drove off in the semi-darkness to scatter my fellow saboteurs. Although dropped blind from the van, I had a good idea of where I was because I was very fond of Orkney by then and had seen every inch of the islands, large and small, from the air. I took to the heather and moorland and, over very rough going, worked my way slowly towards (I hoped) the West. Sometime after dawn, in true Hollywood style, a long line of little figures, presumably soldiers, appeared on the distant skyline and I speeded up my progress. After some time I could see that another lone figure was moving away from the beaters on a course converging with mine. After stalking each other for a while this turned out to be a fellow spy and together we managed to avoid the search party without being spotted.

Around midday Jack (I have forgotten his second name for we had not met before) and I found ourselves in the parish of Stenness lying in good cover at the back of the Standing Stones Hotel which was being used for the accommodation of very senior officers of, I presume, all three services. At that time of day, the area at the back of the hotel was deserted: there was just one official Naval car used, no doubt, for the transport of Senior Naval officers, invitingly parked in a small yard out of sight of the kitchens. After some discussion Jack and I decided that, if we could get possession of the car and perhaps some coats and hats from the hotel, we might be able to bluff our way into Hatston, through the Main Gate, rather than get stuck on the perimeter barbed wire and be eaten by Alsatians. I discovered that I had a small comb I had forgotten about in my shirt pocket and conceived the idea of starting the car with one of its teeth. Accordingly I crawled across the yard while Jack kept watch and, finding the car door unlocked, managed to get the engine going after an agonising fiddle.

Still unobserved, Jack joined me and took the wheel, turning the car round to be poised for a racing approach round the corner of the building to the front door. This we arranged he would do after slowly counting up to ten and meanwhile I strolled around to the front door and into the foyer. To my joy, I saw in a side passage, an impressive array of highly decorated naval greatcoats and hats hanging from pegs among sundry other exalted garments. I therefore grabbed an Admiral's coat and hat and was about to grab another when, down the stairs, came a formidable lady who had manageress written all over her. She let out a series of loud yells just as Jack screeched to the front door with the passenger door open for my immediate embarkation. I bowed silently to the lady, rushed out to the car and we shot off down the Kirkwall road circumnavigating a Naval Commander who tried to stop us and who, we learned later, would have shot at us had he been armed since the Standing Stones Hotel officers had not been warned of the exercise. In fact, this omission was to our advantage since those at the hotel were unaware that we might make for Hatston and did not therefore telephone a warning of our possible arrival. As it was, Jack tore along the Kirkwall road while I tore the lining out of my captured hat (which was too small for me) and got into the greatcoat. I laid my sleeve along the window, turned up my collar to conceal my age (I was 25) and crammed the hat over my eyes. I was certainly flaunting some impressive scrambled egg. There was a pipe in the pocket and that came in handy too.

As Jack and I sped towards Hatston, we agreed that he was dressed just a bit informally for an Admiral's driver even if his navy blue sweater and trousers were unremarkable, so when we neared the Air station, we drew into the kerb beside an unsuspecting and small matelot who stiffened and stood rigid to attention when he saw the weight of gold braid on my sleeve and hat. Beckoning him slightly nearer (Admirals are often deaf), I reached out and, murmuring "Guten morgen mein Freund", removed his cap and we shot off to Hatston. I must confess that I am not entirely certain that this last little twist in my story actually happened but the intention was certainly there and it certainly should have been done. In any event, why spoil a good wartime story for a hap'orth of tar!

Jack and I swept through the Main Gate of the Air Station past the armed guards, slowly enough for them to take note of the seniority of the distinguished passenger but just fast enough for them to be unable to hear clearly my smiling response (in medieval Polish) to their challenge! Fortunately they did not shoot at us and we were able to drive, with pomp and ceremony all round the Air Station slapping our bomb stickers on everything in sight. Nobody was around as everybody was busy catching spies trying to get in over the wire. We finished up in the Wardroom with all officers rising sharply to their feet when we entered!

There was, of course, a considerable celebration of our success but I was later carpeted by the Commanding Officer of the Station who told me that Junior Officers did not further their long term naval careers by mutilating Admirals' caps. However Jack and I received a note of congratulation from our victim and a little parcel containing a broken comb which he had found in the greatcoat pocket.

Mutilating an Admiral's cap was in no way a bar to promotion. John Cooper was appointed CO of 882 Wildcat Squadron shortly afterwards!

Officers and Wrens were generally of the opinion that food on the Orkney stations could not be equalled. Beef production has been for many years the main farming activity in Orkney and the Stations were victualled from local sources wherever possible. Astonishingly, in a county famous for its egg production, the cooks made much use of dried eggs - especially for other ranks. In this respect Jack Holden writes amusingly of the Twatt galley:-

Those who served in the Navy will remember that the Service was steeped in tradition - what Nelson did then must be done now and for evermore! At 12.30 mid-day every Saturday, Nelson must have eaten corned beef, so we had it! One dish that Nelson couldn't have had was reconstituted egg. I understand that dehydrated egg powder was manufactured in America and sent from America by well-meaning Yanks. Had the U-Boats concentrated on sinking egg ships instead of tankers and munitions, they would have earned the eternal gratitude of the Royal Navy. As it was, vast consignments of the stuff got here and, as far as I could make out, authority considered that, since the Navy had conveyed it here, the Navy

Leading Wren Sonia Thorpe (née Morrison) and Wren Jessie Haldane in the Electrical Workshop, Twatt, 10 June 1944 – THORPE

Ann Parker, Audrey Smith, Bulgie and George on Walrus Twatt, March, 1944 – PEMBERTON

Paula West, 'Met' Wren sending up balloon to test wind speed, Twatt, 14 April, 1944 – PEMBERTON

could eat it. Egg powder, when it got into the hands of galley cooks, was lovingly mixed with last week's washing up water, then stirred and churned until it looked and tasted like sludge from the Nile estuary. "Hands to breakfast" blared the Tannoy. Eager matelots rushed to the galley, up went the hatch. "What are we on?" asked the first arrivals. "Ersatz egg", cook would reply, always wearing a long suffering expression of "Don't blame me - I didn't lay the bloody eggs," when this dish was served. The effect on the queue was astounding. Ninety per cent promptly vanished back to the various huts where we all had a private stock of eggs, bacon and farmhouse cheese easily obtainable from the islanders. Those who had spent all their akkers on booze in the NAAFI and had no stock were out of luck - either they ate it or they went without. One stoney broke warrior in our mess, having breakfasted on ersatz egg, came and sat on my bunk. "You know Jack", he said, "if we put that bloody stuff inside bloody bombs and dropped it on the bloody Germans, the bloody war would be over in a week." I must say that I was inclined to agree with him.

<u>Real</u> eggs were extremely rare in Britain during the war but were plentiful in Orkney. King George VI visited Orkney on 9 August 1941, and when he flew south he carried a box of eggs under his arm for the Queen! Egging was a popular pastime among Station personnel. Norwegian Harald Meltzer paints a delightful picture of an evening at Skeabrae:-

. . . we slept two to a room with the exception of the Commanding Officer and the Flight Commander. It would be quite cosy for, with a good fire in the small stove, the room could become surprisingly warm. Then we would sit and smoke or read and talk with friends.

Quite often, one of us had either a bottle of Aquavit or whisky, and another would have fresh farm eggs. So, with some sugar from the Mess and a bowl and whisk, we made eggedosis in the evening. What luxury among such desolation.

Eggs were purchased to take back home and eggs were even sent by post in special boxes! CPO Pilot Eric Haslam of 771 Squadron at Twatt writes that the Station Commander allowed pilots the use of a 10 cwt. truck to go round the farms for eggs. But all kinds of transport were used. Skeabrae pilot Pierre Clostermann ranged far and wide looking for eggs:-

Jacques and I organised an egg round. Using the little Tiger Moth attached to the station, we raided the archipelago twice a week, landing near the farms and snaffling all the eggs. At the end of a fortnight of eggs for breakfast, lunch, tea and dinner, the very sight of an egg made our gorges rise. Ken even made out that feathers were growing down his back.

By 1945 a more sophisticated means of transport was used at Twatt - the Station helicopters - but Orkney farmers were not too keen on them landing in their back yard! True the slipstream from the rotors made a good job of sweeping up the farm courtyard but tended to sweep up the hens too and badly affected egg production!

Another great delicacy savoured by the men and women on the stations was lobster which at that time could be purchased for 5/- (25p.) Twatt and Skeabrae men could, with a little skill and some local knowledge, catch their own lobsters off the rocks at Marwick. The Station Magister from Hatston did a regular shuttle service to the island of Stronsay for lobsters! Hank Rotherham describes an encounter with some Orkney fishermen:-

One of the few boat outings in which I took part happened when the crew of our small motor launch - an old private pleasure launch which bore the name of HMS *Sparrowhawk* - suggested that they take us out fishing, the crew being local fishermen in the Navy. So they prepared and then took us out along the coast, lining up leading marks. Then, when satisfied, they dropped the end of a long line with hundreds of baited hooks and buoyed the end. The line was laid out then, carefully following leading marks until the whole line was laid when they buoyed that end. Then we rushed back and pulled up the first end and on most hooks there was a haddock but, after a bit, dogfish also found the line and we started to get up whole fish, half fish and simply heads, backbones and tails! We were about to throw these useless bits over the side when our crew produced a box and insisted on this being filled. Why we wondered? But then, on the way home, we sighted a lobster boat and closed it and traded those bits of fish for lobsters. They were short of bait so we returned to the Station with plenty of fish for all and lobsters for a feast for ourselves and our friends. A beautiful day and, indeed it had been a lovely day. I should add that, by having a vessel in the water bearing the name of our Station, HMS *Sparrowhawk*, our men were qualified for ship's tobacco and their rum ration!

On the Air Stations men and women of all ranks rubbed shoulders with visiting dignitaries. King George VI visited Orkney five times: on one occasion there were three kings on warships in Scapa Flow. Apart from King George VI, King Håkon VII of Norway was there and King George II of the Hellenes. Other members of Royal families included HRH The Duke of Kent who came to Hatston and HRH Crown Prince Olaf of Norway and HRH Prince Bernhard of the Netherlands who spent some time at RAF Skeabrae. Churchill visited Orkney at least four times. Senior military figures moved shuttle-like between Orkney and London. Admirals and Generals were a common sight in the islands. Admiral Ramsay who planned the Naval side of the D-Day operations visited Hatston. General Montgomery also included Hatston in his exhausting morale boosting tour of Britain before D-Day when he was able to address more than one million men and women. He covered the British mainland by special train but, for the Orkney leg, he travelled in a Dakota of the United States Air Force. This was the only occasion that he addressed personnel on a Royal Naval Air Station. Other visiting Generals included Sir Alan Brooke and Sir Freddie Pile. Air Chief Marshal Sir W Sholto Douglas was rather fond of Orkney and paid four visits to Skeabrae. At least four other Air Marshals visited this Station during the war. Foreign visitors included Admiral Kharlamoff, Deputy Chief of the Russian Naval Staff who inspected Skeabrae. Among civilian dignitaries were A V Alexander, First Lord of the Admiralty, who naturally had to

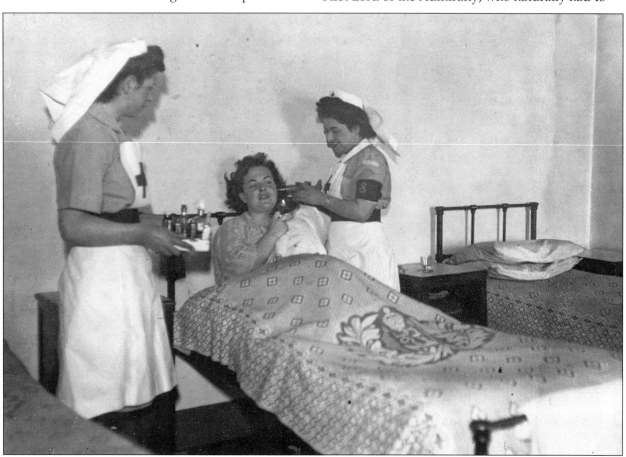

Sick Bay, Twatt, 10.06.45: Nurses Sheila Reed and May Stoddart attending Sylvia Winstanley – PEMBERTON

A Wren Petty Officer gave birth to a child when on Station at HMS Tern, Twatt. She is seen here with Wren First Officer, Mary Foster-Barham and the new, very young member of the ship's company – HILL

Nicolas Horne running the RAF Skeabrae Music Club: all the records in the background have returned to Orkney and are now in possession of BBC Radio Orkney – HORNE

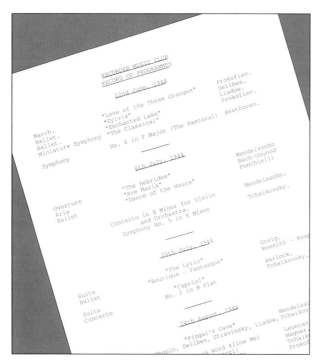

RECORDED MUSIC CLUB
RECORD OF PROGRAMMES

22nd June, 1944

"Love of the Three Oranges"   Prokofiev.
"Sylvia"   Delibes.
"Enchanted Lake"   Liadow.
"The Classical"   Prokofiev.
No. 6 in F Major (The Pastoral)   Beethoven.

March.
Ballet.
Ballet.
Miniature Symphony

Symphony

6th July, 1944

"The Hebrides"   Mendelssohn
"Ave Maria"   Bach-Gounod
"Dance of the Hours"   Ponchielli

                                     Mendelssohn.
Overture
Aria   Tchaikovsky.
Ballet
Concerto in E Minor for Violin
            and Orchestra.
Symphony No. 5 in E Minor

20th July, 1944

                                     Greig. - Resp
"The Lyric"   Rossini
"Boutique - Fantasque"
                                     Warlock.
"Capriol"   Tchaikovsky.
No. 1 in B Flat

Suite
Ballet
                                     Mendelss
Suite
Concerto

24th August, 1944   Mendelssohn, Tchaikov

"Fingal's Cave"   Leoncav
                                     Wagner
Chopin, Delibes, Stravinsky, Liadow, Tchaikovsky Tchaik
            (A Word Allow Me)   Prokof
                  ...ccl)

Programme planned for Recorded Music Club, RAF Skeabrae, June-August 1944; it is interesting to see German music represented: the BBC played German music during the war but all German songs and operas had to be sung in English! – HORNE

make many calls on Orkney. Rev. Tubby Clayton, founder of the Toc H in Ypres during World War I lived near Skeabrae during World War II and was a frequent and warmly welcomed visitor there and at all other stations.

A secret visit was made to Hatston during the war by the American Ambassador to Britain who arrived from London. His mission was to meet Averell Harriman the US special envoy to the USSR who, between 28 September and 4 October 1941, took part in the delicate negotiations at the Moscow Conference on the beginnings of the convoy system to the Soviet Union. Harriman flew from Murmansk to Hatston and found his arrival there more difficult than the Conference. Capt. Herbert St.John Fancourt, Commanding Officer at Hatston was there with the Ambassador when the aircraft, after its mammoth flight, appeared over Hatston:-

I remember one incident of international importance at Hatston that nearly ended in disaster. The United States envoy to the Soviet Union, Mr. Harriman, returned by Catalina flying boat from Murmansk to report after a high powered meeting with the Russians. It was a very long flight with Hatston the first stop. The American ambassador to Britain came up from London to meet Mr. Harriman. We stood on the slip at Hatston and watched the Catalina coming in to Kirkwall Bay. I think the pilot was dead beat for he made three or four extremely dangerous attempts to land, having to put his engines on again and roaring over our heads - almost between the hangars. We were not in W/T touch so could not tell him to land in the outer bay. However he did eventually land and all was well. The American ambassador said to me "I guess the President would not have been too happy if the best we could do was to ask him to send a wreath"!

By contrast many servicemen and women made close and lasting friendships with the local islanders. Norman Brown, Observer with 700 Squadron remembers how his free time was spent:-

It was for me a great pleasure to get inside the Orkney farm houses and experience the genuine warmth of Orkney folk. Sometimes I walked over the hills to Housegarth for I became very friendly with the Linklaters. I can still see Maggie baking at the big table in what is now their sitting room. Jackie was just a boy then but even so he could play tunes on his little melodeon. I couldn't imagine at the time that our adopted holiday home was to be Appiehouse just down the road from them. I also became very friendly with the Spences at Norton. What a fine old man Willie Spence was. We visited him every time we returned to Orkney on holiday. Latterly he was in the Eastbank Hospital and after the usual delightful conversation I said that we would have to be on our way. "But we'll be back again next year and we'll come and see you", I hastily added. But Willie must have had some kind of premonition for he replied wryly, "Yi'll mibbe no ken me address next time though." He died shortly afterwards.

Arthur (Tiny) Small, a Radio Operator at Twatt recalls his associations:-

We made some very good friends when my wife and I were stationed in Orkney, among them Miss Jean Matches and her sister and brother who lived at Gorn in Sandwick and we used to visit them regularly. I always looked forward so much to Sunday afternoon there. Miss Matches used to be able to find four leaf clovers so easily in one little patch of her field and in my little book I still have a four leaf clover that she gave me all these years ago for luck. We needed all the luck we could get at that time. We kept in touch with her for a number of years and it was quite a blow when someone wrote to say she had died for that was the end of our close contact with Orkney. I still have at least two letters she wrote to us. One telling us of an exceptional summer they had in 1946. She says that July and August had cloudless skies and eventually the water ran out. The cattle needed the drink as well as the humans. She told me that they had to go across to Twatt airfield which still had a supply from the Loch of Boardhouse. She says in her letter that there were queues of people and vehicles waiting to load up with water. After spending three years in Orkney I found it hard to believe that the islands could have a water shortage!

TAG Dick Stark of 771 Squadron did not, in the circumstances, expect to find the natives quite so friendly:-

My lasting impression is of the friendliness of the local people in these troubled times. I got to know one family particularly well and that happened by chance. When a drogue was dropped from an aircraft we had strict instructions to release it over the airfield. Occasionally it didn't work out that way. I had to retrieve one of mine from Lower Linklater farm where I had been forced to ditch it. Expecting to be severely upbraided by the farmer for this unwarranted intrusion on his property we were astonished to find ourselves welcomed most warmly. Not only that - we were invited back over and over again. There was always something on the table there for us. We repaid their kindnesses by helping them sometimes with their farmwork. One Christmas I went down there with two of my shipmates and helped them pluck all their turkeys. On 5 March 1943 I was very seriously ill in Kirkwall hospital after our Boulton Paul Defiant crashed into the Bay of Firth. The pilot was killed. My parents were flown up from Nottingham to be at my bedside. My Orcadian friends didn't forget me. Do you know these folks were so kind that, when they heard that I had had a bad accident and that I couldn't eat solid food, they sent some chickens into the hospital so that the staff could make soup for me! And when we went home on leave we always carried a box of eggs. They were worth their weight in gold!

Jack Holden describes the Orkney table:-

One day, after working in the fields, we went in to tea. An Orkney table in war-time had to be seen to be believed. It groaned under the weight of goodies. Mounds of farm butter, cheese, eggs, bannocks, sowan scones, pancakes and that item of Orkney fare that I could never manage - oatcakes. The ingredients (if anyone is interested) are: two parts shore grit, one part cement and a spoonful of latex to bind the lot together. On the table that day were two items that I had never seen before - seagulls' eggs and boiled limpets. I viewed these two gustatory delights with suspicion but my friends were tucking in happily. Oh well - when in Rome. I tucked in also. Over the centuries Orcadian stomachs must have become inured to the devastating effects of gulls' eggs and limpets. Mine wasn't. Half an hour later I nearly died on the farm midden heap. When in Rome it is not always wise to do as the Romans do.

Airmen and women of all ranks based at Skeabrae and Twatt vividly remember the delight of visiting Janet Cooper who kept a small tearoom at The Palace in Birsay. Tea here was often the culmination of a long coastal walk. It was a favourite meeting place for the service personnel of both sexes, fraternisation within the camp perimeter being severely frowned upon. Many a match was made in these surroundings. Lieutenant Keith Remmington writes:-

. . . we would walk to Birsay and have tea provided by two charming ladies in a private house. I can still recall seeing the cake-stands piled high with lovely scones, baps, cakes etc. and we were encouraged to eat as much as we could. Also included in the price

was a boiled egg for a total cost of 1/3 or 1/6 if the tea included two boiled eggs. We really both enjoyed these visits and considering the distance to walk, the teas must have been very good indeed.

For all servicemen and women there came a time to head south again, 'going down the line' as it was popularly known. It would only be fair to say that, for many this was their happiest day! Whether going on leave or to another posting, some were lucky enough to be able to fly south either with the Air Ferry based on Jersey Airlines or with Scottish Airways. Royal Marine Pilot Richard Partridge was amused by the experience of flying to Inverness in a de Havilland Dominie:-

These Dominie trips always used to amuse me because, if the pilot had a full load of passengers, about seven or eight I think, he used to taxi out to the end of the duty runway, and when in position for take-off, he would turn around and casually ask the rear four passengers to come forward and kneel in the passageway just behind him so that it would be easier for him to get the aircraft tail up when taking off. Of course, as soon as airborne, the four passengers returned to their seats.

There was great rivalry between Air Ferry and Scottish Airways. Air Ferry crews wore naval uniform and prided themselves in being able to fly in such diabolical weather conditions that no military aircraft would dare take off.

Lt.Commander Hank Rotherham, Executive officer at Hatston recalls witnessing this:-

I saw a Rapide taxi out to the runway with four men holding the wingtips in 50 knot winds. With the aircraft lined up into wind, the pilot would signal to let go and the aircraft would take off, going virtually straight up.

Rugby at Twatt, 1944: RNAS Twatt in hooped jerseys v. RNAS Grimsetter: the score was 36 - 3 for Twatt, two of the tries for Twatt being scored by Trevor Dole – REMMINGTON

Capt. H St. J Fancourt, CO, RNAS Hatston with rather a cold looking Gracie Fields at Hatston, 1941 – WYLES

Crossing the Pentland Firth by ferry and the long train journey to the south of England was a fearsome prospect for all service personnel. Lieutenant Commander Molyneux, CO of 771 Squadron hated the journey so much that, when going on leave he used to borrow the Squadron Maryland bomber to fly to his home in Sussex. He conveniently parked it at a nearby RAF Station where he had a very good Polish friend! For the lower ranks, no such luxury. Eleanor Robertson, a WAAF stationed at Grimsetter gives an account of a typical departure. Everyone was deliriously happy - for so long!:-

I won't forget leaving Orkney. It was so rough the boat didn't sail so we had to return to the camp and left the following day. Not being much of a sailor I found a bunk before the boat sailed but a lot of the girls went up on deck for a great sing-song. But there was still a tremendous swell on the sea and it wasn't long before they all joined me down below and were being as sick as I was.

Two servicemen going on leave from Hatston were fortunate to get a lift from an aircraft flying from Hatston to Inverness. To their surprise they were then whisked down through Scotland at an alarming rate. Trains were diverted to help them in their progress and staff cars eagerly awaited their arrival at every stop. They could not believe their good fortune. It was only much later that they were told they had been mistaken for two messengers carrying secret codes from an operation off Norway. The messengers had failed to catch the Orkney aircraft and it had not been possible in the time available to change all the specially made transport arrangements!

ENSA Show visits Hatston: comedian Leslie Henson in centre (short and balding with glasses): tall officer behind him is Shea Simmonds, Hatston test pilot and also in charge of recreation at that time – HEWLETT

Sometimes others from the lower deck succeeded in getting air transport home but for some it ended in tragedy. Sam Sephton was a rating at Twatt and was going home on leave:-

In the autumn of 1943 twenty-six of us going on leave had a chance of a flight to Doncaster in a Handley Page Sparrowhawk troop carrier or store carrier. All went well on take off: the flight was bumpy and uncomfortable for there were no seats but we settled down. Some slept, others chatted. Suddenly and with no warning, there was a hellish explosion. I must have blacked out and came to thinking I had been dreaming for I was lying on a piece of rough moorland. Then I realised that some of my shipmates were lying round me all looking rather dazed, some bleeding from facial injuries, others moaning. There was smell of engine oil in the air and I looked up in disbelief to see our plane a total mass of twisted green metal lying about twenty yards away. The plane had hit a hill top. I was lucky: I had only a small cut over my left eye. One of my cabinmates was dead but most of my shipmates were very lucky too: they were all scattered round the hillside and only a few had broken legs and arms. It seemed incredible that twenty five of us survived the impact.

On VE Day there were only three full squadrons left in the whole of Orkney. All ranks including WAAFs had a free pint of beer with their lunch at Skeabrae, the afternoon was free and everyone listened with interest to Churchill's speech which was relayed over the Tannoy. A dance for all ranks was held in the evening. At Twatt, all flying was cancelled and the ship's company assembled in *The Orcadia* cinema for an address by the Commanding Officer, Commander E S Jackson. The magazine *Flight Deck* records that:-

. . . after that the fun began in earnest. The canteens were well patronised and the Chiefs and Petty Officers went up to the Wardroom for a noggin. After lunch, those still on their feet indulged in two soccer matches, England v. Scotland and Wales v. Ireland and also Married v. Unmarried. The results aren't recorded: the official chronicler was one who took his celebrations seriously.

Although flying was cancelled, official station duties still had to be carried out however inefficiently but the top brass humanely turned a blind eye. Twatt Wren Beryl Turner writes:-

I was in the Control Tower as a teleprinter operator along with a sailor named Walter and a Chief Petty Officer who mysteriously disappeared shortly after we came on duty. Feeling sorry for the two of us who were left, friends brought in lots of food and drink of which Walter partook freely. Unfortunately the Captain arrived at midnight. I was quite sober and said "Good evening, sir." My duty colleague, Walter, stood to attention wavering and the Captain asked him, "Where is the Chief Petty Officer?" "Gone to see the Captain, sir", was the reply, whereupon he slumped at the Captain's feet. The Captain looked down at him, looked at me, uttered a mild, "Carry on" and disappeared. With the wisdom of hindsight he probably meant, "What a carry on"!

The Ship's Log for Hatston and Grimsetter have not survived. The last entry in the Operations Book of Skeabrae is 29 June so we have no means of telling how VJ Day was spent at Skeabrae. At Twatt, NAAFI girl Catherine Mair records:-

That night everything that could burn was taken up Yon Bell to make a bonfire. I was coerced into taking the van up as far as I could with refreshments. It was quite a night! After that, the camp wound down until there were only 500 men left, then the NAAFI had to go too. I seem to remember we hung on waiting for the last plane to leave. There was some drama, for the last plane to leave Twatt had engine trouble and when it did go it only just made it to the other side of the Pentland Firth.

By early 1946 all the war-time postings to Orkney had left. Jack Holden has the last word.

In January 1946 came the news that we were to go to Eastleigh, Southampton, pending demob. I went to the farm for what I thought would be the last time. To say goodbye to this family that I had come to love so much was a heartbreaking business. I am a very emotional man and easily moved to tears. When the final moment came, I could not speak. I hope I never have to go through that again. I walked back to the camp. When I reached the top of the hill, I turned and looked back at the silhouette of the farm, clearly visible against the backcloth of the sea. That farm had been my home for three years and emotion crowded upon emotion. I turned away and walked silently back to camp. The world had gone flat and empty. Next day the boat sailed. I stayed down in the hold: I did not want to see Orkney fade into the distance as I wanted no repetition of that sad, sad yesterday.

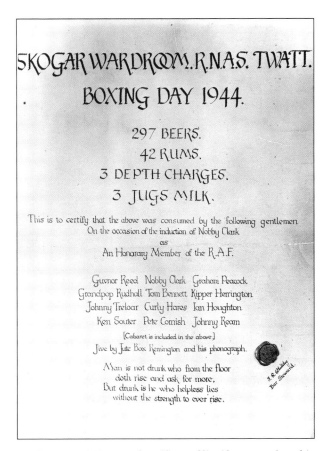

Boxing Day 1944: copy of certificate of liquid consumed on this day: presented to certain gentlemen at Twatt on the occasion of the induction of Lt. Nobby Clark, RNVR, as an Honorary Member of the RAF! – REMMINGTON

Lt. Duncan Hamilton in Irvin jacket on the beach at Hatston with Lt. Shea Simmonds, dog 'Lucky' and the workshop Jeep –
HAMILTON

Lunch at RAF Skeabrae: there were few complaints about the high standard of food for the main meals –
HORNE

John Cooper, CO, 882 Sqdn., Hatston – COOPER

In the dining hall, Skeabrae, Christmas, 1943: Flight Officer Skerman is at the end of the table with the box: others in the photograph are Baker CO, Cpl. Ashton, Cpl. Gonnery, Peggy Borrer, May Burus, Jean Forsyth, Marion Hunter, Cpl. Edwards, Vera Hohnran, Pauline Castle, Rae Ada Royal, Gladys Perry, Kay Hall, Dorothy Nicoll, Dowie – HORNE

What are the Twatt Wrens cooking up in the galley? – HILL

John Fleetwood Morrow, Royal Canadian Air Force, Skeabrae, places a 78 on the gramophone: note the two egg boxes beside him! – HORNE

King George VI inspects Hatston personnel – FAAM

Field-Marshall Montgomery on a morale boosting visit to Orkney takes the salute at Hatston, after arriving in an American C-47 (Dakota), May 1944: on the extreme right of the party is Capt. Geoffrey Gowlland, Commanding Officer, Hatston: an inscription on the back of this photograph, obviously written by RN staff reads 'What a dreadful salute but what can you expect from a pongo?!' – CONDER

Admiral Ramsay, in a Walrus of 700 Sqdn. – HAMILTON

Beechcraft Expediter HD760 arrives at Twatt with Brendan Bracken, First Lord of the Admiralty: 1945 – HILL

Geological expedition in Orkney: on left, Rev. 'Tubby' Clayton, founder of Toc H movement: on right Lt. Donald Hewlett, Hatston: centre possibly a minister? – HEWLETT

Centre: Janet Cooper's tearoom at the Palace, Birsay, a favourite haunt of servicemen and women during the war . . . "and when the occasion allowed, not to mention the weather, we would walk to Birsay and have tea provided by two charming ladies in a private house. I can still recall seeing the cake-stands piled high with lovely scones, baps, cakes etc., and we were encouraged to eat as much as we could. Also included in the price was a boiled egg for the total cost of 1/3 or 1/6 if the tea included two boiled eggs". (Lt. Keith Remmington, RNVR, 771 Sqdn. Pilot, Twatt) – MARWICK

GO BY AIR

AND
ENJOY A LONGER LEAVE

Reduced Fares for all Service Personnel

SCOTTISH AIRWAYS, LTD.

Advertisement in the Hatston Chronicle, the Air Station's newspaper, encouraging servicemen and women to fly to and from the islands

Lt. Comm. Molyneux, CO, 771 Sqdn., Twatt – MOLYNEUX

Chapter Seven

Epilogue; the Return

The war is over and the Churchill Barriers are formally opened to civilian traffic – BALFOUR.BEATTY

The WAAF

Route forms are notoriously erratic documents, taking liberties with time and space but even the hardened R.T.O. was surprised when he saw mine.

"Glasgow to Birmingham via Kirkwall, Orkney. Lumme! Are you ENSA?", he asked. I explained that I was a WAAF in the process of being demobbed and that anyway I'd like to see Orkney again, and why quibble at a few hundred miles at the expense of the Air Force?

"Just as you like: don't forget the eggs," he shouted after me.

I had left Orkney shortly after VE Day when it was still a garrison. Army camps and aerodromes ringed the islands and Scapa Flow was busy with the movements of the Fleet to the Pacific. As soon as the Dominie in which, surprisingly, I was the only passenger, flew low over the Mainland I noticed changes. The Flow was empty. Not even the drifters which, for six years, had run a shuttle service between the Fleet and Kirkwall, steamed across the water. The islands from the plane, a relief map in brown and green, looked deserted. There was little traffic on the roads and the causeways which landlocked the Flow stretched white and empty from island to island.

Arrived in Orkney I had nothing to do but wait for permission to go to Birmingham so I spent my time in nostalgic excursions. Like most sentimental journeys, they were not a success. The island seemed covered with deserted camps. Nissen huts are never decorative but, cleaned and inhabited they have a homely quality. Decaying in an isolation of peat and heather, they presented a scene of dereliction. One Ack-Ack site, famed for its hot punch on cold dance nights, had been converted into a ramshackle smallholding. A black cow peered from the sergeant's mess and hens roosted on the cookhouse shelves.

In Orkney the weather knows no happy mean. There are calm days when sea and sky are luminous with a blue rarely seen outside albums of Swiss views. There are other days when the wind reaches speeds of 60 mph, sea mists swirl over the hills and it rains horizontally. I chose one of those gusty days to visit Stenness, an inland loch famous for the size of its trout. I had visualised myself rowing on the calm water, recapturing the essence of summer days. Instead, cold and bedraggled, I stood in the doorway of the inevitable Nissen hut. A courteous voice interrupted my reverie.

"You would like a lift into Kirkwall?"

An army truck, crowded with soldiers had stopped. I climbed up thankfully and was settled snugly on to a pile of sacks, a greatcoat with a Polish flash round my shoulders. Poles were an innovation.

"How do you like Orkney?", I asked. There was babel.

"Siberia. It could be no worse."

" Why are we here? We do nothing. Here we sit and the wind - it blows - and the rain . . . "

"The Government. It does not know what to do with us. We are - how you say - on the shelf."

I tried to cheer them by describing the luxuriance of the Orkney summer when primroses, wild lupins and spotted orchids all bloom together and night becomes a short twilight. But, looking out on the waste of mist and heather, they were not impressed.

"Anyway, flowers do not help when you are somebody's mistake."

This was something that had changed. During the war, however much we might grumble at the wind and the isolation, the ships safely riding at anchor in Scapa Flow, gave us some sense of purpose. These Poles had nothing but the feeling that they were an embarrassment sent out of sight, out of mind.

That evening, an egg-box under each arm, I walked out to visit my friends who lived in a croft built only a few yards above the high-tide mark. Mrs. I. was gathering in the hens who had been picking along the beach all day. She greeted me very calmly.

"So you have come back. We're glad to have you. Come inside. I'll boil you an egg."

While I ate the egg, flanked by scone spread with Orkney butter and Orkney cheese, she told me the news of the farm. They had a new make of incubator and another cow, an Ayrshire this time. Their eldest son had come back from the Navy so they were beginning to reclaim some of the moor. A few days ago, two young seals had been washed almost to their door. About two feet long, with white fur. Yes, they had been put back. Her daughters returned from work sparkling with their five mile ride.

"There's a dance on at the Hall* tonight, you'd better come," they told me.

The Hall, a grey stone house of many sharply angled wings was approached through the farmyard but leading to a blank wall at the back was a parody of an avenue of stunted pine and fir. Across the cobbled court was a walled graveyard whose grey tombs were lit by two hurricane lamps hanging above the barn door. We climbed up the wooden staircase and watched a dance that might have been described by Hardy. Two fiddlers, one of them most patriarchally whiskered, swayed on a platform at the end of the barn which was intermittently lit by oil lamps set in sconces in the wall. The dancers moved in and out of the shadows to the wail of a Highland Schottische. The dance ended - and there were the men, navy suited and solemn, sitting with their hands on their knees, while opposite, in a long row, sat the girls. The fiddlers, joined this time by an elderly woman pianist, struck up *Two Little Girls in Blue*. There was momentary confusion as the line of men, almost without breaking, slid across the room. Then everybody was turning rhythmically in an old-fashioned waltz.

On my way to Birmingham I remembered that dance. I need not have worried because Orkney was changing. She had scarcely done that in a hundred years. She was simply sloughing her alien war-time skin.

* the Hall of Tankerness [G.L.]

© *The Times*, May 1946: signed I.M.

The Rating

My wife and I came back to visit Orkney forty years after I had left. It looked such a different place. Everywhere looked prosperous, so much of the land had been cultivated, even Yonbell, the hill behind Twatt, was covered in lush grass. We took the car on to one of the runways and I went over to two farmers near the old squash courts and asked if we could walk around.

"Yes", came the reply, "we only graze the land but you can go where you want."

"And can we walk up Yonbell?"

"Why do you want to go up there?" they asked.

"Well I used to work up there at the DF Hut during the war."

"You used to work up there?", one of them remarked in astonishment, "there were only three men ever allowed up there during the war: I was only a boy at the time but I can still remember the name of one of them - Tiny Small he was called."

I couldn't believe my ears! Imagine that 100,000 servicemen and women passed through Orkney during the war and I return after 40 years to find that somebody remembers me! You can't imagine the feelings it brought back. I found out that the man I was talking to was Tom Johnston of Bryameadow. I couldn't honestly say that I remembered Tom but he told me that when he was about eleven or so I would pat him on the head and ask him to help me carry some batteries up the hill! We spent a lovely evening with Tom and his wife and we swopped a lot of yarns. He could remember men that I couldn't!

I told Tom how I could remember the two little ponies that always seemed to stand in the same corner of a field whatever the weather. They often had thick sleet and snow on their backs in winter. This field lay on the route to the DF Hut and, as you can imagine, after three years, these ponies really got to know us and we had always found time to talk to them. In the end we really believed that they could understand what we said to them and I think we also believed that we could understand all their little whinnies and gestures!

Before we left the old airfield I was determined to visit the Control Tower which, at that time, was under sentence of death. I was determined to force my way in through the piles of muck. It was all pitch black: there were strange noises inside, birds beating a hasty retreat and angry at my entrance but as I told them "I was here before you!" It was upsetting to see the building in such a state. Of course as a PCB it wasn't just a Control Tower, it was a communications centre and it had all sorts of office staff inside - met. office and staff, little telephone and exchange. I looked into all the rooms but didn't go up the ladder from the WT office to the Control Tower - it looked a bit dangerous but the structure looked quite sound and I thought "What a shame to destroy it". I felt very happy when I learned later that it was to be saved.

Arthur (Tiny) Small, 1985

Summer 1990: Lynx Mk. 3 (CTS) of 700L Squadron, Portland, pays a nostalgic visit to Twatt Airfield, the proving ground of the Royal Navy's first operational helicopters and where the original 700 Squadron disbanded in March 1944 – JOHNSTON

Aircraft Crash Records
SCAPA
World War II

I sometimes feel that, if I could stop the paperwork caused by accidents, I could then stop the accidents which caused this paperwork which now prevents me stopping accidents
[seen in a Commander (Flying)'s Office]

1939

Date	Aircraft	Base/Squadron	Details
20/09/39	JU88	KG30	Crashed off Hoy.
12/10/39	JU88 4D+EK	Luftwaffe	Shot down over Scapa Flow by AA and crashed Pegal Burn, Hoy: UFF2 Ambrosius, Wireless Operator survived: OB/Lt. Flaemig, Pilot and UFF2 Attenburger, Obergefr.G F R Faust, Air Gunner, killed.
17/10/39	JU88	Luftwaffe	Crashed in sea between Hoy and Stroma: shot down by shore AA during dive bombing attacks on HMS *Iron Duke* with three other JU88's.
28/12/39	Sea Gladiator N5504	Hatston 804 Sqdn.	Mid-air collision in formation: aircraft became uncontrollable, pilot baled out at 6000' and landed safely: Capt. R T Partridge, R.M., O/C 804 Sqdn.

1940

Date	Aircraft	Base/Squadron	Details
09/01/40	Swordfish	Hatston 771 Sqdn.	Took off downwind at Hatston towards Sea Gladiator which was waiting at end of runway: Swordfish got airborne but hit Sea Gladiator which was a write-off: crew abandoned Swordfish 6 miles from Hatston: Sea Gladiator Pilot, P/O G W Peacock *(photographic record of Peacock in a Twatt Hurricane over Scapa).*
09/01/40	Sea Gladiator N5506	Hatston 804 Sqdn.	see above
11/01/40	Skua	Hatston 803 Sqdn.	Spun in off turn at 500', Tor Ness Stronsay; Midshipman (A) John D W Barr *(Merlin)* died in hospital at Kirkwall, buried New Romney, Kent: L/A Ginger Uren, age 22, killed; buried Plymouth Old Cemetery.
08/03/40	JU88	Luftwaffe 2/KG30	Shot down by F/O Dutton, Hurricane, 111 Sqdn., Wick, 40 miles east of Orkney.
16/03/40	Luftwaffe Aircraft	?	Crashed in sea, Scapa Flow.
18/03/40	Rapide DH 82 G-AFEY	Scott. Air	Crashed Kirkwall.
02/04/40	JU88	?	Shot down by AA on raid on Burray and Hoy; in sea?
07/04/40	Skua L3025	Hatston 800 Sqdn.	Reconnaissance, Hatston – Bergen, diverted to Sumburgh on return because of contrary wind: made emergency landing on airfield officially closed due to waterlogging: engine torn off and aircraft a write-off: Capt. R T Partridge, RM, OK: returned to base by Swordfish from Hatston.
08/04/40	He111, H-3 1H+FM	Luftwaffe 4/KG26	Ditched 9 miles SSE of Copinsay Lighthouse after combat with F/O J Edmunds in Hurricane of 43 Sqdn.
09/04/40	Skua L2948	Hatston 803 Sqdn.	Stalled and crashed in sea on turn landing on HMS *Glorious* when joining up for convoy work: P/O Pilot W E Chinn, age 23 killed, buried St. Olaf's, Plot 1, Grave 24: N/A T G L Burgess age 20 killed: buried St. Olaf's, Plot 1, Grave 26.
10/04/40	Do17	Luftwaffe	Fired at off Copinsay by Sub. Lt. Fell and PO Peacock 804 Squadron, Hatston: believed to have crashed into sea after distress call indicated leaking petrol tank.
10/04/40	Heinkel 111 K	Luftwaffe	Shot down by Hurricanes of 43 Squadron, Wick, 10 miles east of Burray: three crew members survived: this aircraft and the one above were two of seven bombers brought down on the same day.
20/04/40	Skua L2999	Hatston 800 Sqdn.	Lost between Lerwick and Orkney on a reconnaisance flight, 59° 81' N, 0° 19' W: Midshipman (A) Pilot John R Crossley, age 19 killed: on Lee-on-Solent Memorial: P/O (A) M Hall age 23, killed: buried Lerwick New Cemetery.
22/04/40	Skua	Hatston 803 Sqdn.	Crashed into sea landing on HMS *Glorious*: pilot picked up.
24/04/40	Walrus L2316	Hatston 700 Sqdn.	Missing on A/S patrol: crashed in Fair Isle Channel: enemy aircraft in vicinity: Pilot P/O (A) C L Smeathers killed: Midshipman (A) Paul L Furbe, Observer, age 19 killed: N/A C E Adams, HMS *Edinburgh*, aged 20 killed.
15/05/40	Do18G	Luftwaffe 1/KO/FL Gr406	Shot down by Skuas of 801 Sqdn, Hatston, east of Orkney.
18/05/40	Swordfish	Hatston 823 Sqdn.	Forced landing in sea with engine trouble: Sub.Lt. (A) Harald D Mourilyan drowned: N/A Roy Parkinson age 21 drowned.

31/05/40	Tutor 1 K3305	Wick Station Flight	Ditched in Pentland Firth.
31/05/40	Gladiator	Hatston 804 Sqdn.	Spun at Hatston from 400' while on training flight, Sgt. Sturgess killed.
19/06/40	Reliant X8521 (formerly G-AEYZ)	1STT	Forced landing in Sanday.
08/07/40	Henley	?	Ran off Hatston runway into Swordfish on take off: Swordfish a write-off.
08/07/40	Swordfish	Hatston 771/770 Sqdn.	see above
14/08/40	Gladiator II N2277	Hatston 804 Sqdn.	Blown into ops. block at Hatston by gale and bent its rear severely.
19/09/40	Vega Gull W9378 (formerly G-AETF)	Hatston Flight	Brakes locked and wheels failed to grip on grass: on landing at Hatston: hit wall: write-off.
22/09/40	Swordfish I L7635	Hatston 821 Sqdn.	Force landed in sea on A/S patrol, 60° 8' N, 3° 23' W: Sub.Lt. (A) Frederick C Saunders DSC, age 21, *Ark Royal*, lost: Sub.Lt. Derek J T Marcus, Observer, age 21, HMS *Sparrowhawk*, lost: body washed ashore Sanday 4-6/11/40: buried Lady Churchyard, Sanday: N/A G H Gaynon killed, body recovered Stronsay, buried St. Olaf's, Plot 2, Grave 6.
26/09/40	Magister I T9769	Castletn. SF	Crash landed on HMS *Furious* in Scapa Flow.
26/10/40	Swordfish I L2794	Hatston 821 Sqdn.	Took off Sumburgh on A/S patrol: landed with engine trouble, took off again, crashed in sea within four miles Quendale Bay, Shetland, 12.35 hrs. Mid. (A) Richard T. Chambers, RNVR pilot age 19, HMS *Sparrowhawk*, killed: body washed up Lerwick, 2/11/40: buried Lerwick New Cemetery, Terrace 11, Grave 14: Sub.Lt. Peter B. Laycock, age 19, HMS *Sparrowhawk*, (Observer?), MPK: N/A B F A Brewster, age 20 killed: buried Lerwick New Cemetery, Terrace 11, Grave 15.
28/10/40	Martlet I BJ568	Skeabrae 804 Sqdn.	Swung on take-off and crashed at Hatston: pilot was attempting to avoid 'B' flight hangar but stalled and hit a mound: Midshipman (A) Birrell slightly injured.
17/11/40	Martlet I BJ	Skeabrae 804 Sqdn.	Flew into ground in landing circuit, Skeabrae: being delivered from Hatston: Pilot Sleigh injured.
20/11/40	Walrus L2257	Hatston 700 Sqdn.	Capsized at Sullom Voe, Shetland: N/A D W Charnock age 21 killed.
03/12/40	Sea Gladiator	Skeabrae 804 Sqdn.	Took off into a Martlet: former burst into flames and burnt out: 2 injured: Pilot Sub/Lt (A) Gunn.
03/12/40	Martlet I	Skeabrae 804 Sqdn.	see above: Pilot Hutchison.
25/12/40	JU88 4N+AL	Luftwaffe 3(F) 22 SOLA W/R 7122	Shot down near Flotterston Sandwick by Grumman Martlet piloted by Lt. L V Carver and Sub/Lt. T R V Parke from Skeabrae at 2.05 pm: Lt. K Schipp, Fw. H Schreiber, Uffz. J Spörtl and Obergefr. K Rotter taken prisoner: first kill of war by UK pilot in US aircraft: aircraft salvaged complete by 15/02/41 and stored in hangar at Skeabrae for some time. *(photographic record)*
??/??/40	Martlet I BJ508	Hatston 804 Sqdn.	Believed to be a write-off at Hatston: details unkown: this aircraft was delivered to 804 Sqdn. on 07/10/40: 804 Sqdn. was based at Hatston from 19/10/40 until 27/10/40 so there is a likelihood that the crash occurred between these dates.

1941

Date	Aircraft	Base/Squadron	Details
02/01/41	Hudson	Wick	Crashed on take off, Skeabrae: port wing engine and undercarriage badly damaged crew one.
09/01/41	Hurricane	Skeabrae 3 Sqdn.	Overshot and overturned on landing after extra long flight: Sub/Lt A N Cole concussed: details uncertain: 3 Sqdn. RAF was at Skeabrae at this time but unlikely to have naval pilot.
13/01/41	Hurricane	Skeabrae 3 Sqdn.	Crashed on landing: extra long flight: Pilot. Officer Muller OK: like the above entry, details uncertain: only 3 Sqdn. RAF in Orkney was equipped with Hurricanes at this time.
24/01/41	Sea Gladiator	Skitten 804 Sqdn.	Crashed on take off, Hatston?: Eyres, Pilot.
04/03/41	JU88 A6+CH	Luftwaffe 1(F)120	Crashed in sea 1 mile east of Westray Sound at 2.35 pm after combat with three Hurricanes of 253 Sqdn., Skeabrae.
19/03/41	Hudson I N7310	? 220 Sqdn.	Flew into Hoy Hills in cloud: 4 killed: army sentry on guard duty at wreck died of exposure.
01/04/41	Albacore N4172	Hatston 828 Sqdn.	U-boat search off Cape Wrath: found nothing: on return to base ran into snowstorm, radio failed, crash landing Whiten Head, Tongue, Sutherland: TAG PO Polmeer slightly injured: Pilot Lt.Cdr. Leon Cubitt and Observer Sub.Lt. Goodger OK: aircraft wreckage recently recovered and now being rebuilt in FAA Museum, Yeovilton.
0?/04/41	Albacore N4155	Hatston 828 Sqdn.	Crashed into sea 50 miles east of Orkney: pilot was only survivor: picked up by Dutch submarine in vicinity: Walrus P1578 from HMS *Shropshire* in Scapa Flow landed beside the submarine to collect the survivor but because of the swell could not take off: Walrus towed by submarine to shelter of Orkney waters!

28/04/41	Hurricane	Skeabrae 3 Sqdn.	Crashed on landing from non-operational flight: repairable off-site.
02/05/41	Albacore	Hatston 828 Sqdn.	Sub.Lt. Stanley W. Everett, RNVR, Observer age 21 killed North Sound during dummy torpedo attacks.
14/05/41	Albacore L . . .	Hatston 828 Sqdn.	Crashed: write-off in emergency landing at Hatston: crew – Bellairs and Paton OK.
31/05/41	Hurricane I V7235	Skeabrae 253 Sqdn.	Crashed in flames 1.25 miles south-west of Crustan, Birsay: Sgt. Pilot H M Cox, RAF, killed: first fatal accident at Skeabrae.
02/07/41	Fulmar N4026	Hatston 809 Sqdn.	Ended up half over the side of *Victorious* landing on, off Orkney: Pilot Sub.Lt. 'Tex' Van Epps OK. *(photographic record)*
12/06/41	Hurricane I P3383	Skeabrae 253 Sqdn.	Crashed 2m east of Wasbister, Rousay, at 16.03: Sgt. Pilot Read, RAF, seriously injured.
04/07/41	Hurricane I V6673	Skeabrae 253 Sqdn.	Crashed near Skeabrae airfield on final at 16.30: write-off.
29/08/41	Hurricane IIB Z5042	Castletn. 124 Sqdn.	Crashed ½ mile west of Skeabrae airfield at 11.45: Sgt. Pilot J M Harris killed.
24/09/41	Spitfire	Castletn. 124 Sqdn.	Flew into ground near Rendall, 5 miles north of Finstown, on flotsam patrol: Sgt. Pilot R F C Pauley, RCAF, killed: buried Sandwick.
10/10/41	Hurricane	Skeabrae 331 Sqdn.	Forced landing at Brough Head, Birsay: pilot uninjured.
05/12/41	Sea Hurricane Z4835	Skeabrae 801 Sqdn.	Crashed: location unknown: write-off: Sub/Lt. H E Duthie, RNZNVR, killed.
03/12/41	Sea Hurricane AF981	Hatston 1st Line Reserve	Overturned on landing at Twatt: pilot, Cdr. H C Ranald spent some time trapped in cockpit until crane arrived from Hatston.
12/12/41	Roc L3186	Hatston 771 Sqdn.	Height finding exercise at sea: Sub.Lt. Jack Tattersfield, RNVR, pilot, killed: L/A G Hall (Wee Geordie) died 13/12/41.

1942

Date	Aircraft	Base/Squadron	Details
10/01/42	Spitfire V B P8729 (call sign 'Green')	Skeabrae 331 Sqdn.	Forced landing near Cleat, St. Ola, ex ops.: write-off: Lt. Hvinden OK.
13/01/42	Swordfish P4222	Hatston 771 Sqdn.	Forced landing in Eday due to low cloud: Pilot Sub.Lt Norris and TAG Richard Stark OK: Lt. Noel Goddard arrived from Hatston to fly off plane: as he took off, tail wheel caught a fence and was ripped off.
24/02/42	Spitfire Mk.II P8580	Skeabrae 132 Sqdn.	Swung off runway at Skeabrae into soft earth and overturned.
15/03/42	Albacore I N 4176/4B	Hatston 832 Sqdn.	Written-off when undercarriage collapsed landing at Hatston from HMS *Victorious*: Sub/Lt. (A) K. Smith OK, but lost off HMS *Victorious* 08/04/43: buried Oatu Cemetery, Honolulu.
01/04/42	Swordfish II W5889	Hatston 833 Sqdn.	North Sound, Orkney. 12.15 hrs. ALT against HMS *Atriah?*: during get-away, aircraft flew into water, bounced off, climbed steeply to 600 feet before stalling and diving vertically into sea: Sub/Lt. (A) A Edward Iveson, RNVR *Jackdaw* RNVR, age 21: L/Photog.(A) Sydney V. Horne F/MX57545, age 23, *Sparrowhawk* both missing presumed killed: on Lee Memorial.
02/04/42	Swordfish II W5924	Hatston	Aircraft being ferried to Crail by RNAS Donibristle: cause of crash unknown: wreckage seen in Pentland Firth: Sub.Lt. (A) Harold Shaw, RNVR, age 21, *Merlin*, 782 Sqdn. missing, presumed killed and also two soldiers going on leave, QMS J. Gallagher, RAOC and Sgt. Drummond.
04/05/42	Spitfire I X4328	Skeabrae 164 Sqdn.	Landed too close on arriving at Skeabrae: chopped tail off R7220: squadron's first day in Orkney.
04/05/42	Spitfire V R7220	Skeabrae 164 Sqdn.	Collided with X4328 on landing at Skeabrae.
31/05/42	Spitfire	?	This is possibly the aircraft which belly-landed on Auskerry in 1942.
15/06/42	Spitfire Mk.V R7267	Skeabrae 164 Sqdn.	Crashed at Dounby due to faulty controls (could turn only to port): plane turned over on its back on impact and pilot thrown out through canopy (which had been opened in an abortive attempt to bale out): Pilot F/L Dowling trapped under wreckage and rescued: pilot only slightly bruised: aircraft a write-off.
26/06/42	Albacore I BF592	Evanton – Aircraft Repair Yard	11.55 hrs. in poor visibility, with cloud base 500', Sub.Lt. (A) James Leggat RNVR, Pilot, HMS *Merlin* ferrying this aircraft Ayr, Evanton, Hatston, hit Old Man of Hoy and crashed Mel Fea aircraft burnt out: pilot's body found Rackwick and buried at sea: on Lee Memorial.
30/06/42	Skua L2951	Twatt 771 Sqdn.	Taxying, swung into hole, X-X damage: Lt. George F Clarke RCNVR, OK: also involved in an accident 23/09/42?
30/06/42	Defiant	Twatt 771 Sqdn.	Landed without tail wheel after hitting obstacle on take off: pilot OK but lost 18/09/45, on maintenance flying, age 30, HMS *Nuthatch*.
08/07/42	Spitfire VA P8706	Skeabrae 164 Sqdn.	Crashed on approach to Skeabrae.
09/07/42	?	Twatt 771 Sqdn.	Pilot Lt. (A) Noel J Cornes, RNVR, age 27 killed: L/A AG Jones killed: buried St. Olaf's Cemetery, Plot 2, Grave 26: L/A A G Jones RNSR age 19 killed: buried St Olaf's, Plot 2, Grave 20.

13/07/42	Swordfish V4593	Hatston 825 Sqdn.	At Woodwick bombing range: failed to recover from dive: Sub.Lt. (A) James H Wood RNVR, age 21 killed (funeral 16/07/42): buried St. Olaf's, Plot 22, Grave 22: L/AM (A) J G Bowick and AM (O) R W Doakin: both bodies recovered.
13/07/42	Maryland AR717	Twatt 771 Sqdn.	Port undercarriage locking gear failed: write-off?: Lt/Cdr. C M Davies, Pilot (photograph of this aircraft at Hatston)
23/07/42	?	Hatston 817 Sqdn. (ex-HMS Victorious)	Flying accident, North Sound, Orkney: L/A G W Howard, age 24 killed: on Lee Memorial: no other casualties reported.
22/08/42	Spitfire VB BL667	Sumburgh 132 Sqdn.	Crashed on training flight off Deerness: Sgt. Pilot Renyard killed.
23/08/42	Spitfire VA P9563	Skeabrae 164 Sqdn.	Crashed at Skeabrae on training flight: wing tip caught workman's hut during low-flying practice; Pilot Officer D B Bridger (Argentinian) killed: buried Sandwick [NB: 164 Sqadron was called the British-Argentine Squadron].
27/08/42	Skua I L3026	Twatt 771 Sqdn.	Spun in off steep turn from 300' and crashed, Houton Head: Pilot Peter K W Nias RNVR age 20 killed: buried St. Olaf's, Plot 33, Grave 2: L/A Alfred L Fletcher, age 29, killed: buried St. Olaf's, Plot 33, Grave 2.
18/09/42	Roc L3177	Twatt 771 Sqdn.	Engine failure in Pentland Firth; Pilot Bill Larkins: ditched off Hoy: pilot picked up by destroyer, HMS Tanaside: L/Phot.Spiller and L/A Benjamin Bassett both killed.
18/09/42	Seafire IIc MA976	HMS Furious 807 Sqdn.	Fell into sea 10 miles west of Hoy due to over-correction of a spin during fighter attacks: sank, leaving no trace: Sub.Lt.(A) Alfred G Harvey, RNVR lost: on Lee Memorial.
24/09/42	Walrus I L2329	Twatt 700 Sqdn. Flight	Mid-air collision in Pentland Firth: Sub.Lt.(A) Maurice G. Clyde, RNVR, Pilot, Sub.Lt.(A) A Ernest H Hardwick, Observer, L/A Charles P Penn-Simkins, AG3, age 20, all killed: on Lee Memorial.
24/09/42	Walrus X94??	HMS Sheffield 700 Sqdn. Flight	Mid-air collision in Pentland Firth with aircraft above: Lt.(A) Neil S Mackenzie, RNVR, Pilot: Sub.Lt.(A) Peter J Wheatley, Observer, age 20, L/A Frederick J P Payne, AG3 all killed: on Lee Memorial.
12/10/42	Seafire MB121	Skeabrae 884 Sqdn.	Barrier crash on Victorious after decklanding trials in preparation for North African landings: damaged propeller: transported by lighter to Scapa hence to Hatston. (Photographic record)
17/10/42	Spitfire VB AD478	Grimsetter 129 Sqdn.	Pilot dazzled by floodlight on landing at Grimsetter: off runway and overturned: write-off.
21/10/42	Spitfire VI BS436	Skeabrae 602 Sqdn.	Swung off runway at Skeabrae into cross wind and overturned in soft ground.
28/10/42	Roc L3187	Twatt 771 Sqdn.	Off runway and tipped on nose: crew unknown.
11/11/42	Spitfire	Grimsetter 129 Sqdn.	Abandoned off Eday: pilot Officer Dixon picked up OK.
27/11/42	Roc L3104	Twatt 771 Sqdn.	Landed with undercarriage up: fuel short and undercarriage wouldn't lower: Sub/Lt.(A) A R Duff Pilot, RNZVR.
15/12/42	Sea Hurricane I Z7089	Twatt 771 Sqdn.	Ex-workshops, Hatston, dived into Peedie Sea from 600': Lt.(A) Thomas N Bush RNZVR, age 27, killed: buried St. Olaf's, Plot 33, Grave 1.
??/??/42	Spitfire	Skeabrae 331 Sqdn.	Plunged into the sea off Orkney when making a simulated attack on a Swordfish: Pilot Ulf Wormdal killed.

1943

Date	Aircraft	Base/Squadron	Details
05/01/43	Defiant DR885	Twatt 771 Sqdn.	Undercarriage collapsed on landing: Sub/Lt. Larkins, pilot: (photographic record).
20/01/43	Spitfire VB BL253	Hatston 899 Sqdn.	Dived into sea whilst circling airfield, 500 yds. north of Hatston: Sub.Lt.(A) Douglas L F Barber RNVR, age 20, Sparrowhawk, killed: buried St. Olaf's, Plot 33, Grave 9.
03/02/43	Spitfire	Grimsetter 234 Sqdn.	Crashed on landing at Grimsetter; pilot OK.
03/02/43	Seafire IB MB362	Hatston 880 Sqdn. (ex Argus)	Mid-air collision at 14.30 near Woodwick bombing range, Evie: on camera gun attacks at 6000', collided with another Seafire: Sub.Lt.(A) Lloyd H Johnson RNZVR, age 21, killed: buried St. Olaf's, Plot 33, Grave 11.
03/02/43	Seafire MB369	Hatston 880 Sqdn. (ex Argus)	Mid air collision (see above): Sub.Lt.(A) Anthony C Smalley RNVR, age 23, killed: buried St. Olaf's, Plot 23, Grave 9.
05/03/43	Seafire IB	Hatston 894 Sqdn.	Pilot Lt.(A) David Wilkinson landed at Hatston with his fitter, L/A Mechanic James Edward Overed on the tailplane: he had taken off from HMS Furious off Deerness and was unaware his fitter was still holding down the tail: after a 15 min. flight in wintry conditions Overed quickly recovered in hospital (compare 30.03.43).
05/03/43	Defiant I DR937	Twatt 771 Sqdn.	In Wide Firth: crashed in sea due to engine failure: Sub.Lt.(A) Jack C Patterson RNZNVR missing, presumed killed: L/A Richard Stark seriously injured.
11/03/43	Henley L3309	Twatt 771 Sqdn.	In bad visibility two aircraft made an identical approach to Twatt: at 300 feet the propeller of the higher aircraft, a Roc, cut off the tail of the lower, a Henley, piloted by S/Lt.(A) Ted Gilberd, RNZNVR: both aircraft crashed: L/A P W Molony was badly injured in the crash – flown to a hospital ship and thence to Aberdeen (Photograph of crashed aircraft).

11/03/43	Roc	Twatt	This aircraft, piloted by Lt. Thackera RN, collided with the Henley above. *(Photograph of crashed aircraft)*.
12/03/43	Spitfire	Skeabrae 66 Sqdn.	Pilot Officer Donald took off from Skeabrae at 10.53 on a sector recce counter – clockwise round Orkney: caught in snowstorm: last message south of Westray "My screen is covered, I can see nothing": extensive search by 4 Walruses, 2 Lysanders and a Dominie: pilot missing presumed killed.
30/03/43	Lysander III T1580	Skeabrae 1494 FG Flight	Took off 09.43 with L/AC L C A Lane on tail: climbed to 200 ft. L/AC Lane fell off and was killed: aircraft crashed: two crew injured: RAF Pilot (name withheld) was court-martialled (compare 05.03.43).
08/04/43	Defiant DR937	Twatt 771 Sqdn.	Hit barrage balloon cable in Scapa Flow and lost wing tip: crash landed: pilot unknown.
08/05/43	Skua 'D'	Twatt 771 Sqdn.	Crashed near Twatt: engine torn from mountings: *(Photographic record)*.
22/05/43	Spitfire VB AB527	Skeabrae 66 Sqdn.	Crashed on take off on training flight at Skeabrae: due to engine failure: pilot F/Sgt. A Hill OK: aircraft a write-off.
23/05/43	Martlet	Hatston 878 Sqdn.	Belly-landed between Field and Berriedale, Westray: pilot OK: transported to Pierowall and, from there by boat to Kirkwall for repair at Hatston workshops. *(Photographic record)*.
28/05/43	Roc L3170	Twatt 771 Sqdn.	Crashed near what appears to be Harray Loch. *(Photographic record)*.
04/06/43	Martlet IV FN288	Hatston 878 Sqdn.	One of three Martlets which took off from Hatston at 02.45 hrs. on a night flying exercise and flew into low cloud: Twatt HF/DF operator, 'Tiny' Small ran half a mile in 3 o'clock in the morning to the transmitter on Yonbell in a desperate attempt to get the aircraft down: one landed safely at Skeabrae: FN288 crashed 400 yds to north of Stymilders in Stenness: Lt.(A) Lonsdale H Wiren, RNZVR, age 26, killed: buried St. Olaf's, Plot 33, Grave 4 (see below).
04/06/43	Martlet IV FN248	Hatston 878 Sqdn.	One of three Martlets (see above): crashed on hillside 4 miles from Skeabrae (the Lyde in Harray?): Lt.(A) Stanley G Brett RNR, age 24, killed: buried St. Olaf's, Plot 33, Grave 15.
07/06/43	Roc L3098	Twatt 771 Sqdn.	Pilot failed to ensure undercarriage locked down for landing and it collapsed: probably a write-off: Pilot Sub-Lt.(A) A D Fyffe RNZNVR.
15/06/43	Seafire IIC MB255	HMS *Indomitable* 880 or 899 Sqdn.	Aircraft landed in sea alongside ship west of Orkney and sank: cause unknown: unknown: Sub.Lt.(A) Robert A Lawson, RNZNVR, age 20, lost: on Lee Memorial.
21/06/43	Walrus II X9467	Twatt 771 Sqdn.	Starboard wheel collapsed on landing: Pilot Sub/Lt. Williams and Observer N. Brown OK.
08/07/43	Chesapeake	Twatt 771 Sqdn.	Crashed near Twatt: Sub/Lt. Mence Pilot: *(Photographic record)*.
27/07/43	Seafire IIC MB187	HMS *Illustrious* 894 Sqdn.	Crashed in sea, 9 miles west of Rora Head: engaged 10.10 hours in fighter direction exercise with ship: Sub.Lt.(A) Robert W D Forbes, RNZNVR, Pilot, age 24, missing, presumed killed.
??/07/43	Boston Havoc	Twatt 771 Sqdn.	Crashed at Twatt: details unknown. *(Photographic record)*.
21/09/43	Seafire IIC LR682	Hatston Reserve	Hit obstruction: undercarriage collapsed: written-off: Sub/Lt. D G Dick, RNVR.
09/10/43	Avenger I (TBF-1) FN787	845 Sqdn. (ex-HMS *Chaser*)	Hatston spun into sea off Old Man of Hoy, 10.05 from 4500 feet after collision with Seafire during fighter evasion exercise: Sub.Lt. Peter C A Heath, RNVR, Pilot, Sub.Lt. Kenneth W Richter, age 23, P/O TAG Gavin Rough (Jock), age 25, missing, presumed killed: all on Lee Memorial.
09/10/43	Seafire	Skeabrae 801 Sqdn.	Collision with Avenger above: no casualties recorded.
22/10/43	Roc A L3159	Twatt 771 Sqdn.	Crashed on South Ronaldsay: crew cut free by Italian Prisoners of War: Sub/Lt. Chadwick TAG D J Cole: Midshipman passenger.
??/10/43	Boston Havoc T8B	Twatt 771 Sqdn.	Landed at Twatt with front wheel unlocked: ran along runway on nose: crew OK: Sub/Lt. Mence pilot. *(Photographic record)*.
22/11/43	Beaufighter TF.X LX415	Wick 144 Sqdn.	8 miles NE Stronsay: 282 Sqdn. located wreck at 1430: high speed launch picked up one survivor, Flight Sergeant H I Shepherd, Observer; Flight Sergeant P G Fletcher, Pilot, missing, presumed killed.
02/12/43	Gladiator	Twatt 771 Sqdn.	Crashed 2 miles SW of Rora Head, Hoy with engine failure; Walrus from Twatt picked up survivor.
09/12/43	Barracuda II DP927	Hatston 830 Sqdn. (ex-HMS *Furious*)	Ramma Stacks, Shetland, 1505 hours: aircraft burst into flames at 3000' during dive bombing attacks with live bombs and dived into the sea: Sub.Lt.(A) Roy D West, RNVR, Pilot, age 22, killed: body recovered: buried Lerwick New Cemetery, Terrace 11, Grave 21: Sub.Lt.(A) James Brown RNVR, Observer, age 20, Lee Memorial: L/A Edward W Kelly, age 21, Lee Memorial.
18/12/43	Spitfire	?	Ditched near Grimsetter.
18/12/43	Oxford MkI HN600	Fraserburgh 14(P) AFU	Crash landing on Auskerry on the only piece of flat land available: Sgt. Franks, RAF, thought the lightkeeper in peaked cap was a German and shouted "Kamerad"! Pilot lifted off by lifeboat, 27/12/43, by which time aircraft had been pounded to pieces by the sea.
??/??/43	Walrus	Twatt 700 Sqdn.	Force landed with engine trouble in Isbister Loch: anchored overnight: next day wheels were lowered and aircraft dragged to road where wheels were lowered, wings folded, and transported by low loader back to station.

Date	Aircraft	Base/Squadron	Details
24/01/44	Martinet TT I MS615	Twatt 771 Sqdn.	Pilot believed he had engine trouble and abandoned take off: aircraft went on to nose; write-off.
25/01/44	JU88	Luftwaffe	Shot down by Bofors gun on Hoy.
28/01/44	Spitfire VB	Skeabrae 602 Sqdn.	Crashed on landing ex-ops. Skeabrae: strong wind and too much throttle on ground caused aircraft to tip on its nose: pilot OK.
20/02/44	Spitfire VII MD114	Skeabrae 602 Sqdn.	Crashed Stronsay due to debris from Bf 109 which Pilot Officer Ian Blair had just shot down: aircraft salvaged, repaired and saw further service certainly until 24/11/48.
22/02/44	Messerschmitt Bf 109	Luftwaffe	Shot down by Pilot Officer Ian Blair, 602 Sqdn. 50 miles east of Stronsay: no survivors.
07/03/44	Spitfire VA EP767	Skeabrae 602 Sqdn.	Landed in front of Skeabrae Control Tower with undercarriage up after night flying exercise: 2nd Lt. P F Clostermann OK: aircraft repaired and saw service until June 1947.
07/03/44	Spitfire VB BL686	Skeabrae 602 Sqdn.	Crashed on Shapinsay: F/O Oliver OK: aircraft salvaged and saw further service until March 1945.
27/03/44	Wildcat V JV350	Hatston 842 Sqdn.	Landed upside down on top of another machine when embarking on HMS *Fencer* to take part in *Operation Tungsten*: damage done to both aircraft.
30/03/44	Skua	Twatt 771 Sqdn.	Ferrying two Air Mechanics to Castletown, skidded on landing in a snowstorm: off runway and tipped on to propeller: PO Pilot Haslam and passengers OK.
11/04/44	Blenheim IV V6173	Twatt 771 Sqdn.	Oil leak in engine: trip aborted: on touchdown undercarriage collapsed and aircraft swung violently to right and ended up off runway: Lt/Cdr. Cyril Burke, pilot and Lt. Bill Larkins, co-pilot OK *(photographic record)*.
19/04/44	Swordfish II	HMS *Fencer* 842 Sqdn.	Crashed on deck while landing to take part in return of Convoy RA59 from Kola Inlet: repaired.
20/04/44	Barracuda II DP983	HMS *Furious* 830 Sqdn.	Struck barrage balloon cable and crashed into Scapa Flow.
25/04/44	Sea Otter I JM 761	Twatt 771 Sqdn.	To Twatt from Abbotsinsch: forced landing in Hoy Sound due to engine failure: Lt. Reid, Pilot: Sub/Lt. W N Brown, Observer: passenger, Gunnery Officer: rescued by High Speed Launch before plane sank.
26/04/44	Skua I L2951	Twatt 771 Sqdn.	Forced landing in sea 6 miles west of Stromness: Sub.Lt. Louis F Weatherall RNZNVR, Pilot, age 22, killed: buried St. Olaf's, Plot 33, Grave 8: L/A TAG Derrick Read, age 19, killed: body sank during recovery.
01/05/44	Martinet	Twatt 771 Sqdn.	Spun into ground, Rousay: P/O (A) Pilot G H Abbott, age 20, killed: buried St. Olaf's, Plot 33, Grave 10: L/A TAG A S Boar, age 20, killed: buried Plot 33, Grave 19: Walrus X9586 Twatt, C.P.O. Crozer, Pilot, and N Brown, Observer, flew out to investigate.
01/05/44	?	?	Stronsay: 118 Sqdn. Spitfire in search.
09/05/44	Oxford I BG555	Skeabrae 598 Sqdn.	Crashed in Scapa Flow east of Cava on Army Co-operative Exercise: W/O D S McGregor, Pilot, T/F/Lt. W O Helm, passenger, LAC H E Haywood, Flt. Mechanic missing, presumed killed.
11/05/44	Hurricane IIb PG483	Twatt 771 Sqdn.	After exercising with HMS *Nelson* and HMS *Argonaut*, crashed on landing at Twatt due to a ground loop: PO Pilot Haslam OK.
12/05/44	Blenheim IV Z6285	Twatt	Off runway and on to its nose in the mud *(Photographic record)*.
23/05/44	Martinett TT I MS684	Twatt 771 Sqdn.	Write-off.
30/05/44	JU88	Luftwaffe	Shot down at 25000 ft. by Spitfires of 118 Sqdn: by F/O J J Parker (Australian) and W/O E Taylor: no survivors.
10/06/44	Warwick I BV417	Wick 281 Sqdn.	Ditched in Scapa Flow due starboard engine failure: lack of pressure: returning from search for Catalina at 62° 22' N, 02° 01' E: Pilot Officer J A J Murray and crew all OK.
11/06/44	Mosquito FB.VI HR133-N	Leuchars 33 Sqdn.	Shot down by two 118 Sqdn. (Skeabrae) Spitfires, BL 718 and BM 423 into Auskerry Sound very close to Stronsay: one killed in Mosquito: Pilot of BL718 (name withheld) cleared by court martial.
17/06/44	Barracuda II BV922	HMS *Furious* 827 Sqdn.	Forced landing Scapa Flow due supercharger or valve gear failure; three picked up.
05/07/44	Hellcat	?	Crashed at Grimsetter.
11/07/44	Corsair JT461	*Formidable* 1841 Sqdn.	Took off from Hatston, 11.40 hours en route to ship: crashed on Hoy: wreckage discovered only one week later: Lt.(A) Edward de E Hewetson, RNZNVR, Pilot, age 23, killed: buried Lyness RN Cemetery, Hoy, Plot H, north border, Grave 6.
14/07/44	Martinet	Twatt 771 Sqdn.	Engine failure on take off with 32 foot winged target in tow: ditched in Loch of Isbister: PO Pilot Eric Haslam concussed and flown to hospital ship: P/O Scougall OK.
08/08/44	Seafire III MkIII LR819	Skeabrae 880 Sqdn.	Crashed (on Skeabrae?): struck contractor's car parked near perimeter track: damage XI-S: Sub.Lt. J C Penfold, Pilot, OK, but lost 10/03/45.
14/08/44	Martinet	Tern 771 Sqdn.	Aircraft struck mast of dockyard drifter and crashed into water: P/O(A) Keith Foster, Pilot, killed: buried St. Olaf's, Plot 33, Grave 13 TAG L/A Donald R Griffiths, age 19, killed: buried Plot 33, Grave 21 *(Photograph of Keith Foster)*.

Date	Aircraft	Base/Squadron	Details
22/08/44	Barracuda II MD647	Hatston 814 Sqdn. – R	Engine failure at 20 feet on take off: belly-landed at Hatston: aircraft written-off: Lt.(A) D M Bell, Pilot.
24/08/44	Avenger Y155	HMS *Trumpeter* 846 Sqdn.	Took off for compass swinging at Hatston from Scapa Flow: did not gain height: crashed into sea and sank in 90 seconds: not recovered: Pilot Sub/Lt. Thomas, A/G David Heath, A/M Arthur Jacobs and Observer (name unknown) OK *(Photographic record).*
09/10/44	JU188	?	Crashed in Scapa Flow, 80 miles ENE of Herma Ness by 611 Sqdn. Skeabrae (flying from Sumburgh?)
16/10/44	Avenger/P	HMS *Fencer* 852 Sqdn.	Stalled and crashed into sea on take-off HMS *Fencer* for anti-submarine patrol on return to Scapa ex-Aarumsund Fjord, minelaying and shipping strike: Sub.Lt.(A) L S Watson Sub.Lt.(A) F Bromilow and P/O Aitken all picked up by dinghy from HMS *Scorpion.*
22/10/44	Bristol Blenheim IV V6251 T8U	Twatt 771 Sqdn.	Tyre burst on landing, aircraft tipped on nose: no casualties: Pilot Lt.(A) Keith Remmington, RNVR: P/O W Jones.
16/11/44	Catalina IVA JX264	Sullom Voe 210 Sqdn.	Flew into sea off Orkney: no other details known.
02/12/44	Wildcat VI MkVI JV751	HMS *Trumpeter* 846 Sqdn.	Crashed over port side of carrier which was around Scapa at time of crash: Sub/Lt.(A) A E Ames RNVR.
03/12/44	Firefly DV122/J	HMS *Implacable* 1771 Sqdn.	Crash landed at Hatston while doing dummy deck landings: Sub/Lt. W R Blatchley RNVR retracted undercarriage by mistake after landing.

1945

Date	Aircraft	Base/Squadron	Details
01/01/45	Liberator GR.V FL949Y	Tain 331 Sqdn.	Crashed near Rora Head, Hoy: failed to heed high ground warning: all eight Czech crew killed: buried Tain.
08/01/45	Spitfire Vc EE772	Skeabrae 441 Sqdn.	Turned off Skeabrae runway after landing and high wind tipped aircraft on to nose.
??/02/45	Seafire III	Grimsetter 880 Sqdn.	Crashed on take off: pilot Midshipman Ian Penfold killed: his glove caught in the cockpit hood while he was closing it on take off, obstructing his vision: funeral held in Orkney *(They gave me a Seafire,* Mike Crosley) but no record of grave.
??/02/45	Avenger I	Hatston 856 Sqdn.	Overturned in cross-wind landing at Hatston: 4 crew OK including a WREN travelling in the turret!
10/03/45	Spitfire	Skeabrae 144 Sqdn. RCAF	Fl.Lt. E W Martin on an exercise, disappeared south of Orkney: extensive search revealed nothing: pilot missing, presumed killed.
??/02/45	Sikorsky R-4	Twatt 771 Sqdn.	Slewed round on take-off and tail rotor struck a parked Blenheim: both aircraft badly damaged: helicopter a write-off but reconstructed at Twatt for pilot/technician instruction purposes: first helicopter crash in Britain.
21/03/45	Seafire LFIII LR856	non-operational	Crashed ½ mile west of Settiscarth, Firth at 17.30 hrs: the aircraft was being ferried: apparent cause of accident – pilot flying into low cloud: struck a ploughed field: aircraft burst into flames on impact: Sub/Lt. Isaac G Cohen, RNVR, age 22, *Merlin*, killed: buried Willesden Jewish Cemetery, London.
31.03.45	Liberator B-24-H-CF 42-50331	42-50331 856 BS (of 492-HBG)	Crashed at Walliwall, ¾ mile SW of Kirkwall: burst into flames on impact: perhaps accidentally shot down: Lt. Pulrang, Co-Pilot baled out at low altitude and survived: 12 killed: believed to have high ranking USAF officers on board.
??/04/45	Reliant I FB542	Twatt	Crashed at Twatt: Pilot Alec Gray: passengers Alex Surgenor and Mary Kiddie from Twatt base all safe *(Photographic record).*
06/04/45	Spitfire LF.IX TB914	Skeabrae 329 Sqdn.	On dawn patrol, crashed in mist at 500' on Skelday Hill, Birsay, at 06.36 hours, 4 minutes after take-off: capitaine Sassard, Pilot, Free French, killed: buried St. Olaf's Cemetery, 10/04/45: some wreckage still visible.
19/04/45	Martinet TT I MS632	Twatt 771 Sqdn. M5632	Undercarriage collapsed on landing: write-off.
23/04/45	Corsair II JS588	Twatt 771 Sqdn.	At Quoyloo, Orkney, 15.20 hours: non-operational aircraft appeared out of haze, hit hillside and disintegrated: Sub.Lt.(A) Alfred J G Playford RNVR killed: buried Norwich Cemetery, Norfolk *(Photographic record).*
27/04/45	Avenger JZ400	Hatston 853 Sqdn.	Arrester hook pulled out after catching No.1 wire on embarking on HMS *Queen* in Scapa Flow: ran into parked squadron aircraft and caused much damage.
10/05/45	Spitfire	Skeabrae 441 Sqdn. RCAF	Disappeared south of Orkney: F/Lt. Martin missing.
01/06/45	Dominie I NR795	Skeabrae Station W. Flight	Hit Nissen Hut, Millfield Camp, Stromness ex-Longman: Pilot F/O T G R Roe died of injuries in Kirkwall: Sgt. Dennis, Sgt. W F Colborne and Cpl. N C Brimmicombe all killed *(Photographic record).*

List of Abbreviations

CAP	Combat Air Patrol
Cdr.	Commander
CO	Commanding Officer
CPO	Chief Petty Officer
D/F	Direction Finding
ENSA	Entertainments National Services Association
FAA	Fleet Air Arm
FAAM	Fleet Air Arm Museum
Fl.Lt.	Flight Lieutenant
FRU	Fleet Requirements Unit
IWM	Imperial War Museum
Lt.Cdr.	Lieutenant Commander
MAC	Merchant Aircraft Carrier
NAAFI	Navy, Army and Air Force Institute(s)
PCB	Protected Control Building
PO	Petty Officer
PRO	Public Record Office
RNAS	Royal Naval Air Station
RNVR	Royal Naval Volunteer Reserve
RNZNVR	Royal New Zealand Naval Volunteer Reserve
Sqdn.Ldr.	Squadron Leader
Sub.Lt.	Sub Lieutenant
TAG	Telegraphic Air Gunner
TBR	Torpedo Bomber Reconnaissance
TT	Target Towing
USS	United States Navy
W/T	Wireless Transmission
WAAF	Women's Auxiliary Air Force
WRNS	Women's Royal Naval Service

References

AIR1 453 15 312 26:   Marine Operations Vol. 5.
1. f100: Scapa 1918, Aircraft Repairs Base and Storage Depot
2. f110: Smoogro, 1918
3. f144: Loch Stenness, 1918: Seaplane Station, Nos. 309, 310 and 311 Flights

AIR20 262:   Photo Index, Scapa Flow

AIR28 712:   Operations Record Book, Skeabrae

AIR28 917:   Operations Record Book, Fighter Sector Headquarters, Wick (later FSH Kirkwall)

ADM1 3574:   Naval Air Stations in Scotland: (report 1942 - 1943)

ADM1 10210:   Fleet Air Arm War Base in Orkney (1938 - 1939)

ADM1 10736:   1939 - 1940: Skeabrae Aerodrome, Orkneys: construction

ADM1 10737:   Defence of Orkney and Shetland: provision of fighter squadrons, 1939 -1940

ADM1 11192:   Construction of Additional Aerodrome at Twatt, Orkney, 1940 - 1941

ADM1 11725:   New Royal Naval Air Stations: fighter direct office, telephone arrangements (1942 -1945)

ADM1 13627:   RN Air Station, Grimsetter, layout

ADM1 13587:   Share facilities for FAA and subsequent transfer to RN

ADM1 16024:   Improvement of Radar Cover in Orkney against low flying aircraft (1944)

ADM1 16427:   MFQ 61/16 RN Air Station, Twatt (Map, 4' X 2½')

ADM1 16427:   MFQ 61/8 RN Air station, Grimsetter

ADM1 16427:   MF 61/18 RN Air Station, Hatston (Map, 18" X 13")

ADM1 16464:   Acquisition of Helicopters by FAA for A/S work, 1942 -1944

ADM1 16481:   RN Air Station, Twatt, Orkney: expansion scheme and layout

ADM1 17033:   Helicopters for the RN, 1943-44

ADM1 17423:   RN Air Stations in the Scottish Highlands and Islands: discussions on post war requirements and future policy (1945)

ADM1 17429:   Decision to close down Scapa as Fleet Base after defeat of Germany and reduce facilities to a minimum: proposals on future use of Orkney Air Stations in the area (1945)

ADM1 65790:   (Chronology): especially Chapter V The Naval Air Stations

ADM53 109896:   Log of HMS Nelson, August 1939

ADM116 3831:   Scapa Flow, Photo Index

ADM116 5790:   Scapa Flow, Photo Index

ADM187 2-4:   Pink Lists: location of HM Ships at 1600 hours each day

ADM 207 8:   804 Squadron Diary

WO199 2712:   Decoy Sites, September 1940 - February 1943

WO199 2713:   Ground Defence of Grimsetter Aerodrome, July 1941 - July 1943

WO199 2715:   Defence of Aerodromes, January 1941 - 1943

Beaver, Paul: *The British Aircraft Carrier*, Patrick Stephens, Wellingborough, Northants, 1987

Brown, David: *Carrier Fighters*, Macdonald and Co. Ltd., London, 1975

Brown, David: *Carrier Operations in World War II Vol.I, The Royal Navy*: Ian Allan Ltd, London, 1968

Brown, Eric: *Wings of the Navy*, Airlife Publishing Ltd., Shrewsbury, 1987

Churchill, Winston: *The Gathering Storm*, Houghton Mifflin Company, Boston, 1948

Clostermann, Pierre: *The Big Show*, Chatto and Windus, London, 1951

Crosley, Cmdr. R Mike: *They gave me a Seafire*, Airlife Publishing Ltd., Shrewsbury, 1986

Department of the Navy, Naval History Division: *Dictionary of American Naval Fighting Ships*, Washington,

Gordon, Dr. T. Crouther: *Early Flying in Orkney: seaplanes in World War I*, BBC Radio Orkney, 1985

Halley, James J: *Squadrons of the Royal Air Force*, Air-Britain, 1980

Hamilton, Duncan: *Touch Wood*, Duncan Hamilton & Co. Ltd., Bagshot, Surrey, 1990

Hewison, W S: *This Great Harbour Scapa Flow*, The Orkney Press, Stromness, Orkney, 1985

Partridge, R T (Major): *Operation Skua*, Fleet Air Arm Museum, Yeovilton, Somerset, 1983

Poolman, Kenneth: *Allied Escort Carriers of World War Two*, Blandford Press, London, 1988

Robertson, Bruce: *British Military Aircraft Serials*, 1878-1987, Midland Counties Publications, Earl Shilton, Leicester, 1987

Rawlings, John D: *Fighter Squadrons of the RAF and their Aircraft*, MacDonald and Co., London, 1969

Roskill, Capt. Stephen W: *The War at Sea, 1939-1945*, HMSO, London, 1976.

Roskill, Capt. Stephen W: *Documents Relating to the Naval Air Service, Vol. I, 1908-1918*, Navy Records Society, 1969

Rotherham, G A (Capt.): *"It's Really Quite Safe"*, Hangar Books, Belville, Ontario, Canada, 1985

Scott, Desmond: *One More Hour*, Century Hutchinson Ltd, New Zealand, 1989

Smith, David J: *Action Stations, 7. Military Airfields of Scotland, the North-East and Northern Ireland*, Patrick Stephens Ltd., Wellingborough, Northamptonshire, 1989

Smith, David J: *British Military Airfields, 1939-45*, Patrick Stephens Ltd., Wellingborough, Northamptonshire, 1989

Sturtivant, Ray: *Squadrons of the Fleet Air Arm*, Air-Britain (Historians) Ltd., Tonbridge, Kent, 1984

Times (The): *Return to the Orkneys*, May 1946

Winton, John: *Carrier Glorious, the life and death of a carrier*, Leo Cooper, 1986

Young, John M: *Britain's Sea War, a diary of ship losses, 1939-1945*, Patrick Stephens Ltd., Wellingborough, Northamptonshire, 1989

N.B. – AIR, ADM and WO references are held by the Public Record Office, Kew: Orkney Archives holds microfilm of some of these references.